Talking Young Femininities

Talking Young Femininities

Pia Pichler
Goldsmiths, University of London

Arts & Humanities
Research Council

First published 2009 by
PALGRAVE MACMILLAN

Palgrave Macmillan in the UK is an imprint of Macmillan Publishers Limited, registered in England, company number 785998, of Houndmills, Basingstoke, Hampshire RG21 6XS.

Palgrave Macmillan in the US is a division of St Martin's Press LLC, 175 Fifth Avenue, New York, NY 10010.

Palgrave Macmillan is the global academic imprint of the above companies and has companies and representatives throughout the world.

Palgrave® and Macmillan® are registered trademarks in the United States, the United Kingdom, Europe and other countries.

ISBN-13: 978-0-230-01328-5   hardback

ISBN-10: 0-230-01328-7   hardback

This book is printed on paper suitable for recycling and made from fully managed and sustained forest sources. Logging, pulping and manufacturing processes are expected to conform to the environmental regulations of the country of origin.

A catalogue record for this book is available from the British Library.

A catalog record for this book is available from the Library of Congress.

10   9   8   7   6   5   4   3   2   1
18   17   16   15   14   13   12   11   10   09

Printed and bound in Great Britain by
CPI Antony Rowe, Chippenham and Eastbourne

For Roger

Contents

Acknowledgements

Above all I would like to thank the girls in all three groups for making this book happen. I would also like to express my gratitude to Alan Durant, Eva Eppler, Janet Maybin and Joanna Thornborrow for taking the time to read draft chapters, and to Jan Blommaert, Judith Broadbent, Anthea Irwin, Claire Lindsay and Siân Preece for their helpful comments, suggestions and feedback which all aided the development of this research project. Above all, my thanks go to Jen Coates for never tiring of reading draft chapters for this book, for inspiring my own research and supporting me on both an academic and a personal level. I am also very grateful to the Arts and Humanities Research Council for supporting this research project (Research Leave Grant AH/E004636/1). Finally, I would like to thank Roger for being my source of calm and sanity at times when I was anything but, and my mother and brother for their continuing support.

This research project is supported by

Transcription Conventions

Spontaneous talk

The girls' spontaneous multi-party talk is represented on an adapted version of the stave system (Coates 1996, 1999; Edelsky 1993). The stave system clearly captures who speaks first (starting on the left) and who speaks at the same time as somebody else (indicated by vertically aligned utterances within one stave). Whereas the traditional stave transcript lists all speakers in each stave, I only list the names of the girls who are actually speaking in a particular stave to save space. Detailed transcription conventions are as follows:

?	identity of speaker not clear
{laughter}	non verbal information
xxxxxx{laughing}	paralinguistic information qualifying underlined utterance
[...]	beginning/end of simultaneous speech
(xxxxxxxx)	inaudible material
(...)	doubt about accuracy of transcription
"..."	speaker quotes/uses words of others
CAPITALS	increased volume
%...%	decreased volume
bold print	speaker emphasis
>...<	faster speed of utterance delivery
/	rising intonation
yeah:::::	lengthened sound
-	incomplete word or utterance
~	speaker intentionally leaves utterance incomplete
=	latching on (no gap between speakers' utterances)
(.)	micropause
(-)	pause shorter than one second
(1); (2)	timed pauses (longer than one second)
.hhh; hhh	in-breath; out-breath
*Bengali	translation of Bengali or Sylheti *utterance* into English

Interviews

For my transcription of interviews I do not tend to use the stave system, as the floor is overwhelmingly held by one speaker. Inserted minimal responses by the other speaker are marked by brackets {...} and the onset and offset of simultaneous speech is marked by stars *...* . E.g.

Hennah   they talk with their mouth full {Pia: yeah yeah *yeah
Hennah   yeah*} *do you* get me and when i- if you go to school

In this extract Hennah (the informant) is speaking and Pia (the researcher) is inserting minimal support. The first two instances of 'yeah' are not uttered simultaneously, but the second two are uttered at the same time as the informant's 'do you...'.

1
Girls' Talk as a Resource for Identity Construction

This book presents the spontaneous talk of three groups of adolescent girls from different socio-cultural backgrounds. My exploration of the girls' talk gives an insight into the range of discursive practices and subject positions/identities which young British women negotiate in their conversations and examines the interactive processes of these negotiations. The book aims to examine the interplay between local subject positions in the girls' talk and larger-scale socio-cultural norms via a focus on discourse, and to integrate a consideration of ethnicity and social class into a discussion of gender and (adolescent) identity. Both aims will be discussed in more detail in the two sections below where I introduce my approach to analysing language/discourse and (gender) identity, drawing on a range of analytic tools from linguistics as well as on research into adolescent identities across different disciplines.

My interest in gender in relation to other situational and macro-social aspects of identity was born out of my comparative exploration of my data which has revealed interesting similarities and differences in the talk and positioning of the three groups of girls. One group consists of five British Bangladeshi girls from a state school in the East End of London, the other of four white English/Irish working-class girls from the same school, and the third group is made up of four upper-middle-class girls from a private school in London's West End. The girls all attended year 11 at the time of the recordings, that is, they were between 15 and 17 years old. All three groups talk about themselves; their parents; friends and friendships; boys or boyfriends; sex; music; school, teachers, homework, grades; and leisure activities. However, the amount of talk dedicated to these topics, and the way the topics are approached varies greatly. For example, when Roberta, Elizabeth, Jane and Nicky from the private school talk about school-related topics it is interesting to observe that on the one hand they clearly foreground their academic selves in their talk about literature, art and scientific topics (such as 'human nature'), but on the other hand they also make a noticeable effort to present themselves as cool and anti-school. Their anti-school stances, however, are very tame in comparison to the truancy or even the resistance to homework which several of the girls in the other two groups are familiar with. At the same time both of the working-class groups also voice pro-school discourses; these are particularly marked in the group of the white East End girls, Pat, Jenny, Susan and Natalie, who frequently try to present themselves as responsible and mature in opposition to their truanting or (allegedly) promiscuous friends. Several girls in the group of Bangladeshi friends, Ardiana, Dilshana, Hennah and Varda, adopt tough anti-school and truanting stances, and support these tough stances with verbal challenges and insults in the form of teasing and boasting. As this example shows, my exploration of the girls' talk frequently focuses on the different positions that the girls take up with respect to similar topics.

Some of these topics will be discussed as parts of individual chapters, others, like the girls' positioning in relation to sexual experience, identities and practices, are explored in more than one chapter (see Part II). Whereas Pat's group produces a great amount of self-disclosing talk about sex-related topics, for example about 'the first time' and contraception, there is very little personal talk about sex in Roberta's group. In their sparse 'sex talk' Roberta and her friends tend to adopt what I define as 'knowing but not doing' positions, that is, presenting themselves as being fully informed and uninhibited about sex, without engaging in any personal self-disclosure. A very different approach is taken in Ardiana's group. Here the sex talk is marked by the girls' switching between playful teasing or boasting and more serious talk, with the former allowing the girls to present themselves as sexually experienced 'bad girls', and the latter as sexually inexperienced 'good girls'.

In addition to the topics which are discussed in all three groups, albeit in different ways, each group also deals with certain topics which are considerably less or not at all prevalent in the other two groups. Thus Ardiana's group often engages in talk about weddings and marriage; Pat's group produces an unusual amount of talk about their mothers; and Roberta's group is the only one to talk explicitly about social class.

As this preview of some of the data shows, my exploration of the girls' discursive construction of identities focuses on how the girls position themselves in relation to specific topics in their talk. The positions the girls take up are frequently associated with certain discourses,[1] that is, different ways of speaking (and thinking, perceiving, representing) which are informed by ideologies or belief systems, and reflect, affect as well as constitute social and cultural practices.[2] This focus on (the girls' interactive negotiation of) different discourses is central to my exploration of the local and supra-local aspects of the girls' positioning in their talk, as I explain in the following section.

The discursive construction of (gender) identities

The primary research context for this book is the area of language/ discourse and gender. Language and gender scholars have generated a substantial amount of research on the interaction of adolescent girls and their friendship/peer groups, investigating a range of accent, grammar, turn-taking and discoursal features of talk (Bucholtz 1999; Coates 1999; Eckert 1993, 2000; Eckert and McConnell-Ginet 1995; Eder 1993; Goodwin 1999; Mendoza-Denton 1999). Much of this linguistic research during the last two decades has been united by a social constructionist approach to gender and by a theorisation of identity as 'a discursive construct that emerges in interaction' (Bucholtz and Hall 2005: 587). The theoretical context of this 'social constructionist-' or 'post-modernist turn' in language and gender research (Cameron 2005a, 2005b, 2009; Swann 2002, 2009)[3] is informed by Judith Butler's (1990) post-structuralist theory of performativity (applied to linguistic discourse analysis for example in Barrett 1999; Cameron 1998; Preece 2009, forthcoming) as well as by Conversation Analytic (CA) notions of 'doing identity' in interaction (e.g. Antaki and Widdicome 1998; Schegloff 1997; Sidnell 2003). Despite their consensus to oppose conceptualisations of identity as biological, fixed or monolithic, the two methodological frameworks differ considerably in their approach to analysis (for an in-depth discussion see Bucholtz and Hall 2005: 588; Cameron 2005a, 2005b; Holmes 2007). Pure CA studies tend to focus on structural/turn-taking features of talk-in-interaction and acknowledge the relevance of social categories only if they are 'oriented to' by participants (e.g. Schegloff 1997). Performativity approaches foreground the interplay between micro and macro contexts and explore power relations, but, due to their focus on the repeated and stylised, that is, 'conventionalised' (Benwell and Stokoe 2006: 33) performance of identity, are at times accused of not offering enough fine-grained analysis of interactional positioning (see Wetherell 1998 for a detailed discussion).

In this book I adopt a perspective which combines a focus on the local, situated identity work of interacting speakers with an exploration of supra-local resources for identity construction. By examining ideological meanings in the form of discourses (but also stereotypes, defined here as representational practices involving reduction and simplification, following Talbot 2003: 471–2 and Hall 1997: 471) I acknowledge the contextualisation of the girls' group talk in the larger-scale, socio-cultural, historical context. My approach to the girls' talk on a discourse level is aimed to encourage an exploration of the girls' discursive positioning, that is, of the stances and identities which the girls take up in their talk. My own, post-modern, conceptualisation of identity as related to discourse is, to some degree, indebted to philosopher and social theorist Michel Foucault, whose understanding of the relationship between identity and discourse is captured in the following famous quotation which characterises discourses as 'practices which systematically form the objects of which they speak' (Foucault 1989 [1972]: 54). My analysis and interpretation of the girls' talk provides evidence for the power of words, which, as Cameron (2001: 16) argues, is acknowledged in the above quotation: different types of discourse form or constrain the identities that individuals 'construct' or produce when they use language. As Jennifer Coates (1996: 261) argues 'more mainstream discourses position us in more conventional ways, while more radical or subversive discourses offer us alternative ways of being'.

However, my analysis of discourses is as much interested in the agency as in the constraint of speakers. I therefore explore not only the 'what' but also the 'how' of the girls' positioning. That is, I examine how the girls negotiate discourses in interaction, how they align themselves with, resist, switch in between, or amalgamate discourses in their talk. My exploration of this process of interactional and discursive positioning focuses on a range of linguistic features (like turn-taking; lexical, grammatical, intonational and paralinguistic cues) and draws on theoretical concepts (like 'cultural capital'; 'voice'; 'interactional frames', etc.) which I shall introduce below and develop throughout the book.

The analysis of my data led me initially to identify several situated identities or local subject positions[4] which are relevant to the girls' friendships groups, such as the 'cool girl', 'sheltered girl' or 'tough girl' positions. However, in addition to these more local positionings, I have also been interested in macro-aspects of identity, and particularly in the connection between one level of identity and another. For example, the 'cool girl' positions adopted by the private-school girls appear to go hand in hand with the girls' efforts to resist stereotypical representations of a posh and socially unaware upper-middle-class femininity, which the girls themselves associate with many of their peers at their private school.

My exploration and interpretation of these micro-macro relations of identity construction are supported by a range of theoretical and analytical concepts, including Michel Bourdieu's concept of 'cultural capital', Michael Bakhtin's notion of 'voice' and Erving Goffman's notion of conversational 'frames'. A more detailed overview will be provided in the overview of chapters, below.

One of the most central arguments in my book is that gender has to be seen in relation to other categories of social identity such as social class and ethnicity. Whereas the rare recent linguistic studies of adolescents and social class focus predominantly on accent and dialect features (Eckert 2000; Rampton 2003), my own exploration of social class in relation to gender is conducted predominantly on a discourse level. This focus on social class and discourse has encouraged me to build on research from sociology, cultural studies and social psychology (Frazer 1988, 1992; Frosh et. al. 2002; Hey 1997; Kehily and Pattman 2006; Skeggs 1997; Walkerdine et al. 2001), situating my work, and particularly Chapters 2 and 3, in a cross-disciplinary research context of social class and gender/adolescent identities.

Similarly, research on language and ethnicity which has built on the concepts of 'new ethnicities' and 'hybridity' (Hewitt 1986; Rampton 1995; Sebba 1993) tends to focus on linguistic style and features of pronunciation, grammar and lexis in analyses of code-switching and crossing, rather than on different discourses. Moreover, although language and gender research has explored a range of femininities, the talk and identity practices of British Asian girls have so far not been studied. My discourse analytic approach to gender and ethnicity is therefore framed by (feminist) cross-disciplinary research on young hybrid British Asian identities (Alexander 2000; Ahmad 2003; Brah 1996; Shain 2003), which I shall review in Chapter 4.

The girls' sex talk, which provides the basis for Chapters 5, 6 and 7 in Part II, will also be approached from a discourse-analytic perspective which combines linguistic tools with insights into adolescent sexuality from a range of cross-disciplinary studies (Holland 1993; Holland et al. 1998; Hollway 1995; Lees 1993; McRobbie 1978; Segal 1997; Tolman 2005). Like recent linguistic publications on language and sexuality (Cameron and Kulick 2003a; Bucholtz and Hall 2004; Sauntson and Kyratizis 2007a) I approach sexuality as constructed in discourse. My analysis will explore how the girls draw on a range of different discourses to position themselves in relation to sexual experiences, norms, practices, orientations and desires and suggests that the girls' positioning in their sex talk bears inflections of gender, ethnicity and social class.

The girls' talk

The girls

This book focuses on the talk of three groups of girls, each of them a pre-established friendship group, who volunteered to tape-record their spontaneous friendship talk for me, after I had made initial contact with their schools. Groups 1 and 2 attended school C, a comprehensive, that is, state-funded school for girls, situated in the East End of London, and recruiting mainly from the surrounding multi-ethnic, working-class communities (which is reflected in the large number of girls at the school qualifying for free school meals). The majority of the girls in this school were bilingual, with more than half of the students from Bangladeshi backgrounds, and less than 20 per cent registering their ethnic background as English/Scottish/Welsh. Group 3 attended School P, a highly selective and successful private school for girls in the West End of London. Although the school offered a number of bursaries, scholarships and government-assisted places (the exact number was not revealed to me), most of the girls' parents were paying high fees. As the school told me that no record was taken of the girls' ethnicity, I am not able to provide any reliable information; however, my own impression was that the majority of the girls were from white British backgrounds. Table 1.1 gives an overview of the three groups. All names are pseudonyms.

Table 1.1   Overview of groups

Group 1	Ardiana, Dilshana, Rahima, Varda and Hennah year-11 students 15/16 years old at time of recording British Bangladeshi girls attend School C, a girls' comprehensive/state school in the East End of London
Group 2	Pat, Susan, Natalie and Jenny year-11 students[5] 16/17 years old at time of recording 3 girls from British/white European background; one (Susan) from black Nigerian/white British background also attend School C
Group 3	Roberta, Elizabeth, Nicky and Jane year-11 students 16/17 years old at time of recording 3 girls from British/white European background; one (Nicky) from Persian/English background attend School P, a private girls' school in London's West End

The ethnic and social class background of the girls in the three groups varied greatly. Four of the five girls in Group 1, and two of the four girls in Group 2 were eligible for free school meals, due to the parents receiving income support or job seeker's allowance. Most of the fathers in Ardiana's group (Group 1) were unemployed, with the mothers being housewives, and the girls' in Pat's group (Group 2) were largely living in single-parent households,[6] with their mothers being employed as home-help for the elderly, or as bakery manager, for example. By contrast, the mothers and fathers of the girls in Roberta's group (Group 3) were all in paid employment, ranging from work in text-book writing and marketing to top-level posts in management as well as in the fields of medicine and the arts. My initial assessment of Groups 1 and 2 as working class and Group 3 as upper-middle class was thus based on the traditional criteria of parental occupation and schooling of the girls. However, my discourse analysis explores how the girls (re-)negotiate the meaning of social class and ethnicity in their local friendship group talk.

The girls in Groups 2 and 3 had received all of their schooling in the UK, whereas the number of years girls in Group 1 had spent in UK education varied between two and eight years, with three of the girls having been born in Bangladesh, and two in the UK. Although there is a certain amount of code-switching, the girls in Group 1 speak mostly in English during their recordings. This may have been partly for my benefit, but my in-group informant, Hennah, explained that the girls in this group 'find it easier to communicate' in English. School records indicated that the 'home language' of all the girls in the group was Bengali. However, according to Hennah, only two girls were fluent in standard Bengali, the official language in Bangladesh. Two other girls spoke Sylheti, a language related, but considerably different from Bengali, but not all the girls in the group understood Sylheti. This complex linguistic situation together with the school context, the larger (British) peer group and the girls' awareness that I did not speak Bengali/Sylheti were probably all reasons for the girls to use mainly English when they recorded their conversations.

The talk

I asked the girls to tape-record themselves in their pre-established friendship groups as I was interested in the everyday spoken interaction of young women with their same-age friends, with a view to exploring the interactive and discursive positioning of adolescent girls from a range of different socio-cultural backgrounds. One additional reason for choosing pre-established friendship groups was that this meant that the girls were used to meeting up and chatting to each other, which, I hoped, would allow them to be less self-conscious in front of the tape recorder.

I had gained access to the two schools in different ways and for different reasons. School C was the only one out of 30 comprehensive/state schools in the Greater London Area which I had contacted that allowed me access to their premises. My relationship to School P was a different one. School P was very protective of the privacy of its students, and the only reason for me to be granted permission to carry out my research was that I had been working there part time as a language assistant (of German). At the time of the recording I had been 'up-graded' to part-time teacher of German, but many of the girls were still on first-term names with me (and very proud of this), unheard of for teachers, but common for language assistants. Although my status as a part-time member of staff may have influenced the girls' talk to some extent, I believe that this influence was lessened by my comparatively low status (as staff), and balanced by the girls' decision to move their recording from the school to the home environment (see below and introduction to Part II). Above all, it is clear that all three groups would have felt an awareness of the tape recorder (and ultimately myself) at some stage. The girls told me that at times they were aware of the tape recorder, at other times they weren't. This is reflected in their recordings, during which moments of awareness stand out (as when the girls address the tape recorder to fill me in on some details) and can therefore be taken into consideration in the analysis.

The data which I will discuss in this book consist predominantly of spontaneous talk recorded by the girls themselves. After receiving my only instruction to fill a tape with their everyday talk, the girls were given full control of these recordings. They were provided with a tape recorder and told that they could switch it off or erase material at any time. However, the girls rarely made use of this offer. In Groups 1 and 2 the recordings tended to be interrupted mostly by fellow students, or by the school pips indicating the end of the break. My intention was for all of the three groups to carry out their recordings during break time at school, partly because I did not want to assume that all girls had the privacy of their own bedrooms at home, and partly because the school environment made it easier for me to meet up with the girls and get to know them a little bit. However Group 3 never managed to find time during their busy school days to carry out the recordings, and therefore moved the recordings to their private sphere, that is, to the house/bedroom of Roberta.[7]

My analysis will draw on the spontaneous conversational data from all three groups, collected over twelve months in 1998 and 1999, as well as on some interview data from my collaboration with one of the girls in

Group 1, collected after the completion of the groups' self-recordings. Hennah helped me to translate the Bengali and Sylheti utterances (the former is the standard language in Bangladesh, the latter is a language spoken in northern Bangladesh) into English and increasingly also acted as my 'in-group informant', providing me with rich and insightful details about herself and the other girls, their families and communities. The sessions therefore developed into ethnographic-style interviews, which, together with other information which I had obtained from question-naires, school records, as well as from observing and talking to the girls in all three groups, provided an additional resource for me to draw on in the interpretation of my conversational data. It is, of course, essential to acknowledge that my informant's views and positions may or may not have been representative of the entire group. Nevertheless, hers is a more 'insider' view than my own, and my interactions with Hennah certainly turned the research process into a more collaborate effort and aided my reflexivity as a researcher (see Chapter 4; Pichler 2008a). She increasingly also adopted the role of data analyst, providing me with her own inter-pretations of some of my material and interpretations, thus enabling a particularly fruitful dialogue between researcher and researched.

Overall, the three groups of girls self-recorded about eight hours worth of spontaneous talk for me. In addition, I met up with Hennah for five five-hour sessions in her house to work on the transcript, another time to have lunch with her and her friends, and on one further occasion I was smuggled into her college.

I chose to represent my data on a stave system, which, similar to a musical score, uses alignment of utterances within a stave to signal simultaneity and thus allowed me to capture multi-party talk more clearly (Coates 1996). All of the Sylheti and Bengali utterances have been converted into Roman script and translations are given at the end of each stave. Transcription conventions are provided at the front of the book.

Analysing girls' talk

This book examines the discursive construction of identities in the talk of adolescent girls. In order to identify different discourses, that is (ideologically loaded) ways of speaking and representing (Fairclough 2003), my analysis focuses particularly on lexical and semantic traces of these discourses in the girls' talk. As Norman Fairclough (2003: 129) argues, 'discourses "word" or "lexicalise" the world in particular ways'. For example, when Ardiana and her friends speak about her 'wedding proposal' several items of vocabulary and their semantic relations (my mum and dad; my sister; related to you; cousins; *their* son's bride) indicate that the speakers at this moment position marriage arrangements as involving families rather than only individuals, highlighting the important role parents and relatives play on behalf of the couple in this practice of arranged marriage.

Extract 1: the wedding proposal (See also Chapter 4)

(1)
Ardiana   they wrote a letter to my s- my mum and dad right
[…]

(2)
Ardiana   my sister was like reading it to me yeah and

(3)
Ardiana   she goes "<they want me to be their bride>" and everything

(4)
Ardiana   and I was like saying (.)   ["EXCUSE ME-"]
Dilshana   wh[o are they]   related to you

(5)
Ardiana   = they just live next door to m[y h]ouse in
Dilshana   (.) cousins =   [ah]

(6)
Ardiana   Bangladesh (.) and they just want **me** (.) as their

(7)
Ardiana   son's bride
Hennah   oh [my God]
Varda   [(Ardiana)] did you see the photo (.)
[…]

(8)
Ardiana   EXCUSE ME I LOVE MY BOYFRIEND here right

(9)
Ardiana   I don't wanna get married to somebody else I don't /**know**

The group position the wedding proposal (and to some extent themselves) in a discourse of arranged marriage, a discourse the speakers show great familiarity with. However, this is not the only discourse in the extract, and lexical and semantic cues are not the only means to identify specific discourses. Grammatical features also help the girls to position themselves, utterances like: 'they want me to be their bride' vs. 'I don't wanna get married to somebody else I don't know', present Ardiana's agency differently on a grammatical and ultimately a discourse level, the latter introducing what appears like a discourse of romantic love at this stage of the transcript.

This brief example (discussed at greater length in Chapter 4) shows how I approach the analysis of discourses and of the girls' positioning in this book. Significantly I do not stop at the identification of specific discourses (on the basis of a range of linguistic features), but I am particularly interested in how the speakers negotiate these discourses. Do they collaborate in their voicing of a discourse, as seems to be the case in staves 1–7, or do they switch between or even resist discourses (as Ardiana in staves 8–9)? A micro-linguistic analysis of a detailed transcript as the one I provide here allows for an exploration of the interactive negotiations that take place when speakers position themselves in discourse, in relation to a specific topic, to one another, or to outsiders of the group. These negotiations can be complex, they frequently result in the speakers' shifting their positions, and they capture differences as well as compromises within the groups.

In order to interpret the girls' discursive and interactive positioning in their group talk I therefore focus on a range of linguistic features (lexical, grammatical, more rarely phonological), prosodic information (intonation, stress – e.g. stave 6), and paralinguistic cues (such as changes of voice quality, speed and volume – e.g. stave 8). I also contemplate the girls' turn-taking behaviour, that is, I consider instances where the girls build on or interrupt each other's contributions, where (and why) the girls hesitate, and, to borrow from Conversation Analytic terminology, how they 'orient' to each other's contributions, that is, how they receive and understand what is going on in a specific conversational extract. The meaningfulness of these features beyond the semantic realm – as cues for interactive and discursive positioning – is partly displayed by the speakers themselves (see CA 'next-turn-proof-procedure', e.g. Hutchby and Wooffit 1998: 15–17). However, I would argue that data is interpreted by the analyst in all cases. For example, Hennah's 'oh my God' (stave 7) clearly signals/indexes (Ochs 1992) her surprise, but whether this surprise indexes a critical position towards the practice of arranged marriage per se or not (as indeed I argue) is more difficult to discern. That is, the relationship between this level of interactional meaning and a higher level of social meaning, or, the relationship between different levels of indexicality (Ochs 1992; see also Bucholtz and Hall 2005; Silverstein 2004), always requires a more complex process of interpretation. In this instance, the remainder of the extract, together with my (ethnographic) knowledge of Hennah led me to reject an interpretation of Hennah's utterance as a criticism of arranged marriage per se. The interpretive role of the analyst is even more significant in the discussion of discourses and their effects on the positioning of the speakers, than in the exploration of interactional roles (Ardiana as the 'story teller') or interactional stances (like Hennah's 'surprise'). As critical discourse analysts remind us in their research, discourses frequently do not appear to speakers as different, ideologically loaded ways of talking about and perceiving the world, but are 'invisible' as they are perceived as commonsensical or factual (e.g. Fairclough 2001: 71).

In this book I draw on participants' and the analyst's understanding of what is going on in a particular extract. In the debate between Conversation Analysts on one side and sociolinguists as well as non-CA discourse analysts on the other, the former tend to focus on the 'oriented-to context' (Schegloff 1997: 184), that is, aspects of social context and identity categories which are 'demonstrably relevant to the participants' at a specific moment in interaction (Schegloff 1991: 50). My own stance is in alignment with many other language and gender researchers who take a constructionist approach to identity and carry out micro-level analysis but 'simply do not accept that social categories need to be observably and explicitly salient for participants in order to be considered relevant to their analyses' (Holmes 2007: 54; see also Bucholtz 2003; Cameron 1998; Weatherall 2000; Wetherell 1998). For my interpretation of discourses and subject positions in the girls' talk I find a consideration of the participants' orientation to categories relevant and necessary but often not sufficient. Particularly in order to establish connections between local meanings and positionings and larger-scale (ideological, socio-cultural, gendered) practices as I seek to achieve in this book, I draw on my own situational, academic, cultural and social knowledge. That is, I draw on my insight into the data gained by comparative analysis, by my observation of and engagement with the participants in my study, but I am also clearly influenced by dominant discourses of post-modern approaches to language, gender and identity, by my training and practice as a feminist sociolinguist/discourse analyst in the UK, and by my position as a white, adult, middle-class woman from Austria living in London for more than a decade at the turn of the twentieth/twenty-first century. I maintain a postmodern approach to (situational as well as gender, ethnic and social class) identity as a discursive process throughout the book, but in order to do justice to the different foci emerging from the data of each of the three groups I draw on a range of different methodological and theoretical concepts, which are made explicit at the beginning of each part or chapter and which will briefly be introduced below.

Overview of chapters

Part I presents three chapters on the interplay of gender and adolescent identities with ethnicity and social class; the first one based on the talk of Roberta and her three upper-middle-class friends from a private school, the second based on the talk of Pat and her three friends from a state school in a working-class area of London's East End, and the third chapter captures the talk of Ardiana and her four Bangladeshi friends from the same East End state school. All of these chapters explore the relationship between local- and larger-scale positionings, between language, gender and other socio-cultural identities.

My analysis of the talk presented in Chapter 2 focuses on the efforts of Roberta, Elizabeth, Nicky and Jane to present themselves as 'cool', 'socially aware' and 'real' in their group talk. The tame non-conformity which is at the heart of the girls' coolness is displayed particularly in the girls' talk about soft drugs, about non-mainstream music, and in their mitigated anti-school stances. Drawing on Pierre Bourdieu (1983, 1984, 1991) the chapter argues that coolness constitutes an alternative cultural capital in this group which allows the girls to position themselves in opposition to their 'posh' friends and school, and to stereotypes of a sheltered, overprivileged upper-middle-class femininity. The girls also reject this stereotype by presenting themselves as both 'socially aware' and as 'real', that is, as ordinary adolescents, in their talk about poems and mines, dance clubs, London's West and East End, state-school and private-school students, A-levels and future university degrees. At the same time this talk indexes social class both directly and indirectly, via 'cultural concepts' (Silverstein 2004) and cultural tastes and capital (Bourdieu 1984). The chapter argues that the girls' efforts to construct alternative private-school, upper-middle-class femininities for themselves locally in their group of friends have to be seen in relation to their dominant or 'legitimate' (Skeggs 1997) cultural capital in the form of their elite education, whose value clearly goes beyond the local context of the girls' interactions.

The talk of Pat, Susan, Natalie and Jenny, which I present in Chapter 3, foregrounds the subject position of the daughter more than in any of the other two groups. Unlike Roberta and her upper-middle-class friends, the girls in this group, who tend to live with their mothers in one-parent families, present their mothers as authoritarian but protective and their fathers as (geographically) distant but caring, frequently constructing themselves as the protected and loved daughter. However the girls also highlight their self-determination or even rebelliousness, presenting different formations of their selves as daughters, and switching in between subject positions of mature adults and rebellious teenagers. In addition to my focus on discourses, which runs throughout the book, the girls' talk led me to pay particular attention to the different voices which they adopt in the evaluation and negotiation of these subject positions. Drawing on the work of Mikhail Bakhtin (1981, 1986) and, more recently, Janet Maybin (2007), I show that the girls frequently quote or even appropriate their mothers' or other authoritative voices to construct themselves as mature and reasonable grown-ups, for example when they object to truancy and vandalism or when they talk about prioritising education over boyfriends. Whereas social class is never topicalised in the talk of this group, I argue with Skeggs (1997: 3–4) that the girls 'recognize the recognition of others' and that their efforts to present themselves in opposition to subject positions like the neglected daughter, the vandalising truant and the future teenage mother, Pat, Susan, Natalie and Jenny demonstrate their awareness of pathologising discourses of (young) working-class femininity and their desire to disidentify from them.

In Chapter 4 I present the spontaneous talk of Ardiana, Dilshana, Hennah and Varda, and some extracts from ethnographic-style interviews with one of the girls. These data provide evidence for how the girls negotiate a range of cultural discourses, practices and identities, presenting themselves as both British and as Muslim Bangladeshi. My interpretation of the girls' talk and positioning is influenced by Stuart Hall's understanding of (ethnic) culture 'not [as] an essence but a *positioning*' (Hall 1990: 226). However, my two sources of data also show that 'essentialising' discourses of culture (-clash) can be significant for the girls' own construction of identities, and therefore led me to reflect on my own and other (romanticised) academic celebrations of hybridity. The influence of cultural studies (as well as anthropology, education and sociology) is evident not only in my theoretical approach to culture and hybridity, but also in the range of empirical studies I review to frame my exploration of what emerges as the girls' hybrid British Bangladeshi femininities. Drawing on the concept of conversational 'frame' (Bateson 1987[1972]: 185; Goffman 1974: 10), I present a detailed exploration of the linguistic and discursive resources the girls use to switch between, manage and even merge culturally different discourses and subject positions. For example, several girls position themselves as 'tough' in their talk about truanting, school and in their tough teasing/verbal duelling. Whereas this position aligns them in many ways with tough British working-class femininities (cf. ladettes) in opposition to stereotypical notions of the studious, quiet, and submissive Asian girl, the group align themselves with notions of *sharam* (shame, modesty, shyness) and *izzat* (honour) in other instances. In the final section of this chapter I explore the girls' talk about traditions of marriage and argue that the discourse of arranged marriage emerges itself as a hybrid in the girls' interactive negotiations.

Part II is dedicated to the sex talk of the girls which reveals a range of different sexual experiences, norms, practices, orientations and desires. There was a considerable amount of sex talk in all three groups: least in Group 3, Roberta's group; most in Group 2, Pat's group. The introduction to Part II gives an overview of relevant existing research on young women's sexuality from different disciplines, and presents an argument for interpreting the groups' different approaches to sex talk from a cross-cultural, discourse analytic perspective. Each of the three (comparatively shorter) chapters shows that the girls in my study use their sex talk not only to identify as heterosexual or to signal varying degrees of sexual experience, orientations and desires, but also to carry out important gender and other identity work.

Chapter 5 presents the richest amount of sex talk produced by the three groups. Pat, Susan, Natalie and Jenny dedicate about a quarter of their total talking time to topics related to sex and sexuality. This talk about their own or their friends' actual sexual activities, about 'losing [their] virginity' or about contraception was produced spontaneously, rather than elicited by a researcher (with a pre-established interest in working-class girls' sexuality). In their talk the girls do not position sex as something that 'just happens' to them (Tolman 2005), instead they highlight their own agency. The girls in this group approach their sex talk predominantly from within a serious frame, in spite of self-disclosing very intimate details about themselves in their conversations. The chapter shows how the girls invoke and negotiate a range of frequently conflicting discourses to balance the strong pro-sex norms they experience in their peer group with their own needs, anxieties/concerns and pleasures in relation to sexual intercourse. Some of these discourses position the girls as moralistic and romantic, others reveal that the girls expect to experience sexual pleasure and desire, yet others highlight the girls' resistance to dominant notions of romance and virginity. In all of their talk the girls present themselves as self-determined, as wanting to determine with whom, where and when they will have sex for the first time to guarantee that it will be an enjoyable, worthwhile experience.

Chapter 6 returns to the talk of Ardiana and her friends, and to their use of playful frames to manage sensitive topics within the group. This chapter provides a rare insight into young British Asian women's discursive positioning in relation to sexual experiences, practices and identities within their friendship group. The girls talk about kissing in public, watching pornography, and about having (or not having) been 'through it' with their boyfriends. Contrary to some (popular as well as scholarly) perception, the group's self-recorded interactions show that Dilshana, Ardiana, Hennah, Rahima and Varda do engage in some personal sex talk, however, mostly in the context of a playful conversational activity or 'frame' such as in their teasing and boasting. The sexualised 'bad' girl identities in playful frames are balanced with non-sexual 'good' girl identities which the girls adopt in most of their talk which is framed as serious. In the chapter I argue that these opposing adolescent identities are to a significant extent informed by two very different discourses, which are not only gendered, but also culture-specific, one celebrating sexual experience as a essential part of British adolescence, the other celebrating female premarital chastity, linked by the girls themselves to their Bangladeshi community and to their 'religion'.

Chapter 7 focuses on Roberta and her friends from the private school. Whereas this group is the only one to talk explicitly about social class, they produce comparatively little talk about gender relations, and even less talk about sex and sexuality. This limited amount of sex talk is, moreover, very impersonal, particularly if contrasted with the other two groups. However, Roberta, Elizabeth, Nicky and Jane engage in some 'academic sex talk', that is, sex becomes a subtopic in scientific discussions about issues like human nature, or in debates about literature and films. Their talk is clearly marked by an absence of the 'pro-sex discourse' which the girls in Pat's group experience in the form of peer pressure. Roberta and her friends are happy to talk about the sexual experiences of others, showing that they are not shocked by active sexuality. Overall, however, they present themselves as 'knowing rather than as doing', they foreground their cool *knowledge about* sex rather than their own sexual experiences or desires (just like they highlight their knowledge about non-mainstream music and drug use). The data extracts I present indicate that for these girls it appears to be less problematic to present themselves as sexually inexperienced than as naïve and unknowing. In Roberta's group the girls feel driven to foreground their rational (academic) mind over their active sexuality (see also Walkerdine et al. 2001), a positioning which aids their discursive construction of a private-school, upper-middle class femininity.

Chapter 8 presents the conclusions to this book, summing up the main findings and highlighting the central argument of the book that a discursive exploration of gender, sexuality and adolescent identities in girls' talk needs to be conducted in relation to a range of local positions and larger-scale social categories such as ethnicity and social class.

Part I

Talking Young Femininities: Identity and the Interplay Between Gender, Ethnicity and Social Class

This section will examine the talk of three groups of adolescent girls from very different socio-cultural backgrounds. The aim of the section is to analyse the talk that the girls produce within their friendship groups with respect to their interactive and discursive positionings. I shall particularly focus on how the local positionings of the girls are inflected with and produce a range of larger-scale socio-cultural meanings, exploring the interplay between different levels and categories of identity in the girls' talk and integrating a consideration of ethnicity and social class into my discussion of gender and adolescent identity.

Recent studies on young women and men have tended to focus on a micro level of identity construction instead of making general statements about working-, and middle-class youths. Many of these studies were carried out in US or UK school/educational contexts, using familiar identity category labels such as 'public school students' and 'state school students' (Frosh et al. 2002), or, differentiating even more locally between 'jocks' and 'burnouts' (Eckert 2000; Eckert and McConnel-Ginet 1995); 'boffins' or 'geeks' and 'hard boys' (Frosh et al. 2002); 'academic achievers', 'real Englishmen', and 'macho lads' (Mac an Ghaill 1994); 'popular dropouts' and 'less-popular achievers', 'Grebos' and 'Trendies' (Kehily and Pattman 2006); 'hard/sporty men' and 'new men' (Edley and Wetherell 1997). Studies focusing exclusively on the self-positioning and representation of young women distinguish between 'ladettes' and 'tomboys' in the UK (Jackson 2006); 'urban' and 'suburban girls' in the US (Tolman 2005); 'can-do-girls' and 'at-risk-girls' in Australia, the UK and US (Harris 2004). These studies are largely undertaken from non-linguistic perspectives, focusing on content and discourse rather than on phonological and grammatical features (except for Eckert 2000; Eckert and McConnell-Ginet 1995; see also Rampton 2001, 2002, 2003 on 'posh' and 'Cockney' stylisations).

The plurality and situatedness of identity positions has also been highlighted in studies focusing on Asian adolescents in the UK. Thus Alexander (2000) discusses a range of different masculini*ties* which young Asian males adopt in a 'gang'; Shain's (2003) research on young Asian schoolgirls from mostly Muslim backgrounds identifies the local identity positions of 'Gang Girls', 'Survivors', 'Rebels', and 'Faith Girls'. Linguistic research on adolescents and ethnic identities (Hewitt 1986; Rampton 1995; Sebba 1993) again tends to focus on (grammatical, phonological and lexical) features of style, code-switching/mixing and crossing, rather than on discourse (but see Preece 2009, forthcoming, for ethnic minority university students in the UK).

Nevertheless, many of the above local identity positions retain connotations of larger socio-cultural categories, and, in several non-linguistic research projects, a discussion of macro categories has remained central. I found this to be truer for studies interested in social class than in ethnicity, perhaps because the latter are still having to defend themselves against homogenising discourses and stereotypical representations of the (ethnic) cultural 'other'. Thus, whereas earlier research on (young) Asian women, such as Valerie Amos and Pratibha Parmar (1981), Avtar Brah and Rehana Minhas (1985), dealt with issues such as racism (but also class, gender, sexuality and education) from a more macro-perspective, more recent studies adopt ethnographic methodologies to counter stereotypes of 'Asianness' by capturing the diversity of (young) Asian femininities (Ahmad 2003; Alexander 2000; Archer 2001, 2002a, b; Brah 1996; Dwyer 2000; Shain 2003). By comparison there have been very explicit expressions of concern about the marginalisation of a more macro-discussion of social class, especially in research taking a sociological or a psychosocial perspective (e.g. Reay 1998; Skeggs 1997, 2004; Walkerdine et al. 2001).

In the following chapters of this section I aim to strike a balance between micro and more macro perspectives on identity. Throughout I will approach identity as a process, and gender, social class, and ethnicity as discursive constructs. As a linguistic discourse analyst my focus is initially very much on a micro-level of the girls' talk, and on the interactional and other local identity positions of the girls. However, my analysis shows how these local identities of the girls, their positionings as 'cool and socially aware girls' (Chapter 2), as 'sheltered but independent girls' (Chapter 3) or as 'tough and respectable' girls (Chapter 4) are frequently influenced by discourses, stereotypes, and larger-scale identity categories which highlight the relevance of gender, ethnicity, and social class. Both Chapters 2 and 3, the former presenting the talk of private-school girls Roberta and friends, the latter the talk of London East End girls Pat and friends, focus on the interplay between gender and social class. Chapter 4, which presents the talk of Ardiana and her British Bangladeshi friends, focuses on the interplay between gender and ethnicity.

2
Cool and Socially Aware Private-School Girls

This chapter explores the talk of Roberta, Elizabeth, Jane and Nicky with a particular focus on the practices, discourses and types of knowledge that are central to the girls' positioning in their friendship group. The talk contains rich evidence of the girls' privileged social background as private-school students from upper-middle-class backgrounds. However, in this chapter I am particularly interested in the girls' considerable efforts to differentiate themselves from their 'sheltered', that is, privileged and socially unaware, peers at their 'posh' school, seeking to align themselves with what they call 'real people' instead. Moreover, in their conversations about drugs, music and school the girls frequently display streetwise knowledge and adopt non-conformist stances, which, I argue, allows them to position themselves as 'cool'. By presenting themselves as cool, socially aware and real in their group talk, the four friends index subject positions or identities which are constructed in opposition to the other girls at their elite school and to (frequently implicit but culturally recognisable) stereotypes associated with an over-privileged private school and sheltered upper-middle-class femininity. However, my discussion of the girls' positioning also shows that their efforts to accomplish what I view as alternative private-school femininities are carefully balanced with a demarcation from what the girls perceive as displays of extreme hardness and 'rough' working classness.

Non-linguistic interview studies by Frazer (1988, 1992), Hey (1997), and Skeggs (1997) found that explicit discussions about social class were more characteristic of upper- and middle-class adolescents, and Walkerdine et al.'s (2001: 38) research captures a heightened sense of awareness about the 'complexity of social stratification' among the middle-class girls she studied. Frazer (1988, 1992) and Frosh et al. (2002)

highlight that pupils at private schools are extremely aware of their private-school pupil identities, and both studies, as well as Kenway (1990), Mac an Ghaill (1994) and more recently Kehily and Pattman (2006), show that this awareness can go hand in hand with a sense of superiority with respect to lower-class and/or state-school pupils. Roberta, Elizabeth, Nicky and Jane tend to avoid explicit displays of superiority, but, on the other hand, they (at times inadvertently) index and reaffirm their privileged background and status by their constant striving for formal knowledge and academic success, and therefore by their continuing accumulation of legitimate 'cultural capital' and (institutional) power (Bourdieu 1984; see also Skeggs 1997, 2004).[1] Thus, on the one hand the girls' talk confirms the findings of Walkerdine et al.'s (2001) psycho-social study of young British women, which highlights the significance of academic excellence for the (re)production of young middle-class femininities. However, on the other hand it also demonstrates that a display of what I see as alternative forms of cultural capital (such as 'cool' non-conformity or streetwise knowledge) can be highly central to the local identities of this particular group of privileged girls.

Unlike many of the sociological, psychological and education-oriented studies on adolescent (gender) identities (such as Frazer 1992, 1988; Hey 1997; Skeggs 1997; Kehily and Pattman 2006; Walkerdine et al. 2001), social class is not foregrounded to the same extent in recent linguistic analyses of the talk and identity practices of young women and men. Many linguistic studies focus more on situated subject positions, describing, for example, US high school identities such as those of the 'jocks', who orient to institutional norms and practices at their school and differentiate themselves from the anti-school and anti-authority 'burnouts' (Eckert and McConnell-Ginet 1992; 1995; Eckert 2000). Bucholtz (1996, 1999) explores another US high school community, the 'nerds', who construct their 'intelligent selves' in opposition to the popularity and/or coolness of jocks and burnouts and therefore avoid current slang, non-standard syntax and colloquial phonological forms. These linguistic and ethnographic studies of adolescent 'communities of practice' acknowledge associations with social class but firmly prioritise the 'level of social organisation at which people experience the social order on a personal and day-to-day basis' (Eckert 2002: 58) and frequently focus on phonological and grammatical variables rather than on a discourse level (see also Rampton 2001, 2002, 2003 on 'posh' and 'Cockney' stylisations). In the vein of these linguistic studies my exploration of Roberta and her friends' social positioning focuses on the girls' negotiation of diverse, shifting and frequently contradictory subject positions. However, I aim to contemplate the girls' local positioning in relation to larger-scale socio-cultural meanings, drawing on theoretical and analytic concepts such as Bourdieu's (1983, 1984) notion of cultural capital, that is, cultural resources including dispositions, goods and (educational) qualifications which are 'helping to determine position in the social space' (Bourdieu 1991: 230) and Silverstein's (2004) notion of 'cultural concepts', that is, 'structures of knowledge about the world', indexed interactionally by certain words and expressions (Silverstein 2004: 632). Thus, the chapter explores the relationship between the situated practices, types of knowledge and subject positions in the talk of a group of elite schoolgirls, and (more macro-level) discourses, ideologies and structures of private schooling and social class.

Socially aware girls

Evidence of explicit discussions of social class is rare in research on spontaneous conversational interaction among adolescents. In my own research on the talk of young British women Roberta and her private-school friends remain unique in their overt orientation to social class, thereby differing from the two groups of London working-class girls. Similarly, Ben Rampton (2002: 1; 2001) found that 14-year-old London pupils from relatively disadvantaged comprehensive schools were 'often far less articulate about social class than about ethnicity and gender'. Unsurprisingly, non-linguistic interview studies interested in social class have been able to provide more evidence on young women's and men's explicit talk about social class (Frazer 1992, 1988; Frosh et al. 2002; Hey 1997; Kehily and Pattman 2006; Skeggs 1997; Walkerdine et al. 2001). My own contribution to the exploration of adolescent positioning to social class foregrounds spontaneous rather than interview data like most linguistic studies on adolescent talk, but unlike those the focus of my study is on discourse rather than on accent/dialect stylisation. In the talk of Roberta and her friends private schooling and upper-middle-class membership are closely linked, with the latter frequently but not exclusively being experienced through the more local identity category of the former.

Extract 1: poems and mines

(1)
Nicky   I was sitting on my bed like (.) a few weeks ago
?   %(xxxxxxxxxx)%

(2)
Nicky   and I just thought "oh my God I have gotta write an

(3)
Nicky   English essay" .hh and I thought "hang on (.) all

(4)
Nicky   I've gotta do is sit down for an hour and **wank** on (.)

(5)
Nicky   about some bollocky poem" yeah   when other people
Jane   mm

(6)
Nicky   have gotta like (.) [go down mines or whatever]{smiling}
Jane   [and this (I find funny)]
Roberta   yeah

(7)
Nicky   how **easy** [have] I [got it]
Roberta   yeah exactly   [like]   [if I don't] do this (.)

(8)
Nicky   yeah{laughing}
Jane   yeah hhhhh{amused}
Roberta   I I I still get my dinner you know   like I'm

(9)
Roberta   still gonna be able to buy those pair of shoes the other

(10)
Jane   yeah exactly (-)
Roberta   week you know whatever

Supported by Roberta, Nicky invokes a range of words and subsequently 'cultural concepts' (Silverstein 2004) which index stereotypical social class categories and identify the girls as members of the privileged group represented by 'poems' rather than 'mines'. Silverstein's work on indexicality investigates how the meaning of words and expressions goes well beyond the denotational level, indexing 'cultural concepts', or (stereotypical) knowledge which is culturally meaningful, and therefore constituting a resource for indexing group memberships and identities. The lexical items 'poem' (stave 5) and 'English essay' (stave 3) index knowledge of and familiarity with academic essay writing and fine art, which in turn highlights legitimate or dominant cultural capital (Bourdieu 1984, 1986, 1991).

The girls show their critical awareness that these lexical items are symbols of their 'distinctive lifestyle' (Bourdieu 1984: 175) as privileged private-school girls. They acknowledge the relative effortlessness of their privileged lives ('all I've got to do is sit down for an hour', stave 4; 'how easy have I got it', stave 7). They are also aware of their lack of existential fears ('I still get my dinner', stave 8) and of their privileged position as (female) consumers[2] ('I'm still gonna be able to buy those pair of shoes the other week', staves 8–9). Although Nicky and her friends here (and in most other instances) do not position working classness as deviant and negative like, for example, Kenway's (1990) Australian elite schoolgirls (see below), they nevertheless invoke a stereotypical or 'mythical' working-class other (Harris 2004: 105; Kenway 1990) by direct reference to manual labour and hardship and by implicitly acknowledging the lack of privileges of 'other people'.

In this extract academic work and refined cultural capital is belittled on the one hand, and presented as classed as well as gendered on the other. Nicky distances herself from her academic self on a lexical level in staves 4–5 when she describes the task of writing an English essay as only having to '**wank** on (.) about some bollocky poem'. Both 'wank on' and 'bollocky' index coarseness/toughness and masculinity, and by employing the two terms Nicky both ridicules and feminises academic work, positioning tough masculinity in opposition to writing an academic essay on poetry. The use of these two slang expressions positions Nicky as somebody who is clearly not worried about refined language, whether it is her own or that of a poem. Nicky's coarseness of expression precedes her reference to the hardship of miners. Thus it seems that Nicky's linguistic and discursive choices are meant to signal some detachment from a sheltered and refined private-school, upper-middle-class femininity, associated with academia, poetry and 'polished' language.

This distancing should not be mistaken for the girls' denial of their privileged background or for an attempt to 'pass as working class' in the way that many of the (young) working-class women interviewed by Skeggs (1997: 91) aim to 'pass as middle class'. The girls are very much aware of their current privileges as well as of their future 'ability to use and capitalise upon their cultural capital' as upper-middle-class girls (ibid.) with university and career paths expected to follow seamlessly from their private school education.

Extract 2: poems and mines – continued

(11)
Nicky   [and the cool thing] is that we go on
Jane   it's just like-
Roberta   it's not [(xxxxxxxxxxxxxxxx)]

(12)
Nicky   to like study history or whatever (the-) <u>it's just</u>

(13)
Nicky   *{slightly amused}*<u>the rest of our lives is just</u> (-) doing

(14)
Nicky   [easy stuff]
Roberta   I mean >I so[rt of think<] it's really weird because (-)

In this extract the girls add a university degree in history to their list of cultural concepts (English essay, poem, dinner and new shoes) which index their identities as carefree and privileged private-school, upper-middle-class girls. Like Walkerdine et al.'s (2001: 38) middle-class girls the private-school girls in my study rarely talk about wealth but they clearly signal their awareness of the significant role of other capital, such as (further) education, for their continuing trajectories towards 'easy', that is, privileged or upper-middle-class lives. This shows that, despite a tendency for idealisation and stereotyping, Roberta and her friends have an understanding of the dominant cultural capital that (re)produces their privileged class position (Bourdieu 1984; Skeggs 1997).

Like the British A-level students studied by Mary Kehily and Rob Pattman (2006: 42) Nicky does not position university education in terms of hardship. However, unlike the young men and women in

Kehily and Pattman (2006: 42), Nicky and her friends do not tend to foreground their future university trajectories in order to highlight their own superiority in relation to others but instead to display their own social awareness, which they contrast positively with the pretentious and sheltered 'mentality' of many other students at their private school.

Extract 3: 'they are just so sheltered'

(1)
Roberta   (.) I'll always feel slightly detached from our school

(2)
Roberta   (2) cause I can't (1) tap into the sort of mentality

(3)
Nicky   =**some** of th- (er) the mentality is (-)
Roberta   sometimes=

(4)
Nicky   totally beyond me
Roberta   we're all down to earth yeah (you)

(5)
Nicky   [we were eating lunch today-]   [and it was-]
Roberta   [just look at like peo]ple who're just so [**sheltered**]

Roberta and Nicky collaboratively position themselves in opposition to the majority of the other girls at their private school. After Roberta indicates that the reason for feeling detached from school is the 'mentality' there (stave 2), Nicky shows her agreement by mirroring and reinforcing what Roberta has said (stave 3). In the following two staves Roberta becomes more explicit about the objectionable 'mentality' of other 'people' (that is, fellow students) who do not share Roberta's and her friends' sense of being 'down to earth' (stave 4) but instead are 'just so sheltered' (stave 5). Roberta thereby creates a pair of meaning opposites which captures the antagonistic relation between her own group and the other girls at her school: being 'down to earth' vs. being 'sheltered'.

In the remainder of this longer stretch of talk Nicky provides an example of the objectionable 'sheltered mentality' of their fellow students.

Extract 4: 'they are just so sheltered' – continued

(6)
Roberta   (I mean) it's just~
Nicky   =we were eating lunch to[day-]
Elizabeth   who=   [who]

(7)
Nicky   and er me and Kim were the
Elizabeth   are you thinking of (xxxx)

(8)
Nicky   only people at [a table of like]   ten people (.) who
Roberta   [Christina Tay/lor]

(9)
Nicky   (-) weren't talking about skiing at Val / d'Isère
Jane   yeah

(10)
Nicky   and I was just like [it wasn't]   [it wasn't]   just
Jane   [I think a]bout [someone like-]

(11)
Nicky   the fact that they were (going) all going skiing at Val

(12)
Nicky   d'Isere it was like the whole mental[ity (about it)
Jane   [no:: you see I

(13)
Nicky   .hh that] sounds like the [most **horrendous**] thing in
Jane   know it's-]   [it's **changed**]

(14)
Nicky   [the world to me]
Jane   [yeah
Elizabeth   [I know I'll] never fit in with that sort of (frie[ndly)

(15)
Nicky   [I am really glad-]
Jane   [and then] the thing] is (that [is) strange about it] is
Elizabeth (xxxxxxx)]
Roberta   [I know it's just~]

Their schoolmates' lunch-break conversation about skiing in Val d'Isère, in itself a cultural concept indexing (French) exclusivity, is interpreted by Nicky and the others as a symbol of this 'sheltered' mentality. Significantly, however, Nicky does not only object to the fact that these 'sheltered' girls spend their holidays at an exclusive resort such as Val d'Isère, but she is critical of 'the whole mentality about it' (stave 12). Although this is not made explicit, it appears that the 'mentality' which Roberta, Nicky, Jane and Elizabeth criticise is characterised not only by their fellow students' display of their exclusive (Val d'Isère) lifestyle but also by their lack of awareness about it. By framing this story with a proclamation of their own 'down to earth' lifestyle and mentality, Roberta, Nicky and the other two girls position themselves in opposition to private-school snobs, who are both unashamed and unaware of their very privileged and sheltered world.

The significance of social awareness (and self-awareness) is explicit in the next extract.

Extract 5: social awareness

(1)
Jane   when you think that people don't seem to have that

(2)
Jane   sort of social (awareness) you know some people
                        {- loud noise -}

(3)
Jane   (what) .hh like know that they are rich or

(4)
Jane   whatever (-) or (that) y'know in the end we are

(5)
Jane   we all go to this posh school yeah (-) hence we are

(6)
Jane   posh sort of (.) by association yeah .hhh and erm you

(7)
Jane   know some people (.) **don't** realise that other people

(8)
Jane   see us that way .hh [and you] so like you know (-)
Roberta   [yeah]

This extract of talk, which was recorded by the girls on a different tape but follows on from the above, contains an explicit description of the difference in 'mentality' which makes it difficult for Jane, Roberta, Nicky and Elizabeth to relate to their schoolmates. Similarly to Nicky's objection to their friends' *mentality* about skiing at Val d'Isère, more than the *actual* skiing at Val d'Isère, Jane constructs a lack of (social) awareness about one's economic and cultural capital as more problematic than the privileged social status itself. This allows Jane to contrast herself favourably with her schoolmates in spite of sharing the same privileged private-school background. Whereas Jane begins her portrayal of the 'rich but aware' group more carefully, by referring to this group as 'some people' (stave 2) and 'they' (stave 3), her own membership in this group of posh private-school girls becomes more evident from stave 4 when she uses the pronouns 'we' and 'us'. It has to be noted, however, that this self-definition as 'posh' is heavily hedged in various ways, not least by Jane's point that 'posh' is a label which is attributed to them because of their 'association' (stave 6) with a 'posh school' (stave 5). This implies that the girls' poshness is not really their own fault, that they themselves do not display or engage in any behaviour which could actually identify them as posh (such as skiing in Val d'Isère). Knowledge, this time in the form of social awareness, is constructed as highly significant capital in this group, which allows the girls to distance themselves from the other girls, despite attending the same private schools.

Extract 6: social awareness – continued

(9)
Jane   but if you might be sort of you know actually quite

(10)
Jane   posh .hh but **know** that other pe- that that's not (2)

(11)
Nicky   [it's like
Jane   you don't (.) it's not good to be perceived [like that

(12)
Jane   (.) and so you might try and **hide** it and [try and
Roberta   [middle

(13)
Jane   be sort of]   [yeah exactly] (.)
Roberta   class (skill)] middle [class school] (.)

(14)
Nicky   (xxxx)
Jane   [but some people just]   SOME PEOPLE JUST DON'T
Roberta   [people who go "oh no no no"] (xxxxxxxxxxxxxxxxx)

(15)
Nicky   you know]   [the way Pam like] (.) (xxxxxx)
Jane   EVEN **REAL]ISE** that [it's **there** (yeah)] (.) >some people<

(18)
Jane   just don't **think** that other people perceive you as sort

(17)
Nicky   [(yeah what everyone)]
Jane   of (-) you know **over-privileged**= [or whatever]
Roberta   (overprim)   = yeah

Jane indirectly suggests that being 'posh' (due to one's economic or
social background) is not as much of a problem as lacking knowledge
about one's own poshness. The social class connotation of the
term 'posh' is now clearly acknowledged by Roberta in staves 12
and 13.

Elizabeth Frazer's (1988, 1992) British upper-/upper-middle-class
private-school girls at times displayed guilt about their privileges but
also reported experience of 'overt class conflict and hostility' (1988:
348) as well as 'fear and dislike of the "lower classes" ' (1992: 106) in
their interviews. Other research provides further evidence of privileged
and/or private-school girls using 'the working class' as a 'negative reference group' (Hey 1997: 106), displaying feelings of superiority towards

'proles' (Hey 1997: 106), 'tarts' (Kenway 1990: 150) and white sock-wearing 'plebs' or 'Sharons' (Frazer 1988, 1992).

Although Roberta and her friends also once use a similarly derogatory term (see extract 21) their positioning is more complex, and they mostly strive to construct themselves as socially aware rather than pretentious, 'down to earth' rather than 'sheltered'. Moreover, Roberta's alignment with a middle-class status, rejected fiercely by Frazer's upper/upper-middle-class girls due to its connotations of nouveau riche (Frazer 1988: 349), also constitutes a performance of 'down-classing', if one considers the extremely high social status of the occupation of her own and the other girls' parents. Jane goes as far as to suggest that their privileged backgrounds should be hidden (stave 12) as 'it's not good to be perceived like that' (stave 11). Jane, Roberta, Elizabeth and Nicky cannot claim that they are any less privileged than their 'sheltered' peers, but they can certainly maintain that they are more socially aware of their economic and cultural capital.

Cool girls

The girls' talk about social class and their privileged private-school lives also provides an interesting and significant background to an interpretation of more local identity practices and positions that characterise their interaction. In their conversations about drugs, music, sex (see Chapter 8), and school, Roberta and her friends frequently adopt what I, and at times even the girls themselves, identify as 'cool' positions. This coolness is indexed by a display of knowledge about, liberal tolerance and even personal experience of street-wise or non-conformist practices, for example in relation to soft-drugs and non-mainstream music, or by an alignment with mitigated anti-school or anti-authority stances. However, the girls make sure that they never come across as trying to be too 'hard' (like fans of Gangsta Rap, 'real' drug addicts or truants).

Roberta and her friends' striving for coolness differentiates them from other pro-academic middle-class femininities, such as Mary Bucholtz's (1996, 1999) nerds, with whom the four girls share an emphasis on intelligent and academic selves, or Eckert's (1989, 2000) middle-class, school/authority-oriented 'jock' girls. Interestingly, Eckert's research in US highschools found coolness to dominate identity constructions of 'burnout' girls who were oriented to working-class rather than higher-education trajectories like Roberta and her friends (whereas the jock girls seek popularity rather than coolness). Penelope Eckert and Sally McConnell-Ginet (1995: 492) define the coolness of the 'burnout' girls as:

a kind of toughness without the added implication of physical power associated with male burnouts. Coolness is a viable alternative to institutional popularity: it asserts independence of institutionally imposed norms, willingness to flaunt the injunctions of authorities and claim all the privileges of adulthood if and when one so desires.

Following Eckert and McConnell-Ginet's findings I define coolness as tame non-conformity. My data suggest that a display of coolness is one of the main ways for Roberta and her friends to distance themselves from posh, privileged and sheltered private-school femininities without aligning themselves with stereotypes of tough working-class identities. The coolness negotiated by Roberta and her private-school friends at times orients to stereotypically masculine subject positions, although sexualised hypermasculinity constitutes a boundary just like extreme toughness.

I argue that coolness is valued as significant local 'cultural capital' (Bourdieu 1984) in this privileged friendship group of private-school girls. Just like their display of social awareness, an alignment with coolness allows Roberta and her friends to present themselves as unlike the other (posh and sheltered) girls at their private school, with whom they share the legitimate cultural capital in the form of their elite education and formal knowledge. I will exemplify and discuss the pursuit of (the 'right' amount of) coolness in the talk of Roberta, Nicky, Elizabeth and Jane in relation to the discourses, types of knowledge and positions that are apparent in their talk about drugs, music and school and, on a lexical level, in relation to their use of slang and swearwords.

Drugs

Roberta and her friends' talk about drugs on the self-recorded tapes is particularly interesting given the complete lack of attention the topic received in the two other (East End, working-class) groups of girls I studied at the same time. Eckert and McConnell-Ginet's (1992: 492) US highschool research found that (working-class-oriented) burnouts used drugs as 'a powerful symbol of their rejection of adult authority and their assertion of adult autonomy' whereas (middle-class-oriented) jocks were associated with an image of 'squeaky-cleanness'. Equally, the academically minded (middle-class) nerds in Bucholtz (1996: 122) did not drink or do drugs. Further evidence for the subversive meaning of cannabis use among teenagers is provided by Kehily and Pattman (2006: 51), whose study of British sixth formers reveals that cannabis is still an important 'marker of deviance and rebellion' when used by younger students and, continues to connote 'streetwise' knowledge even among older students (ibid. 47, 52).

When Roberta and her friends talk about the use of cannabis and other 'substances', they balance their knowledge of and concern about the effects and the taboo status of drugs, informed by dominant discourses about physical and social implications of drug addiction, with a display of nonchalance, 'liberal tolerance' (Kehily and Pattman 2006: 51) and even excitement about drug use/rs, which allows them to signal tame non-conformity or coolness.

In the following story Roberta reveals that her father made an interesting discovery when emptying of the drawers of her brother, who is on a gap-year-trip after his A-level exams.

Extract 7: spliff ends and pill bags

(1)
Jane   [OH MY]
Roberta   **my dad (.) my dad** cleared out his drawers [it just had]

(2)
Jane   GO:[:D]   [SERIOU]SLY=
Roberta   [it] just had l[ike]   =%spliff ends and (.) like%

(3)
Nicky   (.) condoms]
Roberta   (.) empty]   (draw) bags yeah condoms all that kind of

(4)
Jane   [O]H MY GO:D   [how **shock**]ing
Roberta   shi[t]   (-) my dad just [didn't]   my my

(5)
Roberta   brother just said "**I** don't **care** I am so far away they can

(6)
Elizabeth   what did your brother what
Roberta   just find whatever they want"

(7)
Elizabeth   did your dad think
Roberta   (-) I don't think he really ca:red (1)

(8)
Roberta   there were just loads of just **dodgy** things in there just

(9)
Jane   %oh my God%
Elizabeth   Ecstasy]
Roberta   like [p]ill bags and stuff   it's really dod]gy
?   [mm]

(10)
Roberta   yeah *{laughs quietly}* (-) stuff like that (-)
?   (-)*{howls}*

(11)
Nicky   *{laughs}*=
Roberta   quite dodge

Whereas Roberta highlights her brother's coolness (achieved by his positioning as a non-repentant user of soft drugs) and her father's liberal
parenting style (indicated by his alleged tolerance of this son's drug-
taking), the other girls' reactions to the story vary. In staves 1–2 Jane
expresses her shock about what she initially seems to interpret as a viola-
tion of Roberta's brother's privacy and as a display of parental authority.
However, Jane's repetition of 'oh my God' in stave 9 (and perhaps already
in stave 4) is an evaluation of the content of the drawers and, by extension, of Roberta's brother himself. Jane's reaction evaluates the finding of
condoms, spliff ends and pill bags as 'shocking' (stave 4), thereby invoking
a moralising (anti-drug) discourse which positions her very much in alignment with the squeaky-clean middle-class femininity that Eckert (1989,
2000) associates with jock girls and Bucholtz (1996, 1998) with nerds.

    However, although the 'dodginess' or taboo status of the items is
acknowledged explicitly by Roberta in staves 8, 9 and 11 and implicitly
by the howling sound in stave 10, the other girls largely try to refrain
from signalling shock and indignation. Instead they collaborate in the
narration of the event by pre-empting some of the suspicious items
found in the drawers (see stave 3, Nicky: 'condoms' and stave 9:
Elizabeth: 'Ecstasy'). Their ability to understand Roberta's implicatures
and slang terms, that is, to understand that 'pill bags' need to be interpreted as 'bags of a drug called Ecstasy' and that 'spliff ends' means
'remainders of cannabis cigarettes', together with Roberta's use of a very
colloquial or even coarse register ('dodgy', 'that kind of shit') positions

the girls as having the necessary insider or 'streetwise' (Kehily and Pattman 2006: 51) knowledge to 'talk the talk' about class A and C drugs. Similarly to their discussions about sex (see Chapter 8) most of the girls in this group make a conscious effort to distance themselves from naïve, sheltered or moralising young femininities and instead mirror the liberal and cool stances of the two main characters in the story.

In the following staves the girls experiment with less harmful intoxicating substances and the subject positions these experiments offer, after Jane discovers smelling salts in Roberta's brother's room.

Extract 8: smelling salts and spliffs

(1)
Jane   (-) hey listen has anyone smelt these <u>smelling</u>

(2)
Jane   salts*{laughing}*
Roberta   =**don't** do that you'll get a fucking head rush (.)

(3)
?Nicky   let me smell
Jane   THEY'RE AMAZ]ING   (-) SMELL THEM
Elizabeth   let me see
Roberta   they're really erm]

(4)
Jane   [(they're xxxxxxxx)
Elizabeth   are these the things tha[t they always say

(5)
Jane   [yeah yeah]   [imagine]
Elizabeth   ["quick] get the sm[elling salts"]
Roberta   [yeah]   you get fuck[ing **high**]

(6)
Jane   you've just fainted and smell **that** (.)   [unbeliev]able
Roberta   *{faint laugh}*   (.) y[ou get high]

(7)
Jane   *{laughs}* <u>SMELL IT like give it</u>
Elizabeth   (-) **UAGHH***{disgusted}*
Roberta   (.) you'll sneeze

(8)
Jane   <u>back to me it's **amazing**</u>]*{high pitched}*
Elizabeth   that's got amm]onium in it it's **poisonous**

(9)
Jane   (-) no look (I)-   [I don't know but (.) it' s just
Elizabeth   that's ammoni[a

(10)
Jane   *{sniffs and breaths out}* it's (just) so weird]
Elizabeth   it stinks] it's the
Roberta   <u>oh my God] Jane is</u>

(11)
Nicky   let me smell
Elizabeth   most disgus]ting smell that I've smelt in my **life**
Roberta   <u>addicted]</u>*{slightly amused}*

In this extract the girls are playing with subject positions of being
drug consumers, displaying either expert knowledge (Roberta) or
novice exhilaration (Jane) about the effect of the smelling salts.
Roberta's initial 'warning' about the potentially intoxicating effect of
the smelling salts does not act as a deterrent for Jane, Nicky and
Elizabeth. Quite the opposite, it makes them even more determined to
try it out (stave 3). Thus it seems that all the girls initially embrace the
opportunity to experience something 'forbidden' or slightly dangerous. Jane appears particularly thrilled about the intense smell ('unbe-
lievable', stave 6 and 'amazing', staves 3, 8) and gives a playful performance of becoming addicted by inviting everybody to smell the salts
(staves 3, 7) but urging them to return the precious substance to her
immediately (staves 7–8). Jane's performance as a 'drug addict', which
is supported by paralinguistic and nonverbal cues such as her laughter
and delighted voice, is acknowledged by Roberta in staves 10–11, 'of
my God Jane is addicted'.

Although Roberta signals several times that she is aware of the
potential danger of the salts (staves 2, 5, 6, 7), her amused tone of
voice in staves 10–11 contributes to a presentation of herself as both
knowledgeable and unconcerned about this danger. Most importantly,
Roberta again displays her streetwise, insider-knowledge about drugs in
this extract. She uses the appropriate slang 'to get a fucking head rush'
(stave 2) and 'you get (fucking) high' (stave 5 and stave 6) to refer to
the intoxicating effect of the salts and reinforces the strength of her

claims by the coarse slang modifier 'fucking' (staves 2 and 5). Both Roberta and Jane's performances therefore demonstrate that streetwise knowledge and experience is valued highly in this group; it allows the girls to accumulate capital in the form of coolness.

It needs to be noted, however, that this performance of streetwise coolness is not the only form of capital valued in the group. It is countered by Elizabeth's display of more traditional academic/literary knowledge (about the historic use of smelling salts – staves 4–5) and her rational argument about the salt's scientific make-up ('that's ammonia' – staves 8, 9) as well as its dangerous effect 'it's poisonous' (stave 8), which draws on a 'pseudo-scientific discourse' about drugs (Coates 1999). Thus the girls' attempts to highlight their emotional exhilaration and streetwise coolness is balanced by Elizabeth's 'bourgeois rationality' (Walkerdine et al. 2001: 173), which reproduces rather than others their private-school, upper-middle-class femininity (see also Chapter 8).

However, even Elizabeth is not entirely unaffected by the group's struggle for streetwise knowledge.

Extract 9: smelling salts and spliffs – continued

(12)
Nicky   (-) (Jane)   {laughs}
Roberta   (-) yeah (but no) it's really **mental**

(13)
Nicky   %sorry%
Jane   (-) it's like it's strange it's like

(14)
Nicky   why has he got them (1)
Jane   <cotton wool>   (1)
Elizabeth   (1) {deep laugh} (1) God that really was
Roberta   (1)

(15)
Nicky   OH MY **GOD**]
Jane   I KNOW (.)
Elizabeth really unpleasant]
Roberta   on his last night] here (.)   he inhaled]
?   {LAUGHS}

(16)

Nicky	oh my God] it's horrible]	
Jane	it's A**MA**ZING]	it's really scary]
Elizabeth		isn't that ammonium N]icky it's ammonium isn't] it

This short extract contains traces of many of the different discourses and stances that the girls invoked in relation to drugs and the smelling salts earlier. Roberta's cool slang phrase about the effect of the salt 'it's really mental' (stave 12) is countered by Elizabeth's more rational and detached assessment of the sensation of the salt as 'really unpleasant' (stave 15) as well as her request for factual confirmation from 'scientist' Nicky (stave 16). Jane's juxtaposition of 'it's AMAZING' and 'it's really scary' (at the same time interrupted and linked by Nicky's 'it's horrible') in stave 16 shows once more that the danger (and horrible smell) of the salt constitutes a thrill.

The most interesting moment, however, occurs in staves 13–14, when Nicky's question about the purpose of the smelling salts for Roberta's brother results in a significant pause (probably accompanied by a revealing non-verbal sign from Roberta), and then knowing laughter by Elizabeth. In this instance the entire group, including Elizabeth, signals the value of streetwise knowledge (that smelling salts are used to bring about alertness after drug-induced stupor or even unconsciousness), which positions the girls as cool rather than as sheltered and naïve.

The following narrative about the events on the evening before Roberta's brother's departure for his gap year provides an explicit example of the purpose of the smelling salts. Moreover, it shifts the focus from passive to active knowledge of drugs.

Extract 10: smelling salts and spliffs – continued

(17)

Roberta on our last night on his last night here (-) erm

(18)

Roberta (-) it was me and him and we had we had like a couple

(19)

Elizabeth	/mm	
Roberta	of %spliffs yeah%	and I *[laughing]*was going to

(20)
Roberta   <u>school the next morning</u> I remember .hh and erm (.) like

(21)
Roberta   a few of his friends came round and we were all just

(22)
Roberta   oh it was **ridiculous** we were all just sitting here just

(23)
Roberta   I was s::o gone (.) and everyone was just sitting

(24)
Roberta   there going *{laughing}*"<u>oh my God pity</u>)" and he'd (xxxxx)

(25)
Roberta   he'd go *{deep/drowsy}*"<u>shit I've got so much stuff</u> (xxxxx)

(26)
Elizabeth   mm=
Roberta   *{slightly amused}*<u>I'm going in three hours</u>"   =like he hadn't

(27)
Elizabeth   =oh my God
Roberta   **packed** *{laughing}*<u>yeah</u>=   and he just grabs

(28)
Roberta   them and he just goes *{makes sniffing noise}* "SHIT"

(29)
Nicky   *{laughter- - - - - - - - - - - - }*
Elizabeth   *{laughter- - - - - - - - - - - - }*
Jane   *{laughter- - - - - - - - - - - - }*
Roberta   >*<u>and then then he went</u>< "right" and he just shoved *{laughing}*

(30)
Jane   *{laughs- - - - - }*
Roberta   <u>everything into (his bag and just)</u> like sat down again

In this extract Roberta reveals not only her brother's but also her own experience of smoking spliffs, that is, cannabis cigarettes (note the use of slang). This is the first instance in which one of the girls admits to 'doing' drugs rather than just 'knowing' or 'talking' about drugs.

The reduced utterance volume of 'spliffs' suggests that this admission of first-hand knowledge about drugs has to be negotiated carefully. All of the girls were aware of their school's strict no-drugs policy and my connection with the girls' school may be a reason for Roberta to be concerned about admitting to use soft drugs. However, the data show that Roberta is more concerned about her *friends'* opinion about her familiarity with cannabis than about the risk of going on record with her revelation in front of me. In stave 19 Elizabeth produces some brief acknowledgement which conveys a lack of personal indignation about Roberta's admission, and thereby encourages Roberta to proceed (and return to a normal utterance volume and a laughing voice). After her initially hesitant self-positioning as a user of soft drugs Roberta now seems to be very comfortable in this role. Rather than minimising the strong effect of the cannabis on herself and the others, she exaggerates it with a slang phrase containing an intensifier 'I was s::o gone' in stave 23 and with the utterance 'it was ridiculous' in stave 22, which allows her to claim coolness, even more so as she had to go to school the following day (staves 19–20).

In staves 25–30 Roberta then proceeds to paint a picture of her brother's coolness. When imitating her brother in staves 25–26 she adopts a deeper and very relaxed voice which indexes his drowsy state as well as his maleness. Roberta then gives an example of her brother's (drug-induced) carefree state of mind. He is not too worried about the fact that he still has many things to do before his departure three hours later, he has not even packed his bags for his gap year. I would argue that Roberta's re-enacting of her brother's behaviour is also an indirect performance of stereotypical young masculinity, presenting him as carefree, 'a good laugh' (Frosh et al. 2002) and a man of few (and not very refined) words. The brother's coolness is not only signalled by his spliff smoking, but also by his insider knowledge of how to counteract the effect of one drug with another (see Kehily and Pattman 2006. In staves 27 and 28 Roberta describes how her brother achieves a sudden energy boost (or at least a moment of alertness) with the help of the smelling salts. This sharp sniffing sound, followed by another loud interjection, 'SHIT' (likely to be supported by some nonverbal signs that mimic her brother's act of sniffing and its awakening effect), is received with laughter by all the girls (stave 29). The laughter continues (staves 30, 31) when Roberta goes on to describe the unorthodox and funny style of packing which her brother subsequently adopts under the influence of cannabis counteracted by smelling salts.

This narrative shows that soft-drug use indexes coolness in the group and that this performance of coolness, which is evaluated so positively by the girls, can carry connotations of masculinity. However, cool drug-use is very different from hard-drug addiction, as the following extract from the remainder of the girls' conversation about the smelling salts shows.

Extract 11: smelling salts and spliffs – continued

(31)
Jane   that's [(cool)]   [they're] quite~
Elizabeth   *{laughs}*
Roberta   [they they] are quite [cool in]

(32)
Roberta   situations like that (-) we've got murein as well (to go

(33)
Jane   =*fucking hell=
Roberta   go xxxxxxxx we've) got all the kit=   =%it's

unrelated to Roberta's story: Jane has just discovered an interesting book

(34)
Elizabeth   *{laughs}*
Roberta   <u>really awful</u>*{amused}* we are like drug addicts%

In stave 31 Roberta herself chooses the word 'cool' when referring to the useful effect of smelling salts in certain situations. The meaning of the word 'cool' is here closer to 'good' or 'useful', but it still seems to carry a layer of meaning associated with the tame non-conformity and streetwise knowledge that I define as significant for the girls' discursive construction of coolness. Roberta then reinforces her brother's and her own coolness by indicating that they have a selection of smelling salts (staves 32–33). However, Roberta needs to tread a narrow line between being cool and bad, in order not to be perceived as a 'waster' (Kehily and Pattman 2006) or a 'stoner' (Eckert and McConnell-Ginet 1995). By stating that she is *like* a drug addict rather than that she *is* a drug addict in stave 34, Roberta clearly differentiates between being knowledgeable about and experienced in drug use (which is cool) and being addicted to drugs (which is bad). Thus Roberta's display of drug-related coolness, which, in this instance, appears interlinked with her brother's performance of carefree young masculinity and is supported by her friends, allows her to position herself in opposition to a sheltered upper-middle-class femininity, without aligning herself with 'real' drug addicts.

Music

On the tapes the girls frequently speak about, listen, sing and play along to a wide range of (non-classical) music, from the very mainstream to less popular genres and tunes. In this section I focus on the girls' talk about DJing, vinyl records, Rap/Hip Hop music and 'scratching'. In the vein of Bourdieu's (1984) classification of musical tastes I shall interpret the girls' musical allegiances as signifiers of socio-cultural meanings and positionings. However, the taste of music foregrounded by the girls on their tapes is very different from what Bourdieu (1984: 16), in his analysis of 1960s France, defines as 'highbrow' or 'legitimate' and as characteristic of the 'dominant class that are richest in educational capital'. Differently from many of their same-age peers in late 1990s Britain the girls in this elite school are in fact very familiar with these 'highbrow' musical tastes. Their school prides itself in a long tradition of classical music education, with composers of international acclaim as part of its staff, regular concerts and orchestra performances, and 80 per cent of students taking instrumental music lessons. Nevertheless, my analysis shows that Roberta and her friends, who certainly demonstrate their 'highbrow' tastes/cultural capital in many other respects such as their academic debates about literature and science, want to display musical tastes and knowledge which are neither 'highbrow' nor 'popular' (the label Bourdieu uses to refer to 'light' or 'popularised' classical music) but instead non-mainstream and streetwise. I argue that the non-conformist positions that the girls adopt in their negotiation of music imagery constitute further resources for their discursive construction of cool adolescent identities, which stand in opposition to (stereotypes of) sheltered elite school femininities.

Extract 12: "DJ Berta in the house":

(1)
Roberta   I can do scratching with this record *{blows off dust}*

(2)
Nicky   *{laughs}*
Roberta   I bought this in (eight-hundred) (.) (alright)

(3)
Nicky   <u>DJ Berta in the house</u>*{slightly amused}*
Roberta   .hh *{slightly ironic}*<u>I am</u>

(4)
Roberta   <u>fucking wicked</u> (.) when I am in the mood I can do

(5)
Elizabeth   wh[at]   [what]
Roberta   some really good %**sh**it% (1)   [I] need another [deck]

(6)
Elizabeth do [you do Roberta]
Roberta   [then I'm gonna] get really good (-) (xxxxxxxxxxxxx

(7)
Elizabeth <u>what's] she doing are you DJing</u>*{amused}*
Roberta   xxxxx)]   (-) I can do some

(8)
Roberta   (scra-) *{amused}*<u>it's really (shit) though (the) you</u>

(9)
Roberta   <u>sort of muck around it's no **good** but</u>~ (1) oh shit what's

(10)
Nicky   it's all /scratched
Roberta   (the fuck's) happening   *{operates record player}*

In stave 1 Roberta reveals that she is able to do 'scratching' on a vinyl record. Scratching is a DJing technique which consists of a vinyl record 'being briefly moved backwards and forwards during play to produce a rhythmic scratching effect' (*SOED*). Scratching was introduced by (male) African American Hip-Hop artists like Grandmaster Flash, frequently to accompany the boasts and verbal duals contained in the lyrics of their Rap songs. Rap music and scratching constituted the background for competitive street corner performances, 'block' or park parties of Hip Hop DJs (providing the music) and MCs (providing the spoken rhymes) in the socially deprived Bronx of 1980s New York (Gay 2001; Toop 1991: 65). By showing off her scratching and DJing skills Roberta displays coolness, as she signals her familiarity with styles, genres and practices of music (scratching, DJing) which associate her with non-mainstream or even streetwise contexts and subject positions (dance club/street culture; DJ). Moreover, although DJing is certainly not an all-male domain any more, I would argue that the coolness it indexes retains connotations of masculinity, both in the club scene and even more clearly in the Hip Hop scene.[3] Thus Roberta's display of (streetwise and masculine) coolness does not only distance her from a 'highbrow' or even 'popular' taste of music, but ultimately also from a sheltered (white) upper-middle-class femininity.

On a lexical level Roberta signals her coolness and insider knowledge by using jargon like 'scratching' (stave 1) and 'deck' (stave 5). Roberta then increases the informality of her register with the help of slang expressions 'I am fucking wicked' (stave 4), 'I can do some really good shit' (stave 5), and 'you sort of muck around' (stave 9) as well as with swear words 'shit' and 'fuck' (staves 8, 9). This increase in linguistic informality and slang aids her orientation to coolness associated with the subject position of the DJ. Roberta's performance as DJ, which is not lacking in self-irony as her amused tone of voice shows (staves 3–4), is acknowledged and to some extent mirrored by Nicky as early as in stave 3 'DJ Berta in the house'.

The extract captures how Roberta maintains a leading role in positioning coolness as cultural capital for the group. Although most other girls are keen to mirror her coolness, for example by following Roberta's scratching performance, careful negotiations are necessary to establish an acceptable amount of coolness in the group.

Extract 13: stuff on vinyl

(1)
Jane   *{hums beat}*-
Roberta   I love this listening stuff on vinyl (-) you

(2)
Nicky   (-) yeah I buy everything
Roberta   /know (.) I really like it

(3)
Nicky   on vinyl now (.) much be/?/er it's got
?Nicky   [cool]
Jane   s[o much] **cheaper**

(4)
Nicky	good vibes (off] it)	
Elizabeth	%it's a bit sa:d%]	[it's]
Roberta	(-) I think it's pretty [good]	

(5)
| Elizabeth | trying to be cool (.) to buy stuff on vi[nyl] |
| Roberta | [no] but some |

(6)
Nicky	(but loads)]	(xxxxxxxx)
Jane		yeah
Roberta	but come on] you can only get stuff like (xxxxxxxx)	

(7)
Nicky	[yeah]
Jane	some stuff you can real[ly on]ly [get on vin]yl
Roberta	[(xxxxxxxx)] and good

The discussion is about the benefits of vinyl in comparison to CDs, but implicit is a negotiation about the appropriate amount of coolness for the group. Roberta, Nicky and Jane make their pro-vinyl stance explicit from stave 1 onwards, arguing that vinyl is 'better', 'cool', 'much cheaper' (stave 3) and, somewhat ambiguously, that it produces 'good vibes' (stave 4). Apart from the argument about cost, however, the reasons for the girls' preference for vinyl are not made explicit. This lack of explicitness indicates that the girls' main motivation for buying vinyl is not related to the actual attributes of the product, but instead to its symbolic value. Buying vinyl, just like scratching, allows the girls to present themselves as connoisseurs of a non-mainstream or even underground music scene (Fikentscher 2003: 309), which contributes to their performance of coolness.

This discursive performance is again supported on a micro-linguistic level. When Nicky pronounces the word 'better', she does so not with the (standard) voiceless alveolar plosive /t/ but instead with a marked (non-standard) glottal stop /ʔ/. The traditional sociolinguistic association of this non-standard variant with working classness and informality (as well as masculinity) renders the use of the glottal stop particularly interesting in this group of privileged private-school girls. Indeed Nicky is the only member in the group who uses the glottal stop intervocally more frequently, and this is even more striking if one considers the high social status of her parents in the fields of medicine and the arts. It is also noteworthy that Nicky is not accommodating to her friendship group or to the upper-middle-class context of her elitist private school. Nicky's more salient usage of the glottal stop may index her membership in another community of practice, particularly the pop band that she is a member of, and show her awareness of the feature's symbolic value as a marker of coolness, which supports her discursive alignment with a non-mainstream, vinyl-loving subject position in this instance.

The three girls' performance of coolness is both acknowledged and resisted by Elizabeth. According to Elizabeth, buying vinyl records (rather than CDs) is 'a bit sad' (stave 4) because 'it's trying to be cool' (stave 5). Although Elizabeth is the member of the group who is most resistant to a display of tame non-conformity or coolness per se, her utterance here suggests that she is particularly critical of what she perceives as distinct *efforts* being made by the others to *present* themselves as cool. Interestingly, the other girls in the group whose discursive practices clearly position them as cool do also not admit to *aiming for* coolness in their defence. By giving more 'objective' reasons for the benefits of vinyl they implicitly deny Elizabeth's allegations (Roberta: stave 6; Jane: stave 7). Of course, making an effort to be cool would defeat the whole purpose of coolness (see also Kehily and Pattman 2006). Indeed, the following extract confirms that *trying* to be cool is not cool at all.

Extract 14: Gangsta Rap and Pet Shop Boys

(1)
Roberta   I can't understand Christina Howland's taste in music

(2)
Nicky   =yeah her [Gangsta Rap]
Elizabeth   [she tries to be]
Roberta   (can you) explain it to me=

(3)
Nicky   [who does she] (like)
Elizabeth   hard and lis[ten to like-]
Roberta   SHE LIKES like Gangsta Rap (1)

(4)
Roberta   and then she likes like Savage Garden (-) and she likes
Elizabeth   .hhh{amused}

(5)

?Nicky		(1) Five [are cack]	[she really likes the]
Roberta	Five		
Jane		[serio-] no but	[seriously like]

{loud music}

(6)

Nicky	Pet Shop Boys	
Roberta		(-) yeah she like **bought** their album (-)

This brief extract shows how difficult it is to negotiate the boundaries of acceptable coolness in this group. The girls signal their scepticism about a fellow student, Christina, who listens to extremely 'hard' Rap music on one hand and soft or mainstream pop music such as Savage Garden, the Pet Shop Boys and Five on the other. Whereas the group did not find it problematic to appropriate some musical practices associated with Hip Hop culture, such as vinyl scratching, they collaboratively reject Gangsta Rap, which tends to be associated with the violence and criminality of tough street life in poor (African) American urban neighbourhoods (Borthwick and Moy 2004: 159; Springhall 1998: 149). At the same time the girls distance themselves from the safe, mainstream allegiance offered by boy bands, such as Five, and pop bands such as the Pet Shop Boys and Savage Garden. Characteristically, Elizabeth's criticism is directed more towards their fellow student's exaggerated efforts to present herself as hard by listening to Gangsta Rap (2 Staves–3), whereas Roberta, Jane and Nicky seem to find it more worrying that Christina likes mainstream pop music and even bought the album by the Pet Shop Boys (staves 4–6).

It seems that the girls' effort to resolve what they see as contradictions in relation to Christina's taste of music, resisting music that is too soft on the one hand and too hard on the other, is a metaphor for this group's struggle for the adequate type of cool adolescent femininity: not too mainstream, sheltered and upper-middle-class but also not too streetwise, tough and working-class. Although the girls try very hard to present themselves as non-conforming in their struggle for coolness, it is a tame non-conformity that they are aligning themselves with. Thus, just like drug addiction constitutes a boundary for their cool talk about drugs, the hardness of Gangsta Rap constitutes a boundary for the coolness that is indexed by the girls' non-mainstream musical allegiances.

School

The girls even try to position themselves as non-conformist or cool with respect to their school. Their (very tame) anti-school stance needs to be understood in the context of the very pro-academic and elite status of their school and, in relation to that, the girls' own academic striving. School P is a prestigious single-sex private school in London which seeks to establish a partnership between the girls, their parents and teachers to maintain its excellent position in national league tables. Once girls have been selected by the school via entrance exams they are expected to work hard but they also know that they will be rewarded with very good grades and offers from elite universities after their A-level exams. Roberta, Elizabeth, Nicky and Jane identify themselves implicitly with their school's ethos and their own educational capital in many ways by presenting themselves as learned and well read in their frequent debates (see Chapter 8) and by constantly topicalising teachers, exams and academic subjects. This striving for legitimate cultural capital in the form of academic recognition and success, supported by teachers and parents, has been identified as central to the reproduction of young British middle-class femininity by Beverley Skeggs (1997) and Valerie Walkerdine et al. (2001). A number of other empirical studies document the foregrounding of academic selves amongst (British, US and Australian) students on middle-class educational trajectories, whether in elite/private schools or well regarded/successful state schools (Bucholtz 1998, 1999; Eckert 1989, 2000; Eckert and McConnell-Ginet 1992, 1995; Hey 2001 in Harris 2004: 105–7; Kehily and Pattman 2006; Kenway 1990).

My investigation of Roberta and her friends' efforts to adopt a tame anti-school stance therefore needs to be seen in the context of the girls' own awareness of their trajectories as privileged private-school girls, which, differently from other girls at their age, presupposes a successful completion of A-level exams.

Extract 15: Kate

(1)
Roberta   I was speaking to my friend **Kate** and she was going (-)

(2)
Roberta   she said to me "so so are you doing A-levels then"
Jane   (1)
?   (1)

(3)
Roberta   hhh   [and I was] like "yeah" and she's like "yeah
Jane   (yeah) so [(xxxxxxx)]

(4)
Nicky   it's so weird
Roberta   yeah me too" (-) and that was like~ (.)

(5)
Nicky   to think we could (.) like (.) physically [leave] (-)
?Jane   [yeah]

(6)
Nicky   school=   forever [(>cause you know when you think<)]
Jane   I know   [(and) not only do they assume]=

(7)
Nicky   [but-]
Jane   =tha[t we] can do A-levels which (.) I mean **no-one**

(8)
Jane   **doesn't** do A-levels but (.) when I just think about

(9)
Nicky   [yeah]
Jane   them assuming that we are gonna get As (.) [you know]

(10)
Jane   and then you think that some people aren't even **doing**

(11)
Nicky   [yeah]   (ah) it's just so weird
Roberta   GC[SEs] d'you know what I mean
?Elizabeth   [yeah]

The extract is part of a longer conversation in which the girls reveal
their (negative) attitude towards school as well as their social awareness (see also Extracts 1, 2, 16, 17). Roberta's rendering of her
exchange with Kate serves two purposes. Firstly, it signals to the group
(who do not seem to know Kate, as Roberta's explicit introduction of
Kate as her 'friend' suggests) that Roberta's circle of friends is not
restricted to her upper-middle-class, private school context. Secondly,
Roberta implicitly also contrasts Kate (and her educational capital)
with her group of friends from the private school. By simply reproducing Kate's question without framing it as odd (stave 2), Roberta

actually emphasises its oddness, signalling that a question like this speaks for itself. The other girls display their understanding of Roberta's implied meaning and gravity of such a question immediately, if not explicitly, with the help of a meaningful pause at the end of stave 2, a minimal acknowledgement, 'yeah', in stave 3, and an incomplete utterance with a suggestive 'like' in stave 4. In the following staves the girls go on record with their thoughts, revealing that not doing A-levels is inconceivable to them, whereas for other people not doing A-levels or even leaving school before their GCSE exams is the norm. The girls' acknowledgement that they will do A-levels and their realisation that they are expected to do so most successfully, with A-grades, serves as an interesting backdrop for the following extracts, which depict how the girls take great care not to position themselves as too pro-school.

Extract 16: hating school

(1)
Roberta   I used to be so organised >and everything< at primary

(2)
Roberta   school (-) I used to really enjoy stuff and now I just

(3)
Nicky   *{laughs}*   (-) I really [hate school]
Roberta   **hate** it I really **hate** school   [(I could)]

(4)
Nicky   it's it's such don't you feel
Roberta   **so** do without it you /know
?Elizabeth   *{sings along}*

(5)
Nicky   like you're just (-) like (-) it's just (-) dedicating

(6)
Nicky   your life to something (.) that you don't wanna do (-)

This display of 'hating school' suggests that, unlike Eckert and McConnell-Ginet (1992, 1995) Jocks, that is, US high-school students oriented to middle-class lives, the four British elite schoolgirls do not seek to construct their personal identities in full alignment with the institutional norms of their school. In some ways, Roberta's and Nicky's anti-school proclamations even appear reminiscent of the British working-class girls in Angela McRobbie's influential sociological study in the 1970s. McRobbie found that working-class girls emphasise their opposition to school in order to distance themselves from middle-class 'swots' (inverted commas McRobbie, 1978: 103). Of course, 'swots', 'boffins' or 'geeks' are subject positions which are othered by adolescents from a wide range of backgrounds, including state-school boys in pursuit of popular masculinity (Frosh et al. 2002); working-class lads who prefer 'having a laugh' to presenting themselves as school conformist (Willis 1977); and even A-level students who are concerned about being seen as 'teetotal boffs' (Kehily and Pattman 2006: 46). An exception to this list are, of course, students who actively embrace a nerd identity, such as Bucholtz's (1996, 1999) academic and uncool US high-school girls.

However, in the context of Roberta and her friends' private school the teachers' and parents' expectations of hard academic work is shared by the students. Frosh et al. (2002: 207) found that private-school boys were the only male pupils who were not concerned about admitting to working hard, arguing that the high fees that their parents paid and the school's ethos left them 'no choice but to work hard'. Similarly, it does not occur to Nicky or Roberta that there may be an alternative to their life of hard academic work. Thus, when Nicky expresses her dislike of 'dedicating your life to something you don't wanna do' she simultaneously reveals that she *is*, in fact, dedicating herself to school. Nicky's anti-school feelings appear tame in comparison to the resistance expressed by my Bangladeshi girls (from a working-class background), who play truant and refuse to do their homework, or by many state-school students aiming to position themselves in opposition to swots or nerds (Frosh et al. 2002; Kehily and Pattman 2006; McRobbie 1978). Thus, Roberta and her friends' evident acceptance of doing hard work in preparation for A-levels and university education, paired with their interest in acquiring knowledge and displaying academic selves (see also Chapter 8) leaves them few options to construct themselves in opposition to an identity of a swot, and ultimately of a compliant private-school girl. However, Roberta's and Nicky's expressions of anti-school feelings achieve just that. Thus, Roberta and her friends are again engaged in a balancing act: they seek to create some distance from the very pro-school existence that they are expected to lead as students at their high-achieving private school, but at the same time they are not displaying any real resistance like refusing to do school work, truanting or dropping out of school.

Extract 17: hating school – continued

(7)
Nicky   [I know it benefits you >(and all)< yeah::]
Roberta   (-) yeah but [(xxxxxxxxxxxxxxxxxxxxxxxxxxxxxxxxxxxxxx)]

(8)
Nicky   >yeah yeah yeah but-<   [>it's just (that)-<]
Jane   I don't hate [school]

(9)
Jane   cause I like (.) like actually (.) I (.) the I (.)
Elizabeth   *{continues humming}*

(10)
Jane   like lessons I hate but I like the thing of going

(11)
Jane   to school because I can see myself just (-) like (1)

(12)
Nicky   [discipline] *{laughs}*
Jane   [looking] back on school and thinking "I wish I was there

(13)
Jane   again" because when I think about I have such an easy

(14)
Nicky   yeah [I was thi-]
Jane   life going to school   [and li]ke being around my

(15)
Jane   friends and having   [that] like sort of school atmosphere
Roberta   [yeah]

(16)
Jane   just being young and being at school but all hating

(17)
Nicky   [yeah]   [(it's xxxxxx)] >cau[se I was
Jane   school [but li]ke being [(you know)]   [united
Roberta   [yeah]

(18)
Nicky   thinking like<]   [I was like]   [(I w-)]
Jane   in]=   =hating [school it's] just [like ni]ce
Roberta   yeah

In staves 7–8 Nicky signals her awareness of a discourse that praises the benefits of a good school education. Nicky's alignment with this discourse, marked by a more formal and impersonal register ('it benefits you'), highlights her ability to accept 'rational' pro-school/education arguments, which Walkerdine et al. (2001) deem central for the repro-duction of middle-class femininity. On the other hand, Nicky distances herself from this discourse of (middle-class and adult/mature) common sense by producing three fast and dismissive repetitions of 'yeah' followed by a disjunctive 'but' in stave 8.

In the following staves it is then up to Jane to find a compromise in the form of what I interpret as the group's mitigated and 'mature' anti-school stance, both denying and affirming that they 'hate school' (staves 10, 16–17, 18). After admitting that she does not hate school in stave 8 Jane produces multiple hesitations, fillers, repetitions and false starts which show her awareness of the problematic status of an explicit or unmiti-gated pro-school stance in the group. The remainder of the extract captures Jane's subsequent efforts to mitigate further, by introducing a differentiation between the academic and the social side of school. Her dislike of lessons, which she announces in stave 10, creates some distance from the school's pro-academic ethos, which the girls adhere to implic-itly in so many other ways (e.g. their striving for good marks and high academic standards).

Jane's anti-school stance is partially balanced by the mature rationality which is implicit in her argument. She is aware that going to school might be much easier than whatever is to follow later in life and looks forward to some grown-up reminiscing about the good old (school) days, which connote an idyllic, carefree existence (staves 11–14). Jane pro-school argument is that she enjoys school as a social arena which allows her to be with her friends (staves 14–16). However, even this argument about school as a social space for youthful solidarity (staves 16–18) positions her as more anti- than pro-school. Already in 1975 McRobbie found that the rejection of academic success by working-class girls went hand in hand with an acceptance of school as a location for their socialis-ing. McRobbie (ibid.: 104) writes about the girls' 'ability [...] to transform the school into the sphere, *par excellence*, for developing their social life, fancying boys, learning the latest dance, having a smoke together in the lavatories and playing up the teachers'. However, Jane and her friends differ from the girls described by McRobbie in significant ways, most notably by their striving for academic success, which is expected to lead to equally successful upper-middle-class career trajectories (see also Harris 2004; Kenway 1990; Walkerdine et al. 2001). Nevertheless it cannot be ignored that Jane makes an effort to signal a preference for the non-academic side of school life, an effort which is supported by Roberta and Nicky (see minimal support in staves 17–18).

Like McRobbie's working class and unlike Eckert's middle-class jocks, Jane and her friends aim to position themselves against the school as an establishment in this instance. When Jane states that she likes the feeling of 'being united in hating school' she invokes an 'us-against-them' discourse, which highlights her antagonistic position to school. Thus, three of the girls (Elizabeth does not signal any interest in the conversation) clearly make an effort not to present themselves as too pro-school, thereby signalling that they do not want to be perceived as conforming with the ethos and legitimate cultural capital associated with their private-school background in every respect. Again, this tame non-conformity allows the girls to foreground their own coolness and index more normal or 'real' (see below) adolescent identities, and thus to create some distance from the stereotype of a compliant, (upper-middle-class) private school girl.

Real girls

Balancing a display of non-conformist stances and streetwise knowledge (supported by swear and slang words and the occasional phonological non-standard marker) with a demarcation from tough or hard working-classness is the prerequisite for the girls' renegotiation of their private-school, upper-middle-class femininities as cool. Roberta plays a leading role in this balancing act, which is also strikingly apparent in her alignment with the subject position of 'real people', as the final section of my analysis shows.

The following stretch of talk occurred shortly after the girls' conversation about the lack of social awareness of some of their fellow students (Extracts 5, 6). Roberta has just compared her own taste in dance clubs to that of another girl, who prefers more extravagant venues such as the famous Café de Paris in London. Elizabeth then admits that she feels equally uncomfortable in 'rough' places.

Extract 18: 'real people'

(1)
Elizabeth   =I mean I don't I don't like going clubbing with

(2)
Elizabeth   my cousin in Hackney it's just not <u>fun</u>*{laughing faintly}*

(3)
Jane   *{laughs}*
Elizabeth   [that's it]
Roberta   they are probably a bit weird (.)   like th[ese clubs]

(4)
Elizabeth   y- you can't go anywhere without the police

(5)
Jane   *{laughs}*
Elizabeth   <u>arriving</u>*{laughing}*
Roberta   that's quite rough yeah but like (-)

In this extract Elizabeth continues with the depiction of the mythical other from the opposite end of the social spectrum which Nicky had started in her sketching of the stereotypical working-class labourer during her 'poems and mines' conversation (Extract 1). In the course of the girls' discussion about their tastes in dance clubs Elizabeth now cites location as a social class signifier. Elizabeth is not alone in her negative perception of the borough of Hackney in East London, which, despite rising house prices, and regeneration in some of its districts due to their association with the arts and media scene, finds it difficult to shake off its image as one of the toughest and most deprived (working class) boroughs of London's East End.[4] Thus Hackney is itself a signifier or 'cultural concept' (Silverstein 2004) with social class affiliations, indexed by the girls when referring to its 'weird' dance clubs (stave 3), its 'police' presence (stave 4) and its 'rough' life (stave 5).

Elizabeth's and Jane's laughter in staves 3 and 5 captures the girls' awareness of the sensitive nature of their subject, as they are treading a narrow line between differentiating themselves from what they associate with working-classness without invoking a traditional discourse of upper-middle-class superiority. As the talk continues, Roberta takes the lead in negotiating a position in opposition to both tough and posh clubs for the group.

Extract 19: 'real people' – continued

(6)
Jane   [(xxxxxx yeah)]
Roberta   the Blue Moon yeah it's like a [compromise becau]se

(7)
Roberta   you've got like real people who like (.) go to state

(8)
Roberta   school or who like have **jobs** and stuff and you've got

(9)
Roberta   like a few West Londoners yeah (-) and it's just like a

(10)
Elizabeth   %(xxxx)%   (right)
Roberta   mixture of **people** you /know   and it's like (-)

In spite of just having demonstrated her understanding for Elizabeth's concerns about clubs (and areas like Hackney) which are 'rough', Roberta clearly does not signal a preference for exclusive venues and crowds either. Employing dance clubs as 'cultural concepts' (Silverstein 2004) or metaphors indexing social class positions Roberta argues that the 'Blue Moon' constitutes a 'compromise' (stave 6) due to its 'mixture of people' (stave 10).

Central to Roberta's social positioning in this extract is her use and the (shifting) meaning of the noun phrase 'real people'. In staves 7–8 it becomes apparent that Roberta only defines people who go to state schools or who have jobs as 'real'. The 'West Londoners' on the other hand do not appear to count as real people (see repetition of 'you've got' in staves 7 and 8), although they play an important part in the mixed audience that attracts Roberta to her favourite club. Roberta's classification of the club's audience clearly carries social class connotations, relying on more complex signifiers such as socially meaningful 'tastes' (Bourdieu 1984) in clubs, as well as more traditional (but not particularly refined) criteria such as level of education and neighbourhood.

'Real' in this context, appears to refer to 'ordinary' people, that is, people who do not attend West End private schools like the girls themselves. However, the following staves show that Roberta seeks to identify as 'real' despite her private-school background.

Extract 20: real people – continued

(11)
Roberta   it's just real **people** it's just people (who're just

(12)
Roberta   there) they quite like music and stuff yeah
                                        {music on}

(13)
Roberta   and erm (1) but then if you go somewhere like (-)

(14)
Roberta   the Aquarium you get all these Sharoons and stuff

(15)
Roberta   and they're just really **embarrassing** clubs .hh and

(16)
Roberta   then you've got like Café de Paris which is just

(17)
Roberta   a whole other world
                            {playing record}

In stave 12 there is a shift in the meaning of 'real' to include Roberta and her friends despite being West End private-school girls, as now 'real' people are defined loosely as 'lik[ing] music'. A little later it becomes apparent that this redefinition of 'real' still carries social class connotations, albeit different ones, as now 'real' seems to index a mid position on the social spectrum. In staves 14–15 Roberta distances herself from another East End venue and its clubbers, calling the latter 'Sharoons' and the former 'embarrassing'. Although she pronounces the word [ʃəˈruːn] instead of the usual [ˈʃærən] it seems to me that Roberta invokes the derogatory slang meaning of the personal name Sharon. This would imply that like Frazer's (1992) private-school girls, who also used the term in their talk about social class differences, Roberta here distances herself from the girls and women whom she associates with the name Sharon, that is from 'females considered to be working class, unintelligent and vulgarly dressed, generally below the social standards acceptable to the user of the phrase' (Duckworth 2007). But Roberta also dismisses the 'whole other world' (staves 16–17) of the Café de Paris, an (at the time still) exclusive club which is even further removed on Roberta's 'realness' scale. Thus Roberta positions her favourite club, with its 'real' people, in opposition to both extremes of the social spectrum, that is, Hackney clubs and the embarrassing clubs of Sharo(o)ns on one side, and the exclusive world of the Café de Paris on the other. Similar to the girls' discussion of their musical tastes, Roberta's attempt to align herself with 'real' people with these socially meaningful metaphors or cultural concepts of dance clubs therefore constitutes an attempt to take a midway position. Given her own and the other girls' privileged backgrounds, this midway position allows the group to 'play up their ordinariness' (Savage, Bagnall, Longhurst 2001: 889) without aligning themselves with a working-class femininity, just like their self-positioning as cool and socially aware private-school girls.

Conclusion

I have argued in this chapter that social (class) positioning is central to the local identity construction captured in the spoken interaction of Roberta, Elizabeth, Nicky and Jane. Whereas the display of coolness in the girls' talk about drugs, music and school reveals a more covert social positioning (towards a tame non-conformity associated with streetwise knowledge and mitigated anti-authority stances), the girls' awareness of social class is more explicit elsewhere. Their talk about poems and mines, dance clubs and their clientele, London's West and East End, state-school students, A-levels and future university degrees, and public perception of 'over-privileged' private-school girls indexes social class both directly and indirectly, via 'cultural concepts' (Silverstein 2004), cultural tastes and capital (Bourdieu 1984).

The relevance of gender in the spoken interaction of Roberta and her friends is less explicit. Whereas the talk of the other two groups of (English and Bangladeshi working-class) girls contained an enormous amount of spontaneous talk about boys, boyfriends, gender differences, heterosexual relationships and sexual experience (see Chapters 3, 4, 6, 7, this volume, and Pichler 2006, 2007a), these topics play an extremely marginal role in the conversations that Roberta, Nicky, Jane and Elizabeth self-recorded for me. The situation was reversed with respect to the prevalence of the topic of social class in the upper-middle-class and working-class groups. Researchers from non-linguistic disciplines have argued that it should not come as a surprise that working-class girls have rarely been found to engage in talk about social class. Skeggs (1997) attributes her findings to the prevailing 'pathologising representations' of working-class femininity, and Frazer (1988: 53) argues that private- and comprehensive-school girls have different access to 'concepts and vocabularies' of class (see also Hey 1997; Kenway 1990). Similarly, I believe it should not come as a surprise that the private-school girls in my research do not talk about gender and sexuality very much. In Chapter 7 I argue with Walkerdine et al. (2001: 184–194) that the foregrounding of rational mind (e.g. in the girls' frequent academic debates) over sexual/fecund body (e.g. in talk about boyfriends and sex) constitutes an important aspect of the young upper-middle-class femininity that Roberta and her private-school friends negotiate for themselves in their group. The girls highlight their knowledge about sex and sexuality, but they also position themselves as relatively unconcerned about capital associated with active female heterosexuality. It seems likely that Roberta and her friends are affected by a 'dominant educational discourse' which suggests that 'the capital accrued by having a boyfriend often work[s] against other forms of capital – for instance, depleting economic and educational capital' (Archer, Halsall and Hollingworth 2007: 170, 171).

However, in this chapter I also demonstrate that despite the lack of overt orientations to gender it would be a mistake to ignore the gendered connotations of some of the girls' interactional and social positioning. Thus, the academic selves that the girls align themselves with in their intellectual debates are at the same time feminised and othered in Nicky's opposing imagery of poems and mines. Moreover, the coolness that the girls aim for at times has connotations of (stereotypical) masculinity, including the non-mainstream and streetwise masculinity of DJs and the carefree and funny young masculinity associated with Roberta's spliff-smoking, smelling-salt-sniffing brother. Whereas the girls' efforts to 'play up their ordinariness' (Savage, Bagnall, Longhurst 2001: 889) tend to go hand in hand with a positive evaluation of masculine subject positions (including also that of the stereotypical working-class miner), stereotypical working-class femininity (of 'Sharons') is indirectly presented as 'embarrassing' (Extract 20). The subject position of the Gangsta Rapper is, however, equally rejected by the girls, albeit not on the grounds of being 'embarrassing' but because it is associated with 'trying to be hard'. Gangsta Rapp hardness, which is rejected as inauthentic by the girls, carries clear overtones of sexualised masculinity, which may be a further reason why it constitutes a boundary for the girls' striving for coolness.

In this chapter I have interpreted the girls' performance of streetwise, non-conformist coolness and their association with 'real people' not as an attempt to 'pass' as working class (Skeggs 1997) but as a pursuit of alternative cultural capital. This display of alternative capital allows Roberta and her friends to position themselves in opposition to the socially unaware 'Val d'Isère girls' at their own school, and also differentiates them from other elite schoolgirls like the Australian 'ladies' (Kenway 1990) or the Oxfordshire upper(middle)-class girls (Frazer 1988: 1992). I interpret the group's positioning as cool and socially aware as a distancing from a sheltered and posh private-school, upper-middle-class femininity and as an attempt to display some alignment with what they see as more 'real', that is, ordinary, adolescent identities.

I conclude with a caveat about the girls' 'alternative' social positioning. Skeggs (1997, 2004) discusses evidence from recent sociological research which would suggest that my findings in Roberta's group of private-school girls may need to be seen in the context of 'new middle-class lifestyles' as 'cultural omnivores'. These new middle-class 'omnivores' claim status through a display of knowledge about and participation in a wide range of cultural forms, including non-highbrow practices (Skeggs 2004: 141–4; Peterson and Kern 1996). Skeggs (2004: 144), however, warns that cultural omnivorousness should not be seen as a challenge to class distinction, arguing with Warde et al. (2000) 'that the socially privileged do not give up highbrow activities; in fact they pursue leisure activities more assiduously and extend their range, demonstrating evidence of both omnivorousness and persistent distinction among the British middle-classes'. Similarly, the self-recorded conversations of Roberta and her friends shows that the girls do not only value alternative and more localised cultural capital such as 'coolness' or 'streetwise knowledge'. The girls clearly also possess powerful cultural capital in the form of a higher education trajectory, an understanding of poetry, science, history and social class, as well as a knowledge of highbrow literature and the genre of academic debate. Thus the girls have access to cultural capital which will trade into economic and symbolic capital (Bourdieu 1991, 1984) well beyond their local friendship group.

3
Sheltered but Independent East End Girls

This chapter explores the talk of Pat, Jenny, Susan and Natalie, who formed a friendship group at a state school in the East End of London. This school, which was also attended by Ardiana and her friends (see Chapter 4), recruited its students mainly from the surrounding working-class areas, with about 60 per cent of Pat's form group qualifying for free school meals. When I first started transcribing the tapes which Pat and her friends had recorded, it was immediately evident that in their talk the girls attributed a more salient role to their families and especially their mothers than the two other groups. This is evident both on a quantitative and on a qualitative level in my data and struck me as note-worthy also because school records indicated that all of the four girls lived in single-parent families.[1] The girls mention their mums on average about once every 41 seconds of transcribed conversation; by contrast Ardiana, Dilshana, Hennah and Varda only mention their mothers on average once every 11 minutes and 8 seconds and Elizabeth, Roberta, Nicky and Jane speak about their mothers once every 7 minutes.[2]

The qualitative analysis of the talk shows that the girls' relationships with their mothers and families tends to be a very close one but it also indicates that Pat, Jenny, Susan and Natalie frequently position themselves as independent and self-determined. In this chapter I shall explore how the girls construct and balance a range of different and at times seemingly contradictory subject positions, including that of the protected and loved daughter, the self-determined or rebellious teenager and the reasonable and mature grown-up.

Differently from Roberta and her private-school friends Pat and the other girls in her group never discuss the topic of social class explicitly. However, in this chapter I shall argue that this lack of overt orientation to social class does not mean that the macro-category of social class is irrelevant to the positioning of the girls in their talk. As has been argued many times before by feminist scholars in the fields of sociology, psychology and education, it should not come as a surprise that there is little or no explicit talk about social class among working-class women, as working-class femininity tends to be positioned as negative or even 'pathological' in both popular and institutional discourses (Frazer 1989, 1992; McDermott 2004; Skeggs 1997, 2004; Walkerdine et al. 2001). Based on her ethnographic study of 83 white British working-class women Skeggs (1997: 74) argues,

> Class was central to the young women's subjectivities. It was not spoken of in the traditional sense of recognition – I am working class – but rather was displayed in their multitudinous efforts *not to be* recognized as working class. They disidentified and they dissimulated.

My own exploration of the talk of Pat and her friends also leads me to the conclusion that the girls have an (unexpressed) awareness of a range of pathologising discourses about working-class adolescents and families, especially about single mothers. In this chapter I will argue that Pat and her friends position themselves in opposition to these discourses and therefore 'disidentify' from their working-class background in order to gain respectability, which Skeggs identifies as one of the most significant markers of middle-class femininity (Skeggs 1997; see also Walkerdine et al. 2001). They do this by constructing themselves as what I define as being 'sheltered',[3] that is, protected, watched over and cared for by their (single) mothers and (absent) fathers, and by presenting themselves as responsible with regard to their schooling/education, boyfriends and sexual experiences and as compliant with the mostly strict but loving parenting they experience at home.

I shall examine the girls' positioning not only in relation to discourses but also in relation to different voices which emerge in their talk. Whereas I use the term *discourse* to refer to language use that reflects, influences and constitutes ideologies and (socio-cultural) practices, the term *voice* refers to the words and utterances of others that we reproduce in our speech. In spite of providing distinct definitions for these two concepts I would argue that the boundaries between the two are frequently blurred. The reason for this is that the voices of others that we take on in our speech tend to invoke discourses. Thus, the voices of mothers can invoke discourses of discipline and authority, and it can be difficult to differentiate between the two if there are no obvious contextualisation cues, that is, if the voices of other speakers are not marked as 'other' by a change of voice quality or a preceding quotative like 'she said'.

The talk of Pat and her friends encourages a focus on the multi-voiced and dialogic nature of language, which is central to the writings of Mikhail Bakhtin.

> Our speech [...] is filled with others' words, varying degrees of otherness and varying degrees of 'our-own-ness', varying degrees of awareness and detachment. These words of others carry with them their own expression, their own evaluative tone, which we assimilate, rework and accentuate. (Bakhtin 1986: 89)

The voices of others which we report in our own speech are never simply reproduced, but instead 'reworded and reaccented in particular ways by the speaker doing the reporting', as Janet Maybin (2007: 1), drawing on Bakhtin (e.g. 1981, 1984, 1986) and Volosinov (1973), highlights. Bakhtin (1986: 91) sums up the positioning of the speaker ('interlocutor') to the reported utterances of others as follows:

> Both whole utterances and individual words can retain their alien expression, but they can also be re-accentuated (ironically, indignantly, reverently, and so forth). Others' utterances can be repeated with varying degrees of reinterpretation. They can be referred to as though the interlocutor were already well aware of them; they can be silently presupposed; or one's responsive reaction to them can be reflected only in the expression of one's own speech – in the selection of language means and intonations that are determined not by the topic of one's own speech but by the others' utterances concerning the same topic. (Bakhtin 1986: 91)

The transformation of the reported voices/speech therefore always contains some evaluation on behalf of the present speaker, in relation to the people/characters who have been invoked through the reported speech, of their behaviours, stances, perspectives and values (Maybin 2007: 1). In her discourse analytic and ethnographic research Maybin (2007) examines grammatical, prosodic, contextual and ethnographic cues to identify the reported voices in the talk of schoolchildren, as part of the children's evaluation of these voices. My own exploration of the representation and evaluation of voices in the talk of Pat, Susan, Jenny and

Table 3.1   Speech presentation cline

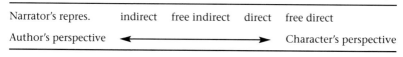

Narrator's repres.	indirect	free indirect	direct	free direct
Author's perspective	←————————————→			Character's perspective

Source: Maybin 2007: 78.

Natalie will focus particularly on prosodic, paralinguistic and grammatical cues. Prosodic cues include for example a change in pitch and/or volume, paralinguistic cues can involve a switch in voice quality, for example from serious to mocking.

The relationship between grammatical cues and the speaker's evaluation of a reported voice has been represented in a cline by Geoffrey Leech and Michael Short (1981), which was adapted by Maybin (2007) (see Table 3.1).

The cline shows that 'the more indirect the speech presentation, the more the perspective of the author dominates; the more direct the reporting, the more the perspective of the character comes to the fore' (Maybin 2007: 77). In order to explain the cline I will briefly provide an overview of some of the examples provided by Maybin (2007: 77–8). By framing a reported utterance in indirect speech (he shouted that he couldn't come just then) the current speaker (the 'narrator') foregrounds their own (the 'author's') perspective more than if they framed the same utterance as direct speech (e.g. he shouted 'I can't come now'), which foregrounds the original speaker's (or the 'character's') utterance. Free direct speech, which is characterised by a lack of a reporting clause, foregrounds the perspective of the character most and is sometimes represented without inverted commas (e.g. I really can't come now) whereas the author's perspective is foregrounded most in the narrator's representation of a speech act (e.g. he shouted). Free indirect speech is a hybrid form in between direct and indirect speech (e.g. he really couldn't come now).

In this chapter I shall draw on Maybin's work on voice to support my examination of the girls' positioning in relation to their mothers and families, and to explore the girls' attempts to balance adult authority/reason and adolescent rebellion/adventure in their friendship talk.

Mothers and daughters

Jennifer Coates' (1999) longitudinal study of a group of white middle-class girls shows that mothers are quoted and referred to very frequently by the girls when they are younger, but that the 'maternal voice [was] to some extent displaced by boys' voices as the girls reach their mid-teens' (Coates 1999: 130). In the conversational data from my three groups of young women the voices, practices and identities of mothers feature most prominently in the talk of the four London East End girls, Pat, Jenny, Susan and Natalie. Although the girls were between 16 and 17 years old at the time of the recording and spent a considerable amount of their talk dedicated to boys and boyfriends, they continued to speak about and invoke their mothers all the time, thereby foregrounding the subject position of daughters for themselves. In the following section I will provide evidence for the extraordinary significance of mother–daughter relationships for the identity constructions of Pat and the other girls in this group, whether they position their mothers as authority figures or as close friends. My analysis of the girls' spontaneous talk about truancy and sex examines the different voices and discourses the girls invoke about their mothers from a micro-linguistic, interactional perspective, but it also aims to establish links to the large body of existing non-linguistic research exploring the positioning and relationship of mothers and daughters in areas such as teenage sexuality and educational trajectories (Aapola, Gonick and Harris 2005; Reay 2000; Lawler 2000; Walkerdine and Lucey 1989; Walkerdine, Lucey and Melody 2001).

Truancy: authoritarian mothers and compliant daughters

One of the dominant subject positions that the girls construct for their mothers is that of the authoritarian mother. This subject position stands in contrast to the liberal and 'cool' parents who feature in the talk of Roberta and her group of private-school friends (Chapters 2, 7). 'Authoritarian mothers' have been discussed at length in educational texts and research. However, as I shall demonstrate, the authoritarian maternal voice that I found in my data is far removed from the pathologising representations of the so-called 'authoritarian' practices of working-class mothers in (liberal) educational/academic discourses (Walkerdine and Lucey 1989; Walkerdine et al. 2001). Walkerdine and Lucey (1989) argue that in these discourses the 'authoritarian' style tends to be contrasted negatively with 'sensitive' parenting, the former associated with working-class mothers and children's educational failure, and the latter with middle-class mothers and educational success. Indeed, whereas middle-class mothers are said to regulate their children by appealing to their reason, which gives the illusion of being more democratic and accepting children's and parents' rights as equal, Walkerdine et al. (1989, 2001: 119) found that the working-class mothers in their sample tended to be more 'explicit about power differentials and about their own position of authority'. Despite finding evidence for a class-related difference in child-rearing practices Walkerdine and Lucey (1989) and Walkerdine et al. (2001) are highly critical of the concepts of 'sensitive' and 'authoritarian' parenting and their supposed 'predictive power' for children's educational success (2001: 114), not least as the two most successful working-class girls in their study had been brought up by what could be referred to as 'authoritarian' or 'insensitive' mothers (ibid. 150).

In this chapter I will adopt the concept of the 'authoritarian mother' without engaging with any of the educational and public debates which aim to evaluate different parenting styles. I had no pre-established interest in the subject position of the authoritarian mother, instead it was made relevant by Pat and her friends in their talk about 'bunking off' school. I will examine the relevance, meaning and evaluation of this subject position in the context of the voices, discourses and identities the girls invoke in their talk in the following extracts of their talk.

Previously to stave 1 in Extract 1 the girls had been talking about one of their schoolmates who tends to be absent from school for no evident or justified reason. In Susan's words 'Hannah just ain't in cause she's never in' (see Extract 13 below). Natalie, who is particularly close to Hannah, had seen Hannah the day before and asked her whether she would be coming to school the following day.

Extract 1: truancy

(1)
?Susan   *{laughing}*(<u>yeah::</u>) *{laughs}*
Jenny   d'you know when you said to her w::hy (c-)

(2)
Jenny   "are you coming into school tomorrow" what did

(3)
Jenny   she say=
Natalie   =she just said "erm I: dunno: I might do"

(4)
Jenny   *{high pitch}*=<u>if I said</u>
Natalie   and I said "ah it's up to you innit"=(xxxxxxxx

(5)
Jenny   <u>to my] mum</u> "mum can I have a day off (of) school"
Natalie   xxxx)]

(6)
Susan   (no if they-)
Jenny   {lower pitch}"<u>no you can't</u>" (-) {squeak}
Natalie   my mum (xx) **would**=

In this extract about Hannah's truanting the girls report the voices of
several speakers, including Natalie's (stave 2 and 4), Hannah's (stave 3),
Jenny's (stave 5) and Jenny's mother (stave 6). Both the content and
the manner of Natalie's reproduction of her exchange with Hannah
shows that Natalie wishes to position herself as non-judgemental and
as non-interfering with Hannah's decision about whether or not to
come to school (see also Extract 13 below). However, whilst Natalie
invokes a discourse of (adult) self-determination or autonomy, Jenny
is less reluctant to problematise Hannah's truanting, albeit indirectly.

When Jenny latches onto Natalie in stave 4 she does so to report what
Maybin (2007: 91) refers to as a 'hypothetical' or 'unvoiced' dialogue
between her own mother and herself on the subject of truanting. By
reproducing this (fictitious) dialogue Jenny invites a comparison between
her own and Hannah's mother and, by extension, between different
styles of parenting. Jenny's high pitched voice when taking the floor
contrasts with the somewhat lower pitch she assumes when reporting her
mother's voice. Although this prosodic cue marks the maternal voice as
different from Jenny's own, the grammatical representation of the
mother's voice in the form of free direct speech: 'no you can't' (rather
than direct speech with a reporting clause, 'and she said: no you can't' or
indirect speech 'and she said that I couldn't') allows Jenny to foreground
the evaluative perspective of her mother without distancing herself from
it (Maybin 2007: 77–8; Leech and Short 1981). Thus, Jenny presents an
overall positive evaluation of her mother's voice and, by extension, her
relatively authoritarian style of parenting, indirectly contrasted with the
absent voice of Hannah's mother. Rather than positioning Hannah as
solely responsible for her actions, Jenny establishes a link between
Hannah's truanting and a lack of parental authority.

Ironically, although an authoritarian parenting style has been patholo-
gised in educational discourses and texts when associated with working-
class families and mothers, it is middle-class mothers who were found
to 'set up rigid boundaries in relation to schoolwork' (Walkerdine et al.

2001: 150; Walkerdine and Lucey 1989). In the words of Diane Reay's (2000: 578) later study on primary-school children, middle-class mothers saw 'academic work in the home as an area which was not open to negotiation'. The voice of Jenny's mother is clearly authoritarian in the sense that it displays her control overtly without engaging in or encouraging 'the art of rational debate' which some educational discourses position as central to more democratic or 'sensitive' mothering (Walkerdine and Lucey 1989: 17). However, this authoritarian voice ultimately associates Jenny's mother with 'good' middle-class practice, that is, strong and even overt 'maternal control' with regard to children's schooling (see also Reay 2000: 578). Jenny's positive evaluation of her mother's voice shows that she does not seek to challenge her mother's authority in controlling her school attendance. I argue that by presenting her mother as strict Jenny indirectly positions her family in opposition to the popular (media) discourse of 'defective parenting' (Hoyle 1998) which attributes truancy and other educational failure of children to a lack of strict boundaries about schooling and is frequently associated with working-class families. Thus, the authoritarian voice/parenting style of her mother allows Jenny to present herself as being protected or sheltered rather than neglected, and thereby to claim an upbringing which is traditional and 'normal', despite living in a one-parent working-class family.

The remainder of this conversation as well as a previous exchange between the girls about Hannah's absences (which will be discussed below) suggests that the majority of the girls in the group distance themselves from Hannah's truanting. Moreover, most girls indicate that their families would not allow them to be absent from school, positioning their mothers as authoritarian in this context of schooling, that is, as setting clear boundaries to the autonomy of their daughters as far as school attendance goes. The only exception is Natalie, who claims that her mother would give her the permission to remain at home in stave 6 'my mum would [let me stay at home]', a claim that is supported by the following brief narrative.

Extract 2: truancy – continued

(7)
Susan   =I'll never get [a day off from school]
Natalie   [my mum (treats) me]   cause it's

(8)
Natalie   (phonxxx) cause I (run) downstairs (>make myself some<)

(9)
Natalie   breakfast (.) she'd **rang** our schools last year (-)

(10)
Pat   (.) [so what]
?Jenny   %she (\was%) (.)
Natalie   [(xxxx %"I ought] to) oughtn't I"

(11)
Pat   {laughs}
Susan   no with
Jenny   {laughs}
Natalie   she went "no it's up to you innit%"

Despite the indecipherable words in this extract it is possible to establish
that on at least one previous occasion Natalie's mother had not only
allowed but actually encouraged her daughter's truancy by phoning the
school with an excuse for her absence. Again, the most interesting detail
about this narrative is the reported dialogue between mother and daughter. Natalie does not change the tone of her voice when she switches
from reporting her own voice in stave 10 to that of her mother in stave
11. Moreover, the voice of her mother is framed as direct reported speech,
which is a further indication that Natalie does not seek to distance herself
from her mother's perspective (Leech and Short 1981; Maybin 2007). The
most interesting aspect of Natalie's reproduction of her mother's voice,
however, is that it mirrors Natalie's own reported voice in her exchange
with her truant friend Hannah in stave 4 (Extract 1) 'it's up to you innit'.
This suggests that Hannah's reported voice (in stave 4) is in fact an
'appropriation' (Maybin 2007: 144) of her mother's voice and stance, that
Hannah has 'internalised the maternal voice' (Coates 1999: 131).
Ironically however, the maternal voice in this instance invokes neither
parental nor institutional authority and does not encourage compliance
with dominant social norms. Instead, Natalie positions her mother as
adopting the same stance of non-interference with regard to her daughter's school attendance as Natalie had taken herself with her truanting
friend Hannah. This suggests that Natalie's mother encourages her
daughter to decide for herself whether or not to go to school, thereby
transferring the responsibility onto Natalie and ultimately constructing
the mother–daughter relationship just as symmetrical/egalitarian as
Natalie's same-age friendship with Hannah.

Walkerdine et al.'s (2001) longitudinal psychosocial research offers a possible explanation for this seeming lack of parental authority in relation to schooling, arguing that 'working-class parents did express more concern about their children's happiness than they did about their performance at school' (2001: 132). Walkerdine et al. and Reay (2000) argue on the basis of their interview data that the prioritising of children's happiness over education can frequently be attributed to working-class parents' own negative experiences with schooling and their desire to prevent their children from the distress they themselves had felt. Like many of the working-class parents in Walkerdine and Lucey (1989), Walkerdine et al. (2001) and Reay (2000), Natalie's mother appears to be less strict in enforcing boundaries in relation to her daughters' schooling, and it is possible that this is because she rates Natalie's happiness as more important than educational success.

However, Natalie's mother's stance is not presented as the norm in this group of London East End girls, as the mothers of the other three girls are taking a more authoritarian approach to their daughter's schooling (see Jenny: Extract 1, stave 6; Susan: Extract 2, stave 7; and Pat: Extract 3, stave 12 below). The girls' positive evaluation of their mothers' authoritarian stance is also implicit in the girls' own positioning: Jenny, Susan and Pat construct themselves as compliant with their mothers' authority, whether this is happening with the full cooperation of the daughters, like in Pat's case, or with some degree of resistance and negotiation, like in Susan's.

Extract 3: truancy – continued

(12)
Pat   my mum makes me [(go to school)]
Susan   my mum er   [if I'm **ill**] for one day (.)

(13)
Susan   they'll let me off but they'll still (.) not believe

(14)
Susan   me like .hh but then they'll I'll (.) convince them=

(15)
Pat   =my mum's never in in the morning=if (I were not-)

(16)
Pat   if I::::'m not well o:::r I say to my mum

(17)
Pat   .hhh I'll say to my mum the night before

(18)
Pat   >"mum I ain't done me homework"< a- m- a quite

(19)
Pat   a few times my mum has said "let me come in in

(20)
Pat   the morning" cause I'm f- .hhh I haven't done me

(21)
Pat   homework or it's been too hard and she-
                                    {bang}

(22)
Pat   [my] mum's never in in the morning though
Susan   =ye[ah]
?   (%xxx%)

(23)
Pat   my mum's out by like (-) six
Susan   (.) [mm]
Natalie   (.) [it's] like my mum

In this extract both Pat and Susan state that they would not be allowed
to be absent from school. Whereas Pat clearly identifies her mother as
the voice of authority in this matter, Susan switches from referring to
her mother in stave 12 to an undefined 'they' in staves 13 and 14. This
suggests that Susan's mother is not the only figure of authority in her
house, although school records indicate that Susan lives in a one-
parent family. Pat and Susan depict their parents/carers in the role of
authority and power, 'making' Pat go to school or 'letting Susan off' if
she is ill only for one day. However, Susan puts up a bit of a struggle to
subvert the adult authority by putting on a convincing performance of
her illness, also signalling some distance between herself and her par-
ents/carers by referring to them solely by third person plural pronoun

'they', without having established a reference for it previously. Pat, on the other hand points out that her mum (who works as a bakery manager in a supermarket) is never at home in the morning. This statement, together with Pat's earlier assertion that her mum makes her go to school, allows Pat to balance discourses of control and independence (Lawler 2000: 92–6) with regard to her upbringing. The implication is that rather than being compliant Pat could in fact easily subvert her mother's authority, as her mother would not be around in the mornings to check whether Pat has really gone to school. Thus Pat positions herself as a reliable daughter, who does not wish to abuse her mother's trust.

Aapola (1999, 2002 in Aapola, Gonick and Harris 2005) highlights how parental trust can be central to girls' managing the frequently contradictory subject positions of good daughters and independent young adults.

> [...] girls frequently positioned themselves as good daughters, who wanted to please their parents, be trustworthy and simultaneously show them that they were reliable and sensible, autonomous individuals... (Aapola et al. 2005: 95)

Thus, although Pat positions her mother as exerting her authority in relation to Pat's school attendance and even homework, Pat really does not need to be regulated in an overtly authoritarian way. In many ways, she is positioning herself as the rational and autonomous subject which is the aim of the democratic parenting styles associated with middle-class mothers (Walkerdine and Lucey 1989; Walkerdine et al. 2001). Moreover, rather than allowing Pat to give up when she faces a difficult situation (like not having done her homework) Pat's mother, like the mothers of all middle-class girls and two successful working-class girls in Walkerdine's research, offers her daughter not only boundaries but also support and encouragement, by 'com[ing] in in the morning', that is, returning home briefly from her work as bakery manger to check on Pat. By presenting a mitigated and supportive version of parental authority with regard to schooling, Pat thus positions her mother as both strict and caring, and herself as sheltered and compliant daughter, subject positions which in many way are in opposition to popular discourses associated with one-parent working class families.

The mothers of Pat, Jenny, and Susan display their authority in different ways, but they all enforce boundaries with regard to their daughters' school attendance. I believe that it is no coincidence that the girls in this group foreground these boundaries and the authoritarian voices of their parents, whereas the privileged upper-middle-class girls from a private school tend to play them down (see Chapter 2). For the working-class girls from one-parent families the association with a sheltered upbringing means a step towards increased middle-class respectability (Skeggs 1997), whether this is in relation to their school attendance or their sexuality.

Sex: protective mothers and self-determined daughters

Pat and her friends do not only highlight their mothers' authority and watchfulness in relation to their daughters' school attendance, but also in relation to their sexual activities. This is particularly interesting as all the mothers of the three girls with boyfriends in this group know about their daughters' boyfriends and, in the case of Jenny and Natalie, are even on very friendly terms with them. I will examine the group's sex talk in great depth in Chapter 5, but in this section I aim to show how, at the same time as asserting their right to self-determination and autonomy, the girls in this group position their mothers as policing and protecting their daughters' sexual innocence. I shall argue that by presenting their mothers as guardians of young female sexuality the girls in this group lay claim to 'respectability' (Skeggs 1997), not only in the sense that they present themselves as sexually respectable, but also in the sense that they highlight their respectable upbringing or family environment. In order to support her argument that working-class girls aim for middle-class respectability by disidentifying themselves from their working-class backgrounds, Skeggs (1997: 82) refers to research by Press (1991) who demonstrates that '[t]heir desire not to be seen as working class are lived through their bodies, clothes and (if not living with parents) their homes'.

My own data show how Pat and her friends present themselves as sheltered by protective mothers and intact/functioning families. I argue that these positions allow the girls to disidentify from dominant pathologising stereotypes about (their) single-parent and/or working-class families. At the same time, however, there is clear evidence that the girls are also very determined to defend their autonomy and privacy in front of their mothers. The following discussion shows how the girls balance these different aims in their talk about sex.

In Extract 4, which I shall discuss in more detail in Chapter 5, Pat's first utterance comes in response to Jenny's previously expressed concern about how her mother would react if she found out that Jenny had had sex.

Extract 4: the first time

(1)
Pat   [I wouldn't **tell** my mum]
Susan   [yeah but then again (now)] but then again if you

(2)
Natalie   yeah but it's up
Susan   think about it it's like~ (-)

(3)
Natalie to **you** it's not what [your mum says]
Susan   [it's **you** at the] end of the

(4)
Natalie   it's what you wanna [do d'you
Susan   day it's you   [and your mum
?   {whispering}%<u>Pat</u>%

(5)
Natalie know what I mean]
Pat   >unless
Susan   ain't gonna know]
Jenny   (.) %yeah I know but (xxxxxxx)%

(6)
Pat   [you have] it written [all over your face<]
Susan   [(if-)]   [if you're close-]

(7)
Pat   [(xxxxxxxxxx] had sex mum {laughs}
Susan   [if you're-]   if you're close

(8)
Susan   to your mum [and every]thing even (.) I'm quite close
?   [(xxxxxxx)]

(9)
Pat   [I] think my mum [would **know**]
Susan   to my mum sometime[(s)-]   [but when (it)-]
Natalie   (but you

(10)
Pat   .hh [when it comes-]
Natalie   ain't seriously thinking that) ["yeah I]*{low pitch}*

(11)
Pat   [yeah but I think but I]   think my
Natalie   slept with [with (xxxxxxxxxx last night")

(12)
Pat   I think my mum would **know**

In staves 1–5 Pat, Natalie and Susan jointly position their sexual
relationships outside their mothers' realm of authority. As I will discuss
in Chapter 5 the girls are determined to decide for themselves, when,
with whom and even where they have sex (for the first time), and this
discourse of self-determination is presented in opposition to their
mothers' policing of their sexuality in the above extract.

The girls agree that they would not tell their mums about having had
sex (Pat: stave 1; Susan: staves 3–5; Natalie: staves 9–11). However, in
staves 7–9 it appears that Susan is ready to modify her earlier stance
that Jenny's or anybody else's mum would not know if they had had
sex. It seems that Susan is about to draw on a discourse of motherly
intuition, arguing that when there is a very close relationship between
mother and daughter, mothers might actually realise what is going on
in their daughter's (sex) life, without being told. This is certainly how
Pat interprets Susan's incomplete utterance, declaring that her 'mum
would know' (staves 9, 12). By foregrounding her mum's intuition Pat
simultaneously highlights the close relationship she enjoys with her
mother, which contrasts her with Susan, whose argument in staves 8–9
that 'even' she 'sometimes' feels 'quite' close to her mum in fact reveals
a lack of closeness.

All the girls position themselves in a discourse which asserts their
right to autonomy and self-determination with respect to their sexual
relationships and experiences, but some girls, like Susan, go further in
protecting their privacy than others.

Extract 5: my mum thinks I'm an angel

(15)
Susan   I wouldn't even like to imagine my mum even (be)

(16)
Pat   [(oh) my]
Susan   thinking I'm **kissing** someone let alone doing an[ything]

(17)
Pat   mum knows **tha:t** like~
Susan   no no I would- .hh like my mum

(18)
Susan   {clicks tongue} {"innocent" voice}my mum thinks

(19)
Susan   I'm an angel anyway so {laughs} (xxxx matter)
                                        (background noise)

(20)
Pat   {- - laughs - -}   (-) ah:
Susan   (2.5) so: (it doesn't) really matter
Natalie   (-) but erm:

Differently from Pat, it appears that Susan does not tend to disclose any
details about her relationship with boys to her mother. Susan positions
her mother as ignorant about her daughter's sexuality and herself as protecting her mother's ignorance. Susan makes it clear in staves 15 and 16
that she does not wish her mother to know or even think that her
daughter might be kissing a boy. In staves 18 and 19 she then indicates
that her mother thinks of her daughter as an innocent 'angel'. Thus it
appears that mother and daughter are co-constructing the subject
positions of (sexually) innocent daughter and protective mother, both of
which 'respectable' femininities, which Skeggs (1997) links to ideologies
of middle-classness. Although Susan reports her mother's thoughts
rather than her mother's actual speech, the paralinguistic and grammatical framing of the reporting still reveals a clear evaluative stance.
Susan's presumed innocence is signalled not just on a content level, by
her identification as an 'angel', but also on a paralinguistic level, by
Susan's adaptation of a tone of voice that underlines her child-like status

in the eyes of her mother (staves 18–19). By reporting her mother's thought in an indirect manner ('my mum thinks that I'm an angel') rather than directly (e.g. 'my mum's like: "Susan is my little angel"') Susan creates some further distance from her mother's voice/thought, signalling that her mother's evaluation does not correspond to her own, that, in fact, her mother's belief is amusing (see also Susan's laughter).

Although Susan clearly ridicules her mother's belief when talking to her friends, in front of her mother she appears to take an active role in the construction of herself as an innocent daughter (staves 15–16). The remainder of the conversation illustrates Susan's belief that by accepting the subject position of the innocent daughter in front of her family she will actually increase her personal agency/autonomy in the context of her family.

Extract 6: my mum thinks I'm an angel – continued

(22)
Susan   I don't like my mum to be in my business like

(23)
Susan   the other day she was going "<u>oh **yeah** so what</u>

(24)
Susan   <u>d'you do"</u>*{high pitch}* (cause) <u>this is her</u>*{amused}*

(25)
Susan   .hhh "whe- erm: *<u>you **came** home when your hair was</u>

{slightly higher pitched and louder than Susan's usual voice}

(26)
Pat   *{laughs}*
Susan   <u>all (.) all out of place and"</u>*{amused}*
Natalie   (oh ∧NO)
Jenny   *{loud laughter}*

In this part of their conversation about their mothers Susan gives an example of her mum's attempts to protect and police her daughter's sexual innocence. Susan positions herself as highly resistant to these attempts, as she signals in a number of ways. On a content level Susan makes it clear that she does not want her mother to interfere with her 'business', that is, as it turns out later, as what Susan considers to be her private matters. This signals that Susan, who has already indicated that her relationship with her mother is not as close as it could be (see Extract 4), actively chooses to maintain some distance between herself and her mother. In this way Susan hopes to protect her privacy and pursue her ultimate goal of greater self-determination in personal matters such as her love-life. Ironically, staves 23 to 26 show that Susan's mother is in fact not altogether convinced of her daughter's innocence as Susan had suggested earlier. The presupposition that is contained in Susan's mother's question 'what did you do?' suggests that Susan did in fact do something, and the following two staves indicate that her suspicion is that this 'something' may have been of a sexual nature. Thus, unsurprisingly, neither Susan's lack of self-disclosure nor her self-positioning as innocent daughter in front of her mother succeed in preventing Susan's mum from casting a watchful eye over her daughter's (sexual) activities and, by extension, her reputation.

In staves 23–24 Susan marks her mother's voice as clearly different from her own by adopting a much higher pitched voice which is mock maternal. Although she somewhat drops her pitch in staves 25 and 26 she still maintains a slightly raised pitch and volume, thus continuing to mark the voice she reports as that of her mother. Leech and Short (1981) and Maybin (1997) argue that the grammatical framing of the reported voice in direct speech ('this is her: "you came home…"') creates less distance between the evaluative point of the reported voice and that of the person doing the reporting than in indirect speech (e.g. 'and she said that I came home…'). However, in this instance the paralinguistic features, that is, the changed tone of voice, together with the initial negative framing of her mother's intervention (staves 22–23) still signal that Susan perceives her mother's inquisitiveness as prying and her attention as over-protectiveness.

The other girls' reactions to Susan's account indicate that they recognise the subject position of the watchful and protective mother; however their opposition to it appears to be less marked and differently motivated from Susan's.

Extract 7: my mum thinks I'm an angel – continued

(27)
Susan   [(and she's going-)]   [she] tried to say my skirt
Jenny   [(when) I'm come in] I [go-]

(28)
Susan   was the wrong way round [but wouldn't go **that** far]
Jenny   ah::   [sometimes she'd]   go (.)

(29)
Pat   "what've you been doing"
Jenny   "what've you been doing"=(but) *{higher pitched}*I ain't

(30)
Pat   *{laughs}*
Susan   [yeah]
Jenny   <u>done **nothing**</u> like (.)   [>d'you] know what I mean< nothing

(31)
Susan   [my mum was going]
Jenny   *{high pitched + innocent}*/**wrong** (.) [(xxxxxxxxx do I]

(32)
Susan   "why is your coat all creas[ed (and this-)"]
Jenny   [[(I am like) "<u>YEAH</u>]" *{high pitched}*

(33)
Jenny   (.) I've been sitting in the car (with three of us)

(34)
Pat   *{laughs}*   *{laughs}*
Susan   [yeah]
Jenny   <u>right</u>*{low pitched}*"<u>I was born yesterday</u>" I forgot
?   [yeah]

(35)
Jenny   <u>you</u> *{amused}*"<u>you've been there you've done it all</u>"

In staves 27 and 28 Susan makes the sexual implications of her mother's reproaches more explicit. At the same time the other girls begin to 'mirror' Susan's story (Coates: 1996), signalling that they had similar experiences with their own mothers. Their contributions frequently overlap, build on and support each other, resulting in a collaboratively constructed account of motherly concern and protectiveness. Jenny introduces her mother's voice in stave 28 with the quotative cluster 'sometimes she'd go'. The utterance is completed simultaneously by Jenny and Pat in stave 29. This jointly constructed utterance shows not only the close relationship between the speakers (Coates 1996, 1999), which allows them to anticipate what is going to be said, but it also highlights the similarities of the girls' experiences with their inquisitive and protective mothers.

Jenny's narrative about her mother becomes also Pat's story about her own mother in stave 29. Similarly to staves 4–5 in the above conversation about 'truancy' (Extract 1), Jenny engages in a reported dialogue to illustrate the relationship between herself and her mother. This dialogue is particularly animated due to Jenny's characteristic use of a wide range of pitch and other paralinguistic features. When she reports her own rejection of her mum's indirect reproach in staves 29–31 she does not state her authorship explicitly with the help of a quotative (e.g. 'I said') but signals it by switching to a significantly higher pitch. In contrast to Susan's earlier mockery of her mother's voice the change to a higher pitch does not signal Jenny's detachment (from her self-reported voice). Instead, it indexes the authorship of the utterance (as Jenny's) and aids her alignment with an 'innocent girl/daughter' position (see also her high pitched/innocent 'wrong', stave 31).

In the remainder of the extract Jenny also uses different paralinguistic and prosodic features to identify the authorship of the voices she reproduces. After Susan quotes another indirect accusation authored by her own mother in stave 32 Jenny completes the reported dialogue, signalling the similarity between the two mother–daughter conversations. Whereas Jenny still employs a quotative 'I am like "yeah" ' to report her indignant (and ironic) defence in stave 32, she does not use any quotatives in the remainder of the extract. Her own explanation (that she had only been sitting in the car with other people) is followed by the mother's ironic 'I was born yesterday' (stave 34), marked by a deeper pitch, indexing an adult voice and conveying the mother's refusal to believe Jenny. Whereas the authorship of the chunk 'I forgot you' is not clear, the following 'you've been there you've done it all' (stave 35) is marked by an amused voice quality and clearly captures Jenny's mocking rejection of her mother's voice, and, at the same time, moralistic stance.

Despite some degree of resistance to their mothers' voices, the collaboratively produced reported dialogue shows that Jenny, Pat and Susan construct the mothers as protective and even moralistic regarding their daughters' sexual innocence. This stands in contrast to Roberta and her private-school friends, who position their mothers as liberal, cool and unshockable in sex-related issues (see Chapter 7).

Although Pat, Susan Natalie and Jenny frequently highlight their independence and their right to self-determination they also position themselves as protected/sheltered by their mothers, and, in fact by their entire families.

Loving families

Their mothers are not the only members of their families that Pat, Natalie, Jenny and Susan position as significant in their lives. The girls frequently signal the importance of family bonds, and although they speak about their fathers considerably less often than about their mothers, they still do so more frequently than the girls in the other two groups. Thus in Pat's group the girls' fathers are mentioned once every 3 minutes 36 seconds, in Ardiana's group once every 5 minutes, and in Roberta's upper-middle-class group only once every 11 minutes 40 seconds.[4] What is particularly interesting about this quantitative comparison is that at the time of my study at least two if not all of the girls in Pat's group lived with their mothers in single-parent families, whereas the girls in my Bangladeshi and in the private-school group all lived with both parents. In this section I shall discuss several extracts of this talk about families and fathers in Pat's group, arguing that it is motivated by the girls' (unexpressed) desire to position themselves and their families as close-knit. I suggest that this desire, which is never expressed directly but is clearly evidenced in my data, needs to be examined in relation to discourses of intact or 'traditional' families. Finch (2007) argues, that a *display* of families or 'family practices' is significant for relationships which do not conform to the model of the traditional nuclear family, especially if these relationships extend beyond one single household as in the case of divorced families (see also Smart and Neale 1999 in Finch 2007). I interpret the girls' 'display' of family practices as signalling their awareness of dominant discourses about the 'intact' family, and, following Skeggs (1997), suggest that these can carry connotations of middle-class respectability. In the words of Skeggs (1997: 90) '[h]omes and bodies are where respectability is displayed but where class is lived out as the most omnipresent form'.

The first extract in this section is taken from the middle of a long stretch of the girls' talk about their mothers, fathers and families, which lasts about three and a half minutes. In this extract the girls have just turned their attention to their families' expectations regarding their educational trajectories.

Extract 8: mums, dads and families

(1)
Pat   oh and my whole family are expecting me to

(2)
Pat   go to university (cause) none of them have (-)
[...]

(3)
Pat   they're not **pressurising** me /though (1)
Natalie   (xxxxxxxxxxx)   (1) (na::)

(4)
Natalie   (.) my sister was the fi::rst out of my fam-

(5)
Natalie   >(all) my (all) my< dad's family not in my

(6)
Susan   (1) I **don't**
Natalie   mum's (in) my mum's family::

(7)
Susan   think my [parents are expect]ing me to go
Natalie   *{hoarse}*   [(<u>oh:: ye::s</u> and-]

(8)
Pat   [(my dad's
Susan   it's jus::t (-) [it's just
Natalie   things like that

(9)
Pat   xxxxxxxx me)]
Susan   that I wanna] go
Jenny   [cause] every mum (.)
?Natalie   (I said [when I)]

(10)
Jenny   mum and dad want their k- (.) kid to do

(11)
Jenny   the best [they] can=   I ph- when
Susan   =yeah
?   [(their)]=dream innit=

(12)
Pat   I phoned my dad yesterday (.)
Natalie   my dad was just

(13)
Natalie   proud just cause I said I was getting me *NRA
*National Record of Achievement[5]

(14)
Pat   {laughs}
Susan   {laughs}
Natalie   next week   he went {raucous voice}"ah::

(15)
Pat   {laughs}
Natalie   well **done**" {faint laugh} (-) I said calm (xxxxx)

Despite their differences, two main similarities in the girls' positioning emerge from the above transcript. One is that a higher education
trajectory is not presented as the norm in Pat's or any of the other
girls' families. The second is that all the group members position
themselves in relation to their families. The girls all comment positively on their families, highlighting their families' high expectations
for (Pat: staves 1–2; Jenny: staves 9–11) and pride in the girls (Natalie:
staves 12–15) at the same time as their lack of pressure (Pat: stave 3;
Susan: staves 6–7). The girls collaborate in aligning themselves with
the subject position of the loved and praised daughter, presenting
themselves as part of supportive, close-knit families.

The girls' positioning towards their higher education trajectory varies.
Although Pat declares that her family 'expect' her to go to university, it
is clear that by stating these expectations explicitly Pat at the same time
reveals that a university trajectory is not taken for granted like in the
families of Roberta and her private-school friends (see Extract 15 'Kate'
in Chapter 2). Pat's declaration is followed by two largely indecipherable
(and therefore untranscribed: [...]) staves in which Natalie and Susan
appear to suggest that their parents do not share the expectations of
Pat's family. But whereas Natalie tends not to express an interest in

university education (in this or other extracts), Susan presents herself as determined to continue her education. Many of the positions the girls adopt above reveal discourses which have been interpreted as classed by Walkerdine et al. (2001) in their long-term study of British working-class girls and their families. Walkerdine et al. found examples of working-class families who took great pride in their daughters' relatively low level qualifications and of girls who were 'constantly praised for the smallest achievement' (ibid. 149). On the other hand they also found that in the comparatively few cases where working-class girls had gone on to university, 'working-class parents' desires and dreams of a better life for their children act as a powerful engine that drives their children's motivation to succeed at education and help to maintain them on the path to higher education' (Walkerdine et al. 2001: 158). Whereas the former stance appears to be represented by Natalie's (mimicking of her) father's proud comments about the NRA report (see note 5), the latter seems to inform Pat's and Jenny's statements in staves 1–2 and 9–11 respectively.

'Dads' are mentioned especially by Pat and Natalie, both of whom live apart from their fathers. Pat begins a story about her 'dad' (who lives in Greece) in the above extract, but she does not get to narrate the content of her phone conversation with her dad because none of the other girls express interest in it at this stage, and Natalie takes over with her story about her own dad's praise for her. Natalie continues to foreground her good relationship with her father as the talk continues.

Extract 9: mums, dads and families – continued

(27)
Susan   I (don't [get it it's no xxxxxx)]
Natalie   [guess who's coming tomorr]ow

(28)
Natalie   (.) guess who is coming tomorrow (no

(29)
Pat   (xxxxxxxxxxxxxxxxxxxxxxxxxxxxxxx)
Natalie   my mum mum and dad xxxxxxxxxxxxx yeah)

(30)
Natalie   my **mum** my dad (-) I think it's nice though

(31)
Natalie   cause (you know) they don't live together like

(32)
Pat   [(on
Natalie   they're getting together just to like y'[know=

(33)
Pat   this day)
Susan   =anyway who else=
Natalie   =my sister and her boyfriend

(34)
Susan   *{mocking}*and m[y baby]
?Jenny   [(are you] coming xxxxxxxxxxxxxxxxx)=
Natalie   and **my** baby

Natalie's attention-grabbing pre-sequence in stave 28 is the first indication
of the importance she attributes to the fact that both her parents will be
attending the NRA reports ceremony. After she repeats 'my mum my dad'
in stave 30 she pauses briefly, as if to invite a comment from the other
girls. When nobody remarks about the fact that both her parents will be
coming to the ceremony together Natalie explains why she thinks it is a
noteworthy event. Natalie explicitly states that she is pleased that her family will be together for this ceremony, despite the fact that her parents do
not live together. Thus, with Natalie's sister and her boyfriend as well as
Natalie's own boyfriend the family will be fully represented at the ceremony. It is interesting to note Natalie's hedging towards the end of stave
32 and the reactions of the other girls towards it. Whereas Pat's completion
of Natalie's unfinished utterance in staves 32 to 33 signals her support for
Natalie's aim to construct her parents' unity as significant, Susan's interruption in stave 33 appears to dismiss it. The reason for Susan's lack of
patience for Natalie's elaborations on her parents' participation in the
ceremony could, to some extent, be attributed to Susan's own family
situation. On one hand Susan's relationship with her mother seems more
problematic as she hints at a lack of emotional closeness (see Extract 4), on
the other hand Susan may be the one member of the group who lives with
both parents or carers (Extract 3), which would make such a display of
parental unity less significant than for girls like Natalie and Pat.
Irrespective of the real-life family situation of the girls, however, Natalie
constructs herself as part of a supportive, loving and close-knit family.

Pat not only acknowledges but shortly afterwards also mirrors
Natalie's discursive construction of her family as a unity. However, Pat's
celebration of her family bond is preceded by a stretch of talk in which

it becomes clear that Pat cannot rely on the physical presence of her family in the same way as Natalie.

Extract 10: mums, dads and families – continued

(35)
Pat   =no one's coming (xxxxxxxxxx) cause my mum will

(36)
Pat   be at work (1.5) [I might I might]
Natalie   (1.5) [your mum's gotta] [**come** for] /you
?   [(at work)]

(37)
Pat   =she'll be at wo::rk I don't wanna drag her

(38)
Pat   away from work **again**
Natalie   (1) you can sit with my

(39)
Pat   {amused}no I sit by myself like
Natalie   with my (erm-) mine then

(40)
Pat   (that)   (faking it) (-)   {laughs} (xxxx
Susan   (-) {laughs}
Natalie   (xxxxxxxx I xxxxxx

(41)
Pat   xxxxxxxxxxx){laughing}   {laughs}
Susan   {laughs} [rented fam]ily{laughing}
Natalie   xxxxxxxx to [my siste:r's]

In staves 35 to 36 Pat states that she will not have any members of her family at the ceremony as her mother will have to work. Pat's mother works very hard as a bakery manager at a supermarket, whereas Pat's father lives in Greece. The reaction of the other girls to Pat's revelation consists of a pause of approximately 1.5 seconds (stave 36). Conversation analytic interpretations of 'significant' pauses like this highlight their potential function as a 'dispreference marker', signalling conversational discomfort caused by face threatening utterances such as disagreements or mitigating a dispreferred turn (Pomerantz 1984). Hutchby and Wooffitt (1998: 46) also point out that 'speakers of second parts can use the dispreference markers strategically as a way of "getting out" of some undesired situation'. Thus the pause in stave 36 allows Natalie to signal the dispreferred status of her subsequent implicit criticism of Pat's mother and at the same time makes it possible for the other three girls to avoid performing the same speech act as Natalie. When Natalie insists that Pat's mother has to join the ceremony for Pat's sake, Pat counters that she does not want to interfere with her mother's demanding work yet again (staves 37–38), indicating that this happens often enough already and implying that she is more concerned about her mother than about the school event. Walkerdine et al. (2001: 152) find that a similar concern about the struggle and hardship of parents was expressed by several of her British working-class girls, arguing that '[o]ne of the effects of the girls' sense of their parents being heavily burdened was they did not want to add to their burden in any way'. Whereas Natalie subsequently offers to Pat to sit with her own family, Pat and Susan defuse the potentially face threatening situation by switching to a non-serious floor. The remainder of the conversation (staves 42–45), which has not been included here, shows that further support for Pat comes from Susan when she dismisses the significance of the entire event. Importantly, Pat never positions herself as neglected but instead constructs herself as an independent grown-up by showing understanding for her mother's work demands. Thus she highlights the importance of her mother's wellbeing at the same time as her own self-sufficiency, positioning herself as the attentive but independent daughter.

However, Pat is clearly aware that her mother's absence at the NRA report ceremony could be (and in fact is) construed as falling considerably short of the dominant model of intact families. The following staves show that in spite of having constructed herself as an independent girl, Pat seeks to mirror Natalie's earlier presentation of herself as part of a caring family.

Extract 11: mums, dads and families – continued

(46)
Pat   when my little siste::r when when she finally learns

(47)
Pat   (.) full blown English she's coming over (xxxxx)

(48)
Pat   my dad said last night .hhh gonna come over .hh and

(49)
Pat   (erm I will be so) proud of her (.) she does **so**

(50)
Pat   much she she does balle::t plays the piano::

(51)
Pat   (-) **does** (.) erm:: you know in Athens like (.) the

(52)
Pat   Olympics started there did[n't it] (.) and
Susan   [yeah]

(53)
Pat   they've got a big (.) track thing she goes

(54)
Pat   track training the::re everything [so it's
Susan   [so >is

(55)
Pat   like)]she's
Susan   she<] really active=
?   =how old (%is /she%)

(56)
Pat   (-) eight (.) she's **nine** (and xxxxx)

(57)
Pat   little brother is six (seven) (-)

In staves 46–57 Pat, who is the only girl in the group without any brothers and sisters in her household, invokes a similar 'happy-family' discourse as Natalie before. She indicates that she spoke to her father just the day before (stave 48), and that her little sister will be joining her in England once she is able to speak English (stave 47). Pat also displays sisterly pride when she speaks about the achievements and the talents of her younger sibling (stave 49–55). Talking about her little

brother and sister as well as about her father in this way allows Pat to
signal that she, too, has strong family bonds in spite of living as an only
child in a one-parent household.

Pat's revelation about her distant extended family is then mirrored by
Jenny, albeit to a different effect.

Extract 12: mums, dads and families – continued

(58)
Susan   {suppressed
Jenny   I have eight brothers and sisters

(59)
Susan   *laughter}*
Jenny   on my dad's side but I don't know
?   (lovely)

(60)
Pat   =I PHONED MY DAD [LAST NIGHT
Jenny   any of them caus::e-=   [they live

(61)
Pat   he (sends me)] money next /week   sending a
Jenny   in Essex]{amused}
?   (%fuck%)

(62)
Pat   hundred pound next {amused}week {laughs}   (1.5)
Susan   /hm (1.5)

(63)
?Pat   OH LET ME HAVE I:::T
Susan   (-) /no:::
                              {loud background talk}

Although Jenny's revelation about having eight brothers and sisters is
clearly triggered by Pat's positive account of her (geographically distant
but emotionally close) siblings, it contrasts sharply with Pat's picture of
a happy extended family, as Jenny does not even know any of her
brothers and sisters, let alone have any contact with them. The only
audible reaction from the other girls following Jenny's revelation about

having eight siblings is Susan's suppressed laughter (stave 58), although it is possible that one of the girls also produces what sounds like a (presumably ironic) 'lovely' in stave 59. Nobody signals any interest in Jenny's revelation or asks her to elaborate. It seems that the group does not evaluate Jenny's large family positively, suggesting that the girls perceive a family of this size to be deviant. In addition, after Jenny explains that she does not know any of her siblings, Pat abruptly changes the topic back to her own family situation in stave 60. Thus she indirectly contrasts her own, close, relationship with her geographically distant father with Jenny's lack of family ties.

Although it now becomes clear that it was Pat who had contacted her father and not the other way round Pat manages to construct her father as responsible as he fulfils his traditional role of providing financial support for his offspring. This utterance, together with the girls' other talk about their mothers and (extended) families suggests that most of the girls in this group, more or less successfully, present themselves as being part of a larger, that is, not a one-parent, caring family. Although it is clear that the families the girls live in do not tend to correspond to the traditional 'ideal' (as in two or more cases the parents are either geographically or, in Susan's case, to some extent emotionally distant) most of the girls make an effort to present themselves as loved and cared for daughters. It is very likely that the comparatively 'untraditional' family backgrounds of Pat, Jenny and Natalie could have encouraged the girls to construct their family bonds as more significant on a discursive level, whereas the aim of the upper-middle-class girls (and the Bangladeshi girls in traditional two-parent families) is the opposite, namely to position themselves and their families as less traditional and sheltered.

Grown-ups or adolescents?

Several of the data extracts from above contain evidence that at the same time as highlighting the significance of their mothers and families, the girls in the group aim to construct themselves as independent grown-ups. As I shall argue in this section, the girls' alignment with the subject position of the grown-up does not necessarily go hand in hand with a rejection of their mothers' voices which I discussed previously. On the contrary, the girls' adult identities are often based on an internalisation/appropriation of their mothers' or other authoritative voices. However, adult voices of authority and reason are set against voices of adolescent adventure and rebelliousness, as the following extracts from the girls' talk about truancy, vandalism and boyfriends show.

Truancy: authoritative adults vs. resistant adolescents

In this section I return to the girls' talk about truancy (see Extracts 1–3).
The following extract precedes the girls' discussion about their mothers'
stances towards bunking off school.

Extract 13: why ain't Hannah in

(1)
Pat   oh no don't stop it don't
Jenny   **why** ain't Hannah in

(2)
Pat   stop it don't stop [(it)]
Susan   [Hannah] just ain't in she's

(3)
Pat   (.) *[bursts out laughing]*
Susan   never in
Natalie   (.) (right=)   =I see her last

(4)
Natalie   **night** on the way home (and she told me)

(5)
Pat   [she needs to come]   in **school** [Nat]
Natalie   [(she can't) come in tomorrow]   [yeah]

(6)
Pat   (.) [(I'm just saying) I'm just saying-
?Jenny   (.) [(and what did she say)
Natalie   (.) [DON'T TELL **ME:::** (XXXXXXXXXXXXXXXXXX ME)

In this brief extract about one of their classmate's absences from school
the girls negotiate a range of voices, discourses and subject positions. In
stave 1 Jenny introduces the new topic by asking the others why
Hannah is not in school. After a brief aside (in which Pat appears to
instruct one of her friends not to stop the tape recorder) Susan is the first
one to reply to Jenny's question (staves 2–3). Susan's reply does not
really provide a direct answer to Jenny's question, but by highlighting
that there is no specific reason for Hannah absence and that she 'just
ain't in' because 'she's never in', Susan implies that Hannah is truanting

and, moreover, that this is not a one-off occurrence. Both the content and the tone of Susan's utterance appear matter-of-fact and signal Susan's reluctance to get involved in other people's affairs. However, although Susan does not evaluate Hannah's behaviour explicitly, her utterance expresses a critical stance at the same time. By suggesting that there are no reasons for Hannah's absences Susan implies that there are no *valid* reasons for Hannah's absences. (The other girls show their understanding of this implicature by their laughter and minimal acknowledgement in stave 3.) Susan's utterance therefore functions both as an acknowledgment of Hannah's right to make her own decisions and as an expression of her critical stance towards Hannah's decision.

Pat's criticism of Hannah's behaviour is neither phrased indirectly nor balanced by discourses of non-interference and self-determination like Susan's. In stave 5 Pat appears to point out the obvious to Natalie when she says that Hannah needs to come to school. However, Pat's utterance does not function as a statement conveying new or non-obvious information but instead constitutes an indirect directive. This is confirmed by Natalie's reaction in stave 6 'don't tell **me**', which indicates that she interpreted Pat's utterance as a directive to take action (to make Hannah come to school). The raised volume and the emphatic stress on 'me' in Natalie's utterance in stave 6 show that she feels that Pat's directive should not have been addressed to her, but instead to Hannah.

Pat's utterance 'she needs to come in school Nat' invokes what I interpret as a voice of authority, which in the group's talk has previously been associated with the girls' mothers (e.g. Extracts 1, 3). I argue that in this utterance Pat's own voice merges with an adult voice which indexes a stance of (parental or institutional) authority and reason. Interestingly, however, Pat does not mark this voice as different from her own with the help of grammatical, prosodic or non-verbal cues. I interpret this example as an instance of voice 'appropriation' where, as Maybin (2007: 144) argues, 'the speaker does not simply repeat someone else but takes on the given words and makes them their own'. Whereas Maybin found many instances of 10–12-year old children's appropriation of teacher's voices and therefore institutional discourses in her classroom research, Coates (1999: 131) provides evidence of mother's voices being 'internalised' by the 12/13-year-old daughters in her diachronic study of girls' talk. By appropriating an adult voice and subsequently a discourse which encourages (parental or institutional) authority Pat thus positions herself as a grown-up. Her adult authority, however, is met with some resistance; it is challenged by Natalie directly and countered by Susan's discourse of non-interference.

Vandalism: reasonable adults vs. rebellious adolescents

The topic of truancy is not the only one which encourages some of the girls to adopt a voice of authority as the following extract shows. Here Natalie had been clowning around during the recordings in one of the empty classrooms during break time, and several noises on the tape indicate that she has damaged something as a result of this.

Extract 14: school vandalism

(1)
Pat   are you going out
Susan   just stop vandalising the school

(2)
Pat   to/night (-) *{very serious}*Natalie did **you** do that

(3)
Pat   on the wall there with the back of your shoes
Jenny   *{- laughs-}*
Natalie   /no

(4)
Pat   alright then (1)   *{laughing}*you did
Natalie   *{suppressed laugh}*
Jenny   *{laughs}*

(5)
Pat   you did*{laughing loudly}*oh:: God
Susan   (Natalie) is vandalising
?   *{laughs}*

(6)
Pat   \yea::::h=
Susan   the school (then)   [d'you] remember
Natalie   =oh SHUT [UP]

(7)
Susan   d'you remember when I got in trouble for that thing

Previously to stave 1 Pat, Susan and Jenny had been laughing about Natalie's clowning around, however then the tone changes. In stave 1

Susan adopts a serious tone of voice to direct Natalie to 'stop vandalising the school'. The fact that Susan voiced a similar utterance in what appeared to be an amused voice just a couple of staves earlier makes it more difficult to assess the seriousness of this directive. By contrast, Pat's tone of voice is sharply marked as serious in staves 2–3 when she asks Natalie whether she had done something to the wall, presumably marking or damaging it, with the back of her shoes.

With regard to both truancy and vandalism Pat appears to have taken on or appropriated a voice of reason and authority which is frequently associated with the perspectives and positions of adults such as parents and teachers. Although her tone of voice is different from her usual, Pat clearly does not wish to mock the voice she thus adopts. On the contrary, the serious tone supports the serious content of Pat's utterance. Natalie both acknowledges and briefly adapts to Pat's self-positioning as an authoritative and authoritarian adult by producing a child-like denial at the end of stave 3. The rising tone on '/no' aids Pat's and Natalie's co-construction of asymmetrical roles during these couple of staves as it renders her denial less challenging than a (high) falling tone. In spite of Jenny's laughter in stave 3, Pat accepts Natalie's denial in the same serious voice as before. However, after a one-second pause, which is likely to have been accompanied by some conclusive facial expressions as well as the subsequent laughter of what appears to be Natalie, Pat abandons her serious voice/position of authority. Pat's laughter in staves 5–6 does not seem forced and her realisation that Natalie had been lying about not having damaged the wall ('you did you did') does not carry a bitter overtone.

It seems to me that this abrupt switch between seriousness and fun goes hand in hand with a switch of subject positions. Whereas the serious voice quality functions as a marker of Pat's mature grown-up identity, the laughter indicates her alignment with her friend's cheeky and rebellious teenage identity. Again, Susan's positioning is more ambiguous. She repeats her earlier reprimand about vandalising the school in staves 5–6 in a rather unmarked voice. However, Susan's repetition occurs after Pat's hearty laughter which signalled the end of Pat's authoritative stance and her re-alignment with a more symmetrical position within the group. This makes it unlikely that Susan intends her utterance about vandalising to function as a serious reprimand. It is more likely that her utterance should be interpreted as an instance of stylisation, which Maybin (2007: 144), drawing on Bakhtin (1984: 189), explains as 'where a voice is reproduced as if it were one's own but with "a slight shadow of objectification" (Bakhtin

1984: 189)'. That is, it seems that (despite not adopting a mocking tone) Susan engages in a stylised and ironic imitation of (Pat's) voice of authority, thereby signalling that she does not seriously seek to align herself with this position of authority. Indeed Natalie's reaction 'oh shut up' and Susan's subsequent self-positioning as rebellious provide further evidence for the playful framing of Susan's utterance about vandalising the school. In the subsequent section of talk (not included) Susan initiates a session of reminiscing about little acts of rebellion against teacher (with teachers' voices being playfully subverted) in which all the other girls join in. This shows that assuming an authoritative adult voice towards a fellow member of the group can be a risky undertaking and needs to be mitigated by alignment with subject positions which put the girls on a more equal footing.

Boyfriends and school: responsible adults vs. adventurous adolescents

In their talk the girls both adopt and challenge adult voices. They construct themselves as reasonable and responsible on one hand and adventurous and rebellious on the other. The following longer extract shows the girls' (complex) effort to balance these competing voices, discourses and stances in relation to heterosexual dating and educational success.

Extract 15: education vs. boys

(1)
Susan   but I reckon it affects school (xxxxxxxxxx)
                                              {banging noise}

(2)
Susan   (1) cause I know that (.) (like) (-) /m/

(3)
Susan   [forever talking about] (.) and yeah f:orever
?Natalie   [(xxxx thinks xxx him)]

(4)
Susan   talking about the actual person (-)
                                              {banging noise}

(5)
Susan   [(%xxxxx%)]   *{laughs}*
?   yeah we know <u>you</u> [a:re]*{amused}{laughs}*

(6)
Natalie   (catch up) a bit on Johnny
Jenny   (-) (<u>Johnny</u>)*{amused}*

In stave 1 Susan invokes a discourse which positions an adolescent girl's heterosexual relationship with a boyfriend as a distraction from her education. Although Susan presents herself as the originator of her utterance '*I reckon* it affects school (my emphasis)' it is likely that her own voice is merged with the voices of parental or educational authority.[6] Evidence for the link between this discourse and the voices of parents and teachers is provided in feminist research from education and sociology by Louise Archer, Anna Halsall, and Sumi Hollingworth (2007: 172). Archer et al. (2007: 170) also highlight the classed connotations of this discourse, arguing that the ' "ideal (female) pupil" is actually a specifically middle-class (and de-sexualised) subject position' whereas 'within dominant educational discourse, working-class femininity is read [...] as both overtly and *overly* sexual and is positioned as antithetical to educational engagement and success' (emphasis in original). This discourse, similarly to another discourse which Harris (2004: 25–36) labels 'young women at risk', positions young people, and particularly young working-class girls, as incapable of successfully balancing their relationship and their education, differently from adults for whom this dual focus is accepted as the norm. Indeed even research which problematises this discourse, like Archer et al.'s (2007) study on young working-class women's educational (dis)engagement, provides evidence to suggest that 'the capital accrued by having a boyfriend often worked against other forms of capital – for instance, depleting economic and educational capital' (Archer et al. 2007: 170, 171). The remainder of the conversation demonstrates Susan's awareness of both forms of capital, one more valuable in her peer group and the other in an institutional and/or adult context.

Natalie's switch into a very brief episode of teasing as a reaction to Susan's self-positioning in staves 5–6 signals once more the difficulty for members of the group to adopt a voice and stance of adult authority or reason. However, the remainder of the extract indicates that, unlike in Ardiana's group (see Chapter 4) the teasing does not prevent other members of the group from engaging in a serious discussion of the topic.

After a brief exchange (not included) in which Jenny, who is in a relationship, and Pat, who currently isn't, join Susan in praising the benefits of being single, but Natalie challenges Susan's stance in a mitigated yet unplayful manner, the ambiguity of Susan's position becomes apparent in the next extract.

Extract 16: education vs. boys – continued

(15)
Susan   but I'd rather (him) he didn't exist like (xxxx)

(16)
Susan   =cause I('d) (.) %I% I'd rather get on with

(17)
Susan   all education and >everything< and then after=

(18)
Pat   [but] if you
Susan   =but then again .hhh (.) I'll be ju[st]

(19)
Pat   [were with] hi::m- (.) yeah=
Susan   [boring]
Natalie   =but then you'll be
?   {very quiet

(20)
Pat   yeah and you don't
Natalie thinking "(well) what if what if"
?   mumbling in background}

(21)
Pat   wanna think that [.hh believe me]
Natalie   [>you don't wanna do that<]

(22)
Pat   [like you regr-]
Natalie (finishing) li:ke [so you just] [***jump** in
**Natalie snaps fingers*

(23)
Natalie   with **two** feet (man) the same's me (-) just hope

(24)
Natalie   for the best (then) (.) so >that's what I (*did)<
*or: 'that's what I('d do)'

Susan's declaration 'I'd rather get on with my education' clearly taps into an institutional discourse which many other students at their school were familiar with. My group of Bangladeshi girls from the same school, who tended to take the most pronounced anti-school stances among the three groups I studied, also voiced this discourse occasionally. Ardiana, who usually positioned herself as bored by school, once even pronounced that 'I wanna finish my qualifications now yeah get a good GCSE grade .hh then get a really good job and then get married'. As I argued above, it is likely that this discourse (about prioritising education over heterosexual relationships) entered the girls' discursive repertoire through their adaptation of their teachers' voices (see also Archer et al. 2007).

However, in staves 18–19 Susan qualifies her earlier objections towards her boyfriend by implying that if she did in fact prioritise her education over her boyfriend she would be 'boring'. This suggests that Susan is very much aware of the voices of her peers and subsequently of what Archer et al. (2007: 171, see above) refer to as 'the capital accrued by having a boyfriend' in her peer group (Chapter 5 provides supporting evidence from my own data). Whereas Roberta and the upper-middle-class girls from the private school position themselves as relatively unconcerned about capital associated with active female heterosexuality, the same does not hold true for Susan and her friends. Susan has to be very careful in her attempts to construct herself as a responsible, mature girl if she wants to avoid the image of a boring swat. The boyfriend appears to gain in significance at this moment, as he is essential in allowing Susan to tread a narrow line between these two subject positions.

The other girls in the group clearly recognise Susan's dilemma. Pat, who previously constructed both herself and Susan as independent girls by highlighting their lack of need for a boyfriend stops short in her utterance in staves 18–19 'but if you were with him' and after a micro pause acknowledges her understanding for Susan's new position (stave 19: 'yeah') Natalie then invokes what I would classify as a discourse of youthful adventure which encourages young people to gain their own experience and determine their own life (rather than being guided by adult reason and authority). Natalie's utterance in stave 20 implies that if Susan prevented herself from being with her boyfriend she would only be left to wonder what it would have been like to be with him ('what if what if') rather than having tried it out herself. Natalie and Pat here highlight the benefits of learning from experience and both refer to their past experiences to back up their argument (staves 20–24). Natalie's utterance in staves 22–24 constitutes a clear and succinct summary of the discourse of 'youthful adventure'.

The remainder of the extract, which is not included here for lack of space, contains more evidence of the girls' negotiation of different voices and stances. Just like their talk about truancy and vandalism, the girls' conversations about balancing their boyfriends with their education allow them to experiment with subject positions of both grown-ups and adolescents in their group, quoting and appropriating adult voices in one moment and opposing them with discourses of youthful adventure in the next.

Conclusion

This chapter has explored some of the most central subject positions which Pat and her friends negotiate in their talk, including loved and protected daughters, reasonable and mature grown-ups, and self-determined or even rebellious teenagers.

The subject position of the daughter is highly significant to the girls in this group. Several girls in the group are being brought up by their mothers in single families and in their group talk most present themselves as close to their mothers. Some of the girls, particularly Pat and Natalie, who both live separately from their fathers, make an effort to present themselves as being part of a larger, caring family, emphasising the (active) role that their fathers and/or siblings play in their lives. My data provides evidence for Finch's (2007) argument that 'displaying families' is a significant practice for all families, but particularly for 'non-traditional' families like single-parent households or families which extend across one household as in the case of several of the girls in this group. Differently from the white upper-middle-class girls who all live with both their parents, Pat, Susan, Natalie and Jenny also do not reject the position of sheltered (that is watched over and loved) girl. On the contrary, the girls tend to position their mothers as protective and at times even authoritarian.

At the same time it is important to the girls in the group to be able to make their own decisions, especially if their private lives are concerned.

However, although the girls criticise their mothers' exaggerated concern for their daughters' sexual innocence, they frequently do not position themselves in opposition to their mothers' voices in less private matters. In fact, several examples indicate that the girls quote or even appropriate (Bakhtin 1981; Maybin 2007) their mothers' or other authoritative voices to construct themselves as mature and reasonable grown-ups, for example when they object to truancy and vandalism or when they talk about prioritising education over boyfriends. A focus on the range of competing voices in the girls' talk and on their negotiation and framing of these voices allowed for a closer examination of the complex process of interactive positioning which takes place in the group. Thus, the data capture the girls' joint efforts to balance adult voices of reason and discipline with teenage voices of adventure and rebellion in an effort to negotiate subject positions which are sanctioned by the group.

Social class is never topicalised in the talk of Jenny, Pat, Susan and Natalie, however, I argue that this chapter contains evidence of the classed connotations and implications of some of the girls' positioning. The comparison of my data from Pat's (working class) and Roberta's (upper middle class) group yielded, together with many similarities, a number of interesting differences in the positioning of the girls. Roberta and her private-school friends tended to position their parents as liberal and cool rather than authoritarian, and tried to align themselves with anti-school stances (countered, of course, by their successful academic trajectories) or other non-conformist or street-wise stances (in their talk about drugs and music). By contrast, Pat and her friends from the East End frequently positioned themselves as protected daughters, mostly of emotionally close, if, at times, physically distant (as divorced) families, and made efforts to adopt pro-school and pro-academic stances in various instances (despite the fact that their academic trajectories were far from certain). With Skeggs (1997) I attribute these efforts to the girls' desire to gain respectability, which, in many ways implies a disidentification from their working-class background. Skeggs (1997:1) argues that 'respectability is one of most ubiquitous signifiers of class' but at the same time acknowledges that 'class connotations may be ubiquitous but they are rarely directly spoken by those who do not want to be reminded of their social poisoning in relation to it' (Skeggs 1997: 77).

I interpret the girls' orientation towards their mothers, their families and other authoritarian voices as attempts to position themselves in opposition to negative stereotypes about working-class adolescents, women or single-parent families. Skeggs (1997) writes about the participants in her study on working-class femininity '[t]he women of this study are aware of their place, of how they are socially positioned, and of the attempts to represent them. [...] they recognize the recognition of others' (ibid. 3–4). In this vein I argue that by positioning themselves in opposition to subject positions like that of the neglected daughter, the vandalising truant, the (pregnant) school dropout, the future teenage mother, the girls demonstrate their awareness of pathologising discourses of (young) working-class femininity and their desire to disidentify from them (see also Frazer 1988, 1992; McDermott 2004; Skeggs, 1997, 2004; Reay 1998; Walkerdine et al. 2001). By constructing themselves as sheltered and responsible both about their education and about boys and sex (see also Chapter 5) Pat and her friends orient to discourses of respectable middle-class femininity (Skeggs 1997). Ironically, it is this femininity which in many ways is countered by Roberta and her upper-middle-class private-school friends in an effort to construct themselves as cool.

4
Tough and Respectable British Bangladeshi Girls

This chapter focuses on the spontaneous friendship talk of a group of adolescent British Bangladeshi girls from the East End in London. The talk of Ardiana, Dilshana, Hennah and Varda is complemented by ethnographic-style interviews which I carried out one year later with one of the girls (see Chapter 1). Both sources of data highlight the significance of ethnic and religious aspects of the girls' construction of cultural identities, intersected with gender and social (class) positionings as well as with situated practices of the girls' friendship group. The girls' conversations about school, dating, love and marriage contain stances and discourses which indicate an alignment with tough ladette or British working-class femininities on one hand, and respectable as well as respectful young Muslim Bangladeshi femininities on the other. My analysis of the girls' talk shows that Ardiana and her friends construct different cultural identities which, as Stuart Hall (1992) argues, 'are not fixed, but poised, in transition, between different positions; which draw on different cultural traditions at the same time; and which are the product of those complicated crossovers and cultural mixes'.

Whereas young British Asians have been at the centre of a wide range of research disciplines, including anthropology, sociology, psychology, education and cultural studies, language and gender research has so far not focused on the informal talk and the identity practices of British Asian girls. Moreover, research on language and ethnicity which has embraced the concept of 'new ethnicities' and 'hybridity' (Hewitt 1986; Rampton 1995; Sebba 1993) tends to focus on linguistic style and features of pronunciation, grammar and lexis in analyses of code-switching/mixing and crossing, rather than discourse. My own exploration of the discourse and identity practices of a group of London Bangladeshi girls therefore draws heavily on cross-disciplinary research on young British Asian identities and aims to provide a space in language and gender research for the voices of adolescent Asian girls. At the same time my discourse analytic exploration of my conversational data seeks to offer to cross-disciplinary research a detailed focus on the complex interactive and situated processes of these formations of cultural identity by linking my analysis of discourse to an exploration of conversational frames, the sequential organisation of the interaction, including pauses, lexical and syntactic features, non-verbal signs such as laughter and paralinguistic features like a change of voice.

The remainder of this section gives an overview of the non-linguistic research on British Asians, exploring empirical studies as well as theoretical concepts such as 'culture', 'ethnicity' and 'hybridity'. The chapter then proceeds to the analysis of my own data, first discussing the group's positioning as 'tough British girls' in their anti-school/truanting talk and their tough teasing, then presenting data which reveals the influence of Bangladeshi Muslim discourses on the girls' negotiations of topics such as love and dating, and finally exploring both discourses of hybridity and culture clash in relation to the girls' frequent conversations about marriage, by comparing my own interpretation of the girls' spontaneous talk with the (at times conflicting) perspective of my in-group informant, Hennah, in our informal interviews.[1]

British Asian identities: a crossdisciplinary overview

Popular media representations of young British Asians continue to perpetuate the stereotype of the suppressed Asian girl as a victim of culture clash (e.g. Cramb, writing in the *Daily Telegraph* 25/04/2002; Kelbie, writing in the *Independent* 30/08/2006). These representations contribute to a discourse of 'cultural pathology' (Brah 1996: 74; Shain 2003: 9), which positions 'Asian culture' in terms of constraints and essentialises the concept of 'culture' itself. Early academic work such as Watson (1977) and the Community Relations Commission (1976) did not present an altogether different perspective, describing the situation of second-generation Asian adolescents in Britain as being trapped 'between two cultures'.

On the other hand, in the last ten years research in anthropology, sociology, cultural studies and education has highlighted that young British born 'Asians' are experienced users of a range of British and Asian cultural practices, thereby developing bicultural or 'hybrid' identities (Anwar 1998; Ballard 1994; Barker 1997, 1998; Brah 1996; Dwyer 2000; Gavron 1997; Gardner and Shukur 1994; Ghuman 1994, 2003; Modood et al. 1994; Pollen 2002; Shain 2003). The heterogeneity obscured by the category 'Asian' has been challenged in larger-scale, comparative studies such as Muhammed Anwar (1998), Paul Singh Ghuman (1994, 2003) and Tariq Modood, Sharon Beishon, and Satnam Virdee (1994). Both Anwar and Ghuman approach their data from a perspective of biculturalism, which views British Asianness more in terms of switching in between two different 'cultures' in alignment with linguistic codeswitching (Ballard 1994: 31) but does not problematise the concept of 'culture' to the extent of later 'hybridity' studies. Ghuman's (2003) psychological study also contains what Archer (2001: 81) describes as pathologising representations of Asian girls, arguing that many of the girls in his research, especially those from Pakistani and Bangladeshi working-class backgrounds, suffer from gender inequality, which may cause 'serious psychological tension' (Ghuman 2003: 168; for a feminist critique of Ghuman see Archer 2001, 2002a).

Pathologising culture-clash theories were challenged as early as two decades ago in the work of feminist scholars who argued that the situation of black/Asian adolescents, and, particularly girls, could not be explained satisfactorily by focusing only on the black/Asian community. Instead, a consideration of macro-social constraints and asymmetries caused by racism, class, gender, sexuality and education needs to be foregrounded (Amos and Parmar 1981; Brah and Minhas 1985). More recent feminist critiques retain this focus on racism but are founded in a constructionist rather than a structuralist argument. The work of Fauzia Ahmad (2003), Claire Alexander (2000), Louise Archer (2001, 2002 a, b), Avtar Brah (1996), Claire Dwyer (2000) and Farzana Shain (2003) challenges earlier studies and conceptualisations of British Asian adolescents for their essentialist approach to culture and identity as fixed and static, with 'Asian-ness' and 'British-ness' as independent, a priori and, moreover, homogenous categories. Much of this work focuses on second and third generation South Asian young women, and rather than being shaped by notions of conflict and oppression, is framed as a 'celebration' of hybridity (Puwar 2003: 31–6; but see also Archer's 2001, 2002 critique of Ghuman 2001, and Ahmad's 2003's critique of Bhopal 1999).

Alexander (2000), Archer (2001, 2002a, b), Dwyer (2000) and Shain (2003) share an ethnographic and/or qualitative approach to their studies of 'Asian' adolescents as well as a focus on the young people's agency in negotiating cultural practices and intersecting ethnic, gender and class identities. Dwyer explores how hybridity is constructed through styles of clothing employed in different ways by Muslim working-class and middle-class girls in two schools. Alexander's (2000) long-term ethnographic study of a small group of South London Asian men challenges the cultural pathology of discourses surrounding stereotypical representations of the 'Asian gang' as both radicalised and hyper-masculine. Providing evidence of aggression as well as friendship and solidarity, Alexander presents a picture of 'Asian' masculinities in a 'gang' as complex, heterogeneous and flexible. Whereas Alexander's analysis of discourse tends to be content-driven, Archer's feminist discourse analytic approach to her interview data draws on the tradition of discursive psychology, which, just like conversation analytic or linguistic ethnographic approaches to identity, highlights the co-construction of meaning in spoken interaction, and foregrounds the role and positionality of the researcher (Archer 2002b; see also Pichler, 2008a). Archer (2002a) highlights the importance of introducing a focus on the discursive positioning of young gendered and ethnic identities into discussions of British Muslims' educational 'choices'. Shain's (2003) research also explores the construction of gendered identities in the context of schooling, identifying different strategies adopted by four groups of mostly working-class Muslim girls ('Gang Girls', 'Survivors', 'Rebels', and 'Faith Girls') to cope with their experience of schooling. In her discussion of these strategies Shain highlights the girls' active role in negotiating gender, class and 'cultural' aspects of their identities, a focus which will be shared by the present study.

Many of these recent studies from anthropology, cultural studies, education and sociology adopt a (feminist) poststructuralist approach to culture, conceptualising it 'not [as] an essence but a *positioning*' (Hall 1990: 226), or, in other words, viewing culture not as a reified, homogenous entity (Bauman 1997: 211) but instead as a 'process' and as a 'semiotic space with infinite class, caste, gender, ethnic or other inflections' (Brah 1996: 234, 246). The spontaneous talk of the Bangladeshi girls in this study contains what I would interpret as rich evidence for the process of invoking, challenging and synthesising cultural practices and discourses with various 'inflections' and thus, for the local negotiation of 'cultures of hybridity' (Hall 1992: 310). However, my interview data suggest that this performative notion of culture and the celebration of cultural hybridity are not always shared by the research participants themselves. This combination of data sources and the contextualisation of my linguistic research in a cross-disciplinary research context has therefore encouraged me to develop a critical and reflexive approach to my analysis, building both on academic theorisation and my participants' lived experience of culture and hybridity, and even considering the possible limitations of my own work.

Tough girls: truanting and teasing

Differently from the stereotype of the timid Asian girl, and, in fact more so than the other two groups of girls whose talk I explored, the group talk of Ardiana, Dilshana, Hennah, Varda and Rahima often features a display of toughness. This toughness is achieved both on a content level, by the adoption of anti-school and truanting stances, and on a formal/stylistic level of language, by the girls' verbal challenges and insults in the form of teasing and boasting.

Truanting anti-school girls

Although the girls do engage in some talk about school work and grades (see Extract 3) and Hennah even tends to position herself as a diligent pupil, the group frequently adopts an anti-academic stance, complaining that school is 'boring', boasting about their attempts to escape this boredom by 'bunking off' (truanting), and forging their parents signatures in order to be able to 'bunk off' some more.

The following extract captures Varda's attempt to skip a couple of her classes by forging her father's signature in a fake letter of excuse to her form teacher. The extract begins with Ardiana reading out the draft letter that Varda has been working on.

Extract 1: Dear sir/madam

(1)
Ardiana   *{reading}*"dear sir/madam [could you please allow]
Varda   [I need her signature]

(2)
Ardiana   my daughter Varda 11A to leave school at two:: pm

(3)
Ardiana   .hhh   [because] she has (.) =[/WHAT dental]
Varda   CAL[M down]
?Dilshana   (she=[is calm xxxxxx)]

(4)
Ardiana   treatment [at two forty-five] p.m. (.)   [she]
Rahima   (.) oh [man]
Dilshana   [(this is xxxxxxx)]

(5)
Ardiana   needs to <u>come home</u>/*staccato*/ (and collect my wife)
Rahima   LET ME GO HO:::ME
?   (XXXXXXXXXXX)
[...]

(6)
Varda   *doro! Shashima sign kori desil on nia ame puram na* look
Bengali: "doh! Shashima signed it for me and now I can't do it"

(7)
Ardiana   (1)
Varda   this one is erm a bit sus**picious** but this one is good (1)

(8)
Ardiana   [you're **mad**]
Varda   [(>Hennah can you] come and do it<) (-) *Shashmia ola

(9)
Ardiana   =let me see let me try
Varda   koriya zeya ki mola*   I swear=
                              {scribbling}
Bengali: "Shashmia goes like this somehow"

(10)
Ardiana   if I ca[n]   (-)   [forge] *korai ko*
Varda   [he]re (-) (so) this [one is-]
                              {shuffling paper}
Bengali: "you are forging"

(11)
Ardiana   >you're out of order< (to forge xxxxxxx)

In this extract Varda, whose contribution to the group's self-recorded talk tends to be less frequent but more in Bengali/Sylheti faces a dilemma. The dilemma consists of the fact that Shashmia, who usually forges the signature of Varda's father, is not present.[2] This time Varda's excuse for missing school is an alleged dental appointment, as the content of the letter, read out aloud by Ardiana in staves 1–5, reveals. Varda's forging attempts are clearly seen as problematic by Ardiana, as her comments in stave 8 and staves 10–11 certify. However Varda is not the only member in the group who wishes she could end her school day now (see Rahima, staves 4–5). Moreover, Varda herself is more pre-occupied with the quality of the forged letter or signature (staves 6–7) and calmly demands help from the most pro-school girl in the group, Hennah, whose nickname in the group is 'Miss Education' but who is also a close friend of Varda.

This extract shows that the anti-school stance which characterises much of the group's talk is different from the one that is evident in the group of private-school girls. Although the girls do occasion-ally, especially following the lead of Hennah, take a more positive stance to a teacher or to education, talking for example about want-ing to complete their GCSEs successfully (see Pichler 2007b), their frequent expression of anti-school stances is not equally balanced by pro-education positions and discourses, as in the private-school group. Moreover, truanting is not part of the private-school girls' repertoire, whereas planning of and reminiscing about truanting episodes is central to the anti-school stance of the Bangladeshi East End girls. All of the girls in the group had truanted in the past, as the following extract shows.

Extract 2: it was a laugh man

(1)
Hennah   can you remember all- (-) (but) **she** remembers it .hh

(2)
Hennah   (innit) all the time we (1) %bunked% {laughs}
Varda   yeah I
?   (what)

(3)
Hennah   (remember xxxxxxx) Stratford we went Forest Gate
Varda   (know xxxxxxxxxxx)

(4)
Hennah   yeah loads of places (man) .hh
[…]

(5)
Ardiana   we never got caught me I used to bunk off every time every

(6)
Ardiana   lesson Bengali::: [(Rahima and me)]
Rahima   [yeah we used to hid] in (the) toilet

(7)
Ardiana   yeah we used to hid in the toilet=[do you know where
Rahima   innit   =[(we used to hide

(8)
Ardiana   where (our old)] do you know where Miller School Miller
Rahima   in rooms]

(9)
Ardiana   Girl was   you know where the cafeteria is=
Rahima   yeah   =yeah we know=

(10)
Ardiana   we used to climb the tree and get over the walls but

(11)
Ardiana   [= since]   since we got caught yeah (.) cause one of the
Hennah   [=oh my] God

(12)
Ardiana   caretakers saw us   and we done a runner*(laughing)* (.) and
Hennah   *ya
*Bengali: "oh no"

(13)
Ardiana   (any]thing) yeah (.) that's because (we're **so**) after that
?   (/hm)]

(14)
Ardiana   yeah they took the tree off cause no one could go away

(15)
Ardiana   then   [and then we] were on report for two
Hennah   oh::: *(laughs)* [no wonder]

(16)
Ardiana   weeks   (-) but still it was a laugh man
Hennah   (.) oh my God

This extract is from a longer episode in which the girls boast about their truanting. In the first three staves Hennah constructs herself and the others as a truants, first more tentatively (see reduced utterance volume of 'bunked; in stave 2), then, with the support of Varda: 'yeah I know', with more certainty. This performance is mirrored shortly afterwards by Ardiana and Rahima. During Ardiana's following mini-narrative Hennah offers encouragingly shocked and equally delighted audience feedback in staves 11, 12 and 16. Adopting a linguistic marker in the form of the common non-standard past-tense form 'done' Ardiana, who usually uses standard past tense forms, signals her toughness both in language content and form. Ardiana tends to lead the group in taking up an anti-school stance but her performance is supported even by Hennah. Like the 'Gang Girls' in Shain (2003) Ardiana and her friends like to position themselves as truants, and like the Gang Girls they frequently signal that having 'a laugh' (stave 16) is more important than academic achievement.

Having a laugh is a central practice in the group in many ways. Ardiana and her friends rely significantly more on playful speech activities such as teasing to create solidarity and friendship than the other two female friendship groups I studied. In addition to describing this truanting adventure as 'a laugh', the girls in this group repeatedly express their concern about not being bored.

Extract 3: school's boring

(1)
Ardiana   {whistling}
Dilshana   but you know she done the Higher Paper (that's why she's got

(2)
Ardiana   {keeps on whistling}
Hennah   if I (did-) if I've got e::rm (.) in the Foundation Pape::r (-)
Dilshana   a U)

(3)
Ardiana   {keeps on whistling}
Hennah   forty-eight (-) (then I would've got an::) (1.5) %(E)% (-) I guess

(4)
Ardiana   OH:: yous lot are **boring** man [talking about school]
?Hennah   [no she's got a U]
?   (xxxxxx)

(5)
Ardiana   *{tuts}* school'[s bori]ng
?Hennah   [(well)] this is not boring=[sing]ing
Dilshana   =[I know]

(6)
Ardiana   [excuse me (we] weren't)
Hennah   boring *<u>songs</u> *{laughs}*
Dilshana   IT'S NOT BO[RING SONG]
*{*laughing voice}*

(7)
Ardiana   singing songs [are /we]
Hennah   <u>EXCUSE **ME**</u> and I am*{amused}*
Dilshana   [\innit] (.)

(8)
Ardiana   yeah you **are deaf**
Hennah   <u>supposed to be deaf</u>

(9)
Hennah   (-) [excuse me (xxxx)] thinking about some
Rahima   (-) [you mean YOU ARE]

After Ardiana's boasting about having the lowest marks in her form
group a few minutes earlier this short extract captures Ardiana's growing
impatience with talk about school and exam results. The first three staves
show how Ardiana uses whistling to indirectly demonstrate a lack of
interest in the conversation of Hennah and Dilshana. In stave 4 she
finally challenges the rest of the group directly and makes her anti-school
stance explicit, followed by a tough challenge of Rahima in stave 8. Thus,
whereas skipping school is a laugh, talking about school is boring.

Stephen Frosh, Ann Phoenix, and Rob Pattman (2002: 104) show in
their interview-based research that adolescent boys position '[m]essing
around and having a laugh' as typical of young, unconscientious boys,
contrasting this popular and laddish masculinity with femininity,
maturity and academic achievement. Frosh et al. (2002: 104) also appear
to align themselves with Paul Willis' (1977) study on adolescent
working-class boys, 'the lads', for whom 'having a laugh' signals non-
conformity with adult or school authority and therefore constitutes an
important part of an 'anti-academic culture'. Moreover, Frosh et al.'s

popular boys, Willis' working class 'lads' and Mac an Ghaill's (1994) working-class 'Macho guys' all appear to suggest a (more or less direct) relationship between young masculine anti-school stances and social class, with the former two studies positioning 'having a laugh' as a strategy to accomplish adolescent working-class masculinities.

Thus, Ardiana's and the other girls' preference for 'having a laugh' can be seen as an expression of their anti-academic stance, and by extension, as an effort to construct themselves in opposition to the goals and authority of the school. Although the above studies associate anti-school and tough stances with tough and/or working class masculinity, research on ladette culture suggest that these behaviours and practices are not the sole domain of young men. Siân Preece (2006: 148) identifies 'having a laugh, acting cool and being tough' as characteristics of ladettes. Preece (2006), Imelda Whelehan (2000) and Carolyn Jackson (2006) see ladette femininities as orienting to laddish masculinity, with Jackson also highlighting associations with stereo-typical working classness. Jackson (2006: 354) argues that although there are clearly middle-class ladettes, the '[...] disruptive (school classes, social order), crude (swearing, rudeness), aggressive (verbal and occasionally physical) [...] behaviours attributed to "ladettes" remain associated with the "least desirable", "unrespectable" elements of working class lifestyles' (Skeggs, 1997, 2004).

My own data suggest that non-seriousness, toughness and anti-school stances are not only valued by groups of young men or white British ladettes. Like Shain's (2003) Gang Girls, Ardiana and her friends frequently position themselves in opposition to the stereotype of quiet, conscientious Asian femininity. The girls' rebellious, anti-school stance, combined with their prioritising of 'having a laugh' may well constitute an emulation of British lad culture practices. Certainly these practices and stances index toughness, and, I would argue, this toughness is indi-rectly accomplishing femininities with inflections of British youth- and lad(ette) culture, the latter carrying connotations of working classness.

Tough teasing

The following example explores the girls' display of toughness on a formal/stylistic level by focusing on several examples of teasing. My spon-taneous conversational data first highlighted the importance of teasing in the group of the five Bangladeshi girls by revealing that Ardiana and her friends produce on average 1 tease every 2 minutes, whereas Pat's group engage in teasing approximately every 3.4 minutes and Roberta's group as rarely as every 9.4 minutes. Although there is a substantial body of research on teasing (Alberts 1992; Boxer and Cortés-Condes 1997; Drew 1987; Eder 1990; Eisenberg 1986; Günthner 2000; Keltner et al. 2001; Miller 1986; Straehle 1993; Yedes 1996), Donna Eder's 1993 paper remains unique in its exclusive focus on teasing in girls' talk. Eder (1993) demonstrates that 10–14-year-old white American girls use teasing to maintain friendship, communicate romantic feelings to boys and subvert traditional gender roles. There is no comparable account of teasing in Britain, although Coates' (1999) diachronic study of a group of white British middle-class girls shows that playful language is central to girls' friendship talk at the age of twelve. However, Coates' girls stop experimenting with subject positions in a playful manner at the age of fourteen/fifteen and instead rely on mirrored self-disclosure to signal solidarity and friendship.

Eder (1990: 17) defines teasing as 'any playful remark aimed at another person, which can include mock challenges, commands, and threats as well as imitating and exaggerating someone's behaviour in a playful way'. Eder's definition emphasises the playful nature of teasing and therefore the need to differentiate teasing from serious challenges, insults and complaints. This distinction between 'play' and 'nonplay' was first made by Gregory Bateson (1987/1972: 185), who also introduces the concept of a (play) 'frame', which was developed by Erving Goffman (1974: 10) to refer to the 'principles of organisation which govern events [...] and our subjective involvement in them'. I shall define frames as (speakers' understanding of) different speech activities such as joking, teasing, discussing and arguing (Gumperz 1982; Tannen and Wallat 1993).

Whereas my closer, functional analysis of teasing in this group of girls also draws on ethnographic information, I identified teases on the basis of linguistic and paralinguistic information and cues contained in my recorded data. Thus, firstly, I established which provocative utterances were framed as playful by the speaker with the help of 'contextualisation cues' (Gumperz 1982: 131) such as laughter, a mocking or provocative tone of voice, exaggerated intonational patterns, contrastive stress, raised volume and faster speed of utterance delivery, syntactic and lexical repetition (see Eisenberg 1986: 184; 186 and Miller 1986: 203; Straehle 1993: 214–5) as well as formulaic expressions like 'shut up' and 'yes dear' (Drew 1987: 231; Straehle 1993: 219) and exaggerated lexis (Drew 1987: 231). Secondly, I explored the target's and other participants' interpretations of the challenge and of the teaser's intent by analysing their reactions in the turns following the teasing utterance, investigating the contextualisation cues that framed the responses to the tease. Thus, I classified any response that was framed as playful as evidence that the target had recognised the previous tease and was attempting to sustain the teasing frame. Eder (1993: 21) highlights the importance of a playfully framed response in a teasing sequence, '[i]n order for a teasing activity to remain playful the target of the teasing needs to respond in some non-serious manner'. If, however, the recipient defended herself in a serious voice I considered the dispute to have moved into a more serious frame.

My functional analysis of the numerous teasing episodes in the group of British Bangladeshi girls revealed that the girls used teasing as an extremely versatile, multifunctional linguistic resource to manage their friendship and negotiate identities (for a detailed discussion see Pichler 2006). The following extract will show how the girls use teasing to position themselves as tough. Just prior to this sequence the girls were complaining about a teacher who had given them too much homework. Only Hennah showed understanding of the amount of homework as she accepted the teacher's explanation that the form group needs to work harder as they 'are behind'. The other girls argued that this is not their own fault, but the teacher's, however staves 1–2 show that Hennah disagrees and defends the teacher's decisions.

Extract 4: I don't think so

(1)
Rahima   instead she goes *{contemptuous}*"<u>oh: the (sto[ry)</u>]"
Hennah   [ye]ah but

(2)
Hennah   if you don't understand the story [((from the beginning)]
Rahima   [but we do understand]

(3)
Hennah   (so she should [come xxxxxxxx)]
Rahima   the story don't /we   *{mocking}*[WE AIN'T **THAT**] **DUMB**

(4)
Ardiana   [we know Rahima you are]
Rahima   <u>we're (in comprende)</u>*{mock Spanish/French accent?}*
Varda   YOU WAS TAL[KING QUITE DUMB]

(5)
Ardiana   (1)   <u>we know you are</u>*{teasing}*
Rahima   (1) /what   (-) **oh::** that's because **you** are

6)
Ardiana   <u>I don't think so somehow I (get) **good** grades</u>*{sl. provoc.}*
?   *{faint chuckle}*

(7)
Ardiana   <u>in English you know (.) I've got A-star</u> (.)   [/right]
Rahima   *{mock impressed}* (.) <u>wo:[::w]</u>

(8)
Ardiana   .hhh*{nasal}* [I think] I (said yo[u:-)]   [(are
Rahima   [wow]   [yeah] that's [why

(9)
Ardiana   you doing that)]
Rahima   you're doing *Found]ation yeah I understand (-)
Dilshana   *{laughs}*
*foundation level of exam

(10)
Ardiana   I did *Higher **tu janishne (-)   =really >what do
Rahima   *{higher pitch}*\really=
?   *{yawn}*
*higher level of exam; **Bengali: "do you know?"

(11)
Ardiana   you [mean really<]   [REALLY REALLY] =did /I::
Rahima   [you done Founda]tio[n with me /right]=

(12)
Ardiana   ><u>I don't [think] so (somehow)</u><*{teasing}*   ><u>I don't think</u>
Rahima   [yeah]   <u>yeah you di::d</u>*{teasing}*

(13)
Ardiana   <u>so::</u><*{teasing voice}*   well that ain't
Rahima   <u>well that's you and your thing</u>*{amused}*

(14)
Ardiana   my:: me and my thing
Rahima   (-) (it i::s) (.) (*just saying it) *{amused voice}*
Dilshana   *{starts singing quietly}*

(15)
Ardiana   *{clears throat}* .hhh*{nasal}* (am I) *{starts humming}*
Dilshana   sing a song

The exchange starts as a serious dispute about a teacher between Rahima and Hennah. However, Rahima's second interruption, in stave 3, moves the exchange onto a more playful frame and appears to be aimed at bonding the group together rather than emphasising differences between them. When she says 'we ain't that dumb we're (in comprende)' (staves 3–4) in a mocking tone Rahima positions the entire group in opposition to the teacher's alleged opinion about the girls' lack of academic abilities and thus in opposition to the teacher herself. However, Varda's and Ardiana's next turns render the exchange more confrontational. Rather than aligning themselves with Rahima against the teacher they position themselves in opposition to Rahima, making her the target of their mockery and accusing her of being exactly what she denied in the name of the entire group, namely, 'dumb' (stave 4). Ardiana and Varda assume a non-playful tone of voice when addressing Rahima, which makes it difficult for her to decide whether the challenges are serious or whether they are introducing a playful confrontation. Her doubt is clearly expressed when she falls silent for one second and then produces a request for clarification 'what' (stave 5). (Note the rising tone, as a marker of her surprise.) Ardiana then repeats her challenge, this time in a slightly changed, teasing voice. Rahima's following utterance shows that she has now understood and accepted the new frame and she presently counters Ardiana's tease.

What follows is an extended teasing activity, which in many ways seems similar to episodes of ritual insulting, that is, episodes of verbal duelling in which each participants tries to 'top the previous insult with one that is more clever, outrageous, or elaborate' (Eder 1990: 67). Both Donna Eder (1990) and Marjorie Goodwin (1990) describe ritual insulting in the talk of American working-class girls, and Goodwin, like William Labov (1972), argues that ritual insults are not used to release tension about a real issue. In the above extract the teasing about Rahima's alleged 'dumbness' is certainly face-threatening, although Ardiana is not really suggesting that she is more intelligent or higher achieving than Rahima.

The challenge has to be interpreted in the context of the group's knowledge that Ardiana is far from being an A-star student; in fact, just a few minutes later Ardiana boasts that in a different subject she even received the lowest mark in the class. In addition to the playful contextualisation cues from stave 5 onwards, this background knowledge is significant for the participants' evaluation of the dispute as playful. For most of the remainder of the exchange the girls manage to stay within a playful frame. Thus, they try to refrain from taking each other's claims seriously, as this would move the dispute closer to a real conflict. For example, in staves 7 and 8 Rahima reacts to Ardiana's false claim of being a good student not with an open challenge, but instead with a mock expression of admiration 'wo:w'. Even when Rahima reveals her knowledge of Ardiana's true and somewhat less glamorous academic abilities in staves 8–9 she does so with the help of irony: 'yeah', 'yeah I understand', to maintain the teasing frame. Dilshana's following laughter (stave 9) confirms the success of Rahima's move. Rather than justifying themselves the girls continue to recycle each other's prior challenges in their counters, that is, 'turn [them] on [their] head' (Goodwin 1990: 185). Recycling is a strategy Goodwin (1990) observed in ritual insult episodes by African American working-class children in order to sustain rather than to close an argument (Goodwin 1990: 158–63, 185–6). Recycling appears to be used for the same purpose in this teasing episode, as staves 10–11 'really' or staves 13–14 'you and your thing' demonstrate. Significantly, the girls frequently employ teasing or amused voices to contextualise the dispute as playful (staves 6, 12–14) and they also lengthen their vowels in a manner that is reminiscent of child-like playground interaction (staves 11–13: 'did I::', 'yeah you di:d', 'I don't think so:::').

Similarly to Goodwin's (1990) young research participants, who showed a preference for escalating both serious and playful conflicts, the Bangladeshi girls seem to enjoy the teasing in this episode as an activity in its own right which is as entertaining as singing songs. However, one of the most interesting ways in which the teasing functions in this extract is as a resource for the girls to construct themselves as tough. Despite their playful, non-serious framing the insults and accusations contained in the teases potentially threaten the girls' positive face wants (see Brown and Levinson 1987: 66) and serve as a display of competitive verbal skills. The face threatening acts as well as the verbal competition position the girls in opposition to being timid, nice and polite girls and instead allow them to display toughness.

The girls were very much aware of their form group's reputation as 'not nice' and their feelings about it were ambivalent. In the final group interview with all the girls Hennah explained to me 'that's why it's fun in our class we don't communicate with each other we go wild'. On the other hand, on the tape there were also instances of the girls distancing themselves from their 'loudmouth' classmates. The over-assertive outspokenness that earned the form group their reputation meant that in class it was difficult for some of the Bangladeshi girls to get heard.

Extract 5: keep everyone else quiet

(1)
Hennah   Miss McDonald she does it better (.) if she wants any of us to

(2)
Ardiana   [mmmm]
Hennah   talk she'd just pick on us and [say i]t   (.) and keep

(3)
Hennah   everyone else quiet (.) but- (.) er b- because Chantalle

(4)
Hennah   and them are still loudmouth they would even talk when

(5)
Ardiana   I know
Hennah   we're talking (.) like did you see like (.) erm::

This extract captures Hennah's and Ardiana's distaste of their loudmouthed classmates, and their appreciation of one of their teacher's efforts to control the class and allow other girls to speak. But they cannot always rely on their teacher to get their voices heard. Thus, I argue, that they need to develop competitive verbal skills to assert themselves in their class environment. Their ability to display verbal toughness is demonstrated in many of their extracts of teasing and is particularly noteworthy in the following extract, which occurs within seconds of a girl from a different friendship group entering the classroom in which Ardiana and her friends had been recording themselves during their lunch-break. The relationship between Helen, one of three Somali girls in the form group, and several members of Ardiana's friendship group was frequently tense, partly as they perceived her to be one of the most notorious loudmouths of the form group.

Extract 6: your man

(1)
Ardiana   did you see your man (-) didn't [you]   that man over
Helen   [which] man is that

(2)
Ardiana   **[the:re]**   [(xxxxxxxxxxxxxxxx)]
Hennah   [UH:::]*{teasing}*[(are you trying to)] say you have millions
?   [which man]

(3)
Ardiana   [she's got **loads**]
Hennah   *{laughs}*
Helen   that's not– e- exactly I've got **loads** [>you know what I mean<]

(4)
Ardiana   don't [you **know** she's got] **loads** one after o:[:ne]*{teasing}*
Helen   [I've got (loads)]*{laughing}*   *{staccato}*   [I don]'t

(5)
Helen   need some ugly guy who whose (.) career is in giving

(6)
Ardiana   *{laughs}*
Helen   crappy food at schools   uah:

This extract of teasing with an outgroup member highlights the girls' implicit awareness that verbal toughness can constitute symbolic capital for them (Bourdieu 1991). Just like Penelope Eckert's (2000) burnout girls in an American high school use non-standard forms, the Bangladeshi girls in my study use teasing as a resource to claim status as tough girls in their peer group. This type of 'toughness' has been linked to working classness and contrasted with middle-class 'politeness' by a number of researchers dealing with girl talk. Donna Eder (1990: 74), Ingrid Hasund and Anna-Brita Stenström (1997: 129) argue that ritual insults allow working-class girls to develop communicative self-defence skills, required by the 'toughness' of working-class culture at the same time as expressing closeness and friendship. My data demonstrate that teasing can serve the same purpose as ritual insults as it allows the girls both to express friendship and solidarity within their group and to rehearse tough femininities that allow them to assert themselves with some of their peers. The link between ladettte/working-class femininities and verbal toughness which I propose here is neither fixed, nor does it capture the reality for all working-class girls. For my other, predominantly white, working-class group (Group 2) a display of toughness is less central than an alignment with middle-class norms and stereotypes (for similar findings see Walkerdine et al. 2001). I do not claim that the girls explicitly self-identify as working class, but, again I suggest that the girls' habitual performance of tough femininities indexes (stereotypical) British lad(ette)/working-class youth culture. The Bangladeshi girls in this group do not use teasing or present themselves as rebellious and anti-school because they *are* working-class girls but because they use it as a resource to accomplish tough femininities, which are valued in the context of their peer group at school. Significantly, I believe that for Ardiana and her friends a display of tough and anti-school stances in fact offers alternative subject positions, locating them in stark opposition to the stereotype of the timid, quiet and studious Asian girl (Shain 2003).

Respectable girls: balancing discourses of love and dating

Teasing is used by the girls in a number of different ways and as a resource to adopt a range of different stances which accomplish social action and index social identities (Ochs 1992; Pichler 2006). In addition to being a fun or bonding activity, and to signal toughness, teasing is also used by the girls to release real tension in a relatively non-confrontational, face-saving way. The next extracts show how the girls make use of teasing when approaching a range of sensitive topics which have to be negotiated carefully in the group in order to signal respect for face needs within the group as well as for larger-scale cultural norms. The topics of dating and love, and even more so the topic of sexual experience (see Chapter 6), are sensitive, as they are regulated by dominant cultural discourses which the girls both indirectly and directly associate with their Bangladeshi/Muslim community, and which shape the girls' alignment with culture-specific variations of 'respectable femininity' (Skeggs 1997; see also Chapter 3).

Boys and dating

Talk about dating and boyfriends is very common in this group, moreover three out of the five girls in the group date boys. However, although this topic is so prominent not all members of the group are equally comfortable with it. The following extracts exemplify this, but they also show how the teasing is used as a strategy to balance different (cultural) discourses and positions in the girls' talk.

Extract 7: that's all we talk about

(1)
Ardiana   I don't **know** these songs
Hennah   *tura ze boring
Dilshana   I love that song %(xxxxxxxx)%
Bengali: "you lot are making it sound boring"

(2)
Ardiana   (.) yeah **so::** (-) *hamra only otha mati
Hennah   malara
Rahima   (.) {laughs}
Bengali: "that's the only thing we talk about"

(3)
Ardiana   **no:: we** [normally] **don't**
Hennah   [(we-)]
Varda   [WE DO:::]
Dilshana   innit that's all we talk a[bout]

(4)
Ardiana   we talk about *Ran Magi and (what else){laughing}
Dilshana   {marked laugh}ha ha ha
names of Ardiana's and Dilshana's boyfriends

(5)
Hennah   (yeah w::ell) **we** li]sten {amused}**you talk** {laughs}
Dilshana   (innit xxxxxxxxxxxxxx)]

(6)
Ardiana   yeah go on then we talk they('ll) listen
Dilshana   (-) I'm gonna

(7)
Hennah   =oh WHAT ARE YOU **WEAR**ING{excited}
Dilshana   ring Ran up tomorrow=

Hennah makes two challenges in this extract (staves 1–2 and stave 5). The lack of laughter or other playful contextualisation of Hennah's first challenge about her friends' (earlier) boring delivery of songs is likely to be the reason for Ardiana's confrontational next turn, which constitutes an admission ('yeah') and a counter challenge ('so::') at the same time. Ardiana's denial in stave 3–4 changes the referent of 'we' (marked by contrastive stress in stave 3) from 'the entire group' to 'Dilshana and Ardiana', thereby distancing herself and Dilshana from the rest of the group. At the same time, however, Ardiana's denial also constitutes a self-tease about her preferred conversational topic, boys, framed by laughter. In her second challenge in stave 5 Hennah mirrors Ardiana's teasing tone as well as her categories of inclusion and exclusion, though not without having reversed them first. She now presents herself as being part of the powerful 'we' and excludes Ardiana from the group: '**we** listen **you talk**'. Importantly, the exchange is now clearly marked as a playful one by the accompanying laughter and the amused tone of voice.

Although the girls use cues from stave 4 onwards which signal that this is play, the teasing this times reveals some more serious issues and releases underlying tensions. Despite Hennah's playful frame in stave 5 and Ardiana's acknowledgement of this teasing frame in stave 6 (by countering Hennah's tease rather than justifying herself), and despite Hennah's efforts to mitigate further by signalling a keen interest in Dilshana's next date with her boyfriend Ran in stave 7, Hennah expresses her critical view on the topic of boyfriends, which Ardiana and Dilshana raise so frequently. Other extracts of data clearly show that the group is aware of Hennah's dislike of this topic.

Extract 8: let's talk about boys

(1)
Ardiana   how about- no >let's talk about< **boys /Hennah**{*teasing*}

(2)
Ardiana   have [**you** seen that *(xxxx)]=oh shut u[p Rahima]
Rahima   [(BUT THAT BOY:::)]   [FUCKING HELL] MAN
boy's name

(3)
Ardiana   [no we are] mates yeah we should find out the
Rahima   why [do we (xxxx)-]
Varda   (Hennah do you know where he lives)

(4)
Ardiana   truth a[bout *them two]   [cause they-]
Hennah   [SHUT UP SHUT] UP [I'm not go]ing out with
*Hennah and Varda

(5)
Ardiana   [cause]   [they cause they] never talk about any **boys**
Hennah   [anyone]
?Varda   [right but]

(6)
Rahima   but HELLO [they don't go out with any]one
Varda   [(I know) Hennah's going out] (.) she's

(7)
Varda   not going out she fancies one boy

Ardiana's and Varda's teasing as well as Rahima's defence of Hennah show that the group are aware that Hennah dislikes the topic of boys. Interestingly, although Varda usually adopts a similar stance to Hennah, remaining more quiet when the other girls talk about boys or even expressing her discomfort about the topic (see also stave 3 in the extract above), here Varda joins into the teasing. This move could be explained by the fact that this is Varda's strategy to avoid becoming another target of the tease, a scenario which would have been likely as Ardiana threatens to extend her playful challenge also to Varda in stave 4. It is equally interesting and revealing that Rahima, who herself has a boyfriend, defends both Hennah and Varda on the grounds that neither of them do actually date. Although this reason goes some way to explain Hennah's discomfort about the topic, it does not sufficiently capture her stance. In the other two groups I studied a lack of dating experience did not necessarily go hand in hand with a reluctance to talk about boys. Rather, Hennah's dispreference of this topic needs to be seen in relation to dominant cultural and religious discourses in the Bangladeshi community, which position dating as incompatible with young respectable Muslim Bangladeshi femininities. Evidence for these discourses about dating is provided in non-linguistic research on British Asian girls as well as in my interviews with Hennah in the role of my in-group informant.

Evidence for some British Asian girls' resistance to non-dating rules goes back a long time (Wilson 1978: 104–5; see also "Mina" 1997). Although some 'parents are beginning to turn a blind eye (or even accept) dating' (Ghuman 1994: 145), research has found evidence for Asian parents' continuing opposition to their children's dating before marriage, especially when daughters are concerned (Ghuman 1994: 60). Shain's (2003) more recent research of adolescent Asian girls shows that the members of 3 out of 4 groups of girls in her ethnographic study are not involved romantically with boys, and only the girls in the remaining group, termed 'the Rebels', defied religious and cultural requirements about mixing with boys, however even they did this only without the knowledge of their parents (Shain 2003: 121). Similarly, my spontaneous conversational data suggest that none of the girls' parents were in fact aware of their daughters having boyfriends, and the informal interviews with Hennah, my in-group informant, confirm this. The following extract captures Hennah's answer to my question whether parents were aware that their daughters had boyfriends. (For conventions of interview transcripts please turn to pages x–xi of this book.)

Extract 9: did their parents know?

1) Hennah: you /know you're not supposed to have it *yeah*
2)   {Pia: *yeah* yeah} they think that in our religion
3)   yeah {Pia: yeah} they say that .hh y- you can
4)   choose the guy yeah but they don't mean
5)   you go out and look for him {Pia: yeah yeah} and you
6)   go out with a hundred boys and then {Pia: yeah *yeah*}
7)   *you* decide .hh 'oh yeah he's {slightly amused}
8)   the right one *for me*' {Pia: *yeah yeah*} they just say
9)   like you know erm first you let your parents
10)   choose {Pia: yeah} then the parents will say {slightly formal}
11)   'I suggest he is a (good boy)' .hh and then
12)   erm you sit there and you talk to them to find
13)   out about their personality {Pia: mm yeah} d'you get
14)   me and then (.) if you're thinking 'right-'
15)   it's not for one day thing you /know (-)
16)   {amused} one day you get to know him {Pia: alright}
17)   and then you go 'oh my gosh my life is ruined'
18)   {Pia: *yeah yeah*} *d'you get me* it's up to you how
19)   long you want to talk to that person {Pia: yeah

20)	yeah} and then you do .hh and then you tell
21)	them if whether you like them or not {Pia: yeah
22)	yeah} d'you get me {Pia: yeah yeah} and that's it

23)Pia:	OK so bu- but basi[cally]
24)Hennah:	[otherwise] you're not supposed

25)Hennah:	to do that stuff {Pia: yeah yeah} d'you get me

26)Hennah:	{Pia: yeah yeah} and then
27)Pia:	so the parents like wouldn't

28)Pia:	have (-) have been happy about (.) about
29)Hennah:	no:::

30)Pia:	them
31)Hennah:	you know what they would **do** yeah

32)Hennah:	if they found out their daughters do that
33)	they would get her .hh immediately married to
34)	**that** person .hh o:r take her aboard .hh
35)	cause they {yeah} *don't* wanna face the shame
36)	because the *community* {*yeah*}

This rich extract from our interviews captures what Hennah positions as 'religious' norms about dating in her community.[3] Hennah makes an effort to highlight that a lack of dating does not necessarily mean a lack of agency or 'choice' (line 4) for the girls, only that this choice follows a pre-selection by the parents. It seems that in this extract Hennah indirectly challenges the widespread portrayal of arranged marriage as forced marriage in the British or European public and press (e.g. Cramb, writing in the *Daily Telegraph* 25/04/2002; Kelbie, writing in the *Independent* 30/08/2006). My position as an outsider of her community, who asks Hennah questions about this issue may be one of the reasons why at this stage she feels the need to correct this pejorative image of this process which for many girls and their families replaces the western practice of pre-marital dating. (However, note that later on during the interview Hennah suggests that this process is not unproblematic or conflict-free for several of the girls in their group, see below.) In the final lines of this extract Hennah suggests that if parents discover that their daughter is dating they would arrange a marriage for her immediately, which indicates that the parents perceive dating as a threat to the reputation of an unmarried girl. In fact, Hennah directly addresses this threat, the 'shame' (line 35) that the family would suffer on behalf of their daughter in the community. Hennah was not familiar with the (originally Persian/Urdu) terms 'sharam' or 'izzat', but she was clearly aware of the concept and the associated discourse. Many studies of Asian women in Britain found *sharam* (shame, modesty, shyness) to be essential for women's good reputation, which in turn is linked to the *izzat* (honour) of the entire family (Jamdagni 1980: 11; Ballard 1994: 13, 15; Bhopal 1999: 120; Dwyer 2000: 478; Ghuman 1994: 72; Hennink, Diamond, Cooper 1999: 876; Wilson 1978: 99–104). Although Ahmad's (2003) Muslim feminist work rightly warns against an overemphasis on these concepts by (white) researchers and members of the public, my data provides evidence that the relevance of these terms cannot be entirely dismissed. I interpret Hennah's reference to the shame that she says parents would feel on behalf of their daughter as evidence of a (culture-specific) discourse of respectable femininity, linked to notions of *sharam* and *izzat*.[4]

This was not the only occasion during our interviews on which Hennah highlights that dating is not considered appropriate in the Bangladeshi community. Again, she links these dominant norms about mixed-sex interaction not to ethnic but to religious inflections of culture, emphasising the significance of the category 'religion' for her identity:

Extract 10: we are Muslims

1)Pia: is there a difference between what you see: English
2)   people do: and what you .hh your your like your
3)   parents would expect you to do: and stuff

4)   [you know that difference in behaviour a- a-]
5)Hennah: [yeah it's different it's because-]

6)Pia: and how do you deal with [it]

7)Hennah: [it's] because of the erm
8)   (.) (dyknow) most English are Chr- are Christians
9)   or {Pia: mm} Hindus *do you get* {Pia: yeah yeah} me (.)

10)	and we are Muslims (-) there is not much
11)	(.) difference but *there* {Pia: yeah} is a **lot**
12)	do you get me *.hh* {Pia: yeah} (>and dyknow<)
13)	Christians allow their children to go out and
14)	everything and my parents like .hh they prefer
15)	to b- be like (-) the **same** as the old religion
16)	{Pia: yeah yeah} like (xxxx) things were like in olden
17)	times {Pia: yeah} but because of k- society and all
18)	the changes {Pia:=yeah} you can't really **stick** to it
19)	{Pia: yeah *yeah*} *but* they try as hard as they can
20)	to stick to it {Pia: yeah} and they want **us** to try
21)	as well {Pia: yeah} (.) and I do try I do *try* {Pia: yeah}

Shortly before this extract I made a first, unsuccessful, attempt at formulating the question in lines 1–4, offering the concept of 'culture' as a potential resource for the identity construction of my informant based on my findings from the girls' spontaneous talk. The above extract captures my re-formulation of this question, now introducing the category of ('English') ethnicity, but Hennah rejects these resources and instead chooses religion as the central defining aspect of her identity. Thus, in lines 8–10 Hennah distances herself from both Christians and, interestingly, Hindus and self-identifies as Muslim. From line 13 on Hennah gives an example to support her emphasis on religious identity, suggesting that she does not attribute her parents' objections to their children 'going out' to cultural norms in relation to ethnic customs but instead to religious norms. The relevance of this distinction between religion and ethnic culture, which I adopt for this chapter, is also emphasised in critical research on multiculturalism (Mirza, 2006) and in the anthropological and sociological work of Asian Muslim feminists on hybridity (Ahmad, 2003; Shain, 2003). However, although I adopt this conceptual distinction, I feel it is significant to acknowledge that research participants may not share this distinction, or may interpret norms and practices in relation to religion rather than ethnic culture.

Love and romance

Similarly to the above extracts on dating, the girls also tease each other about their romantic feelings. Although this could be seen as romantic teasing, common amongst young girls from all socio-cultural backgrounds (Eder 1993), my ethnographic interview data suggest an additional layer of interpretation. Again, the teasing allows the girls to manage popular discourses of love and romance at the same time as discourses of respectable young femininity with inflections of religious and ethnic culture.

Extract 11: thinking about Tom

(1)
Ardiana   (-) what's **wrong** (.) *ne ray keneya=
Rahima   =nothing (-)
*Bengali: "why're you so quiet?"

(2)
Ardiana   THINK]ING ABOUT **TOM** [(all this) romantic stuff)
Rahima   {laughing}[NO]   {laughs}

(3)
Ardiana   you said right (YEA::H){amused} {laughs}

(4)
Ardiana   {teasing}yeah yeah (.) that's what I am
Rahima   no no nono{amused}

(5)
Ardiana   thinking right {laughing}now about **my** guy {laughs} as if

(6)
Rahima   (-) I'm thinking sometimes life [can be so you know]
Dilshana   (-)   [I'm thinking]

(7)
Rahima   =yeah I'm thinking what
Dilshaa   what I am gonna do on Monda::y=

This extract provides an example of how the girls in this group tend to avoid serious self-disclosure about their romantic feelings (but see Extract 14 for an exception). In stave 1 Ardiana expresses her concern that something might be wrong with Rahima because she is so quiet (see translation of Bengali utterance). After Rahima's brief answer, which denies that anything is wrong, Ardiana switches into a teasing frame. She playfully suggests that Rahima's silence is due to her mind being engaged with romantic thoughts about her boyfriend. Both her own and Rahima's voice identify this episode as teasing. Ardiana first increases the volume of her voice in stave 2 and then slightly alters the tone of her voice, signalling that she is only joking. Rahima's repeated denials of this mock accusation in stave 2 and then in stave 3 equally assume a non-serious tone. The laughter of both girls also contributes to the contextualisation of this exchange as non-serious.

Drawing on my overall knowledge of the group which I gained from the girls' spontaneous conversational talk as well as from the interviews with Hennah, I believe that Ardiana's switch into teasing when engaging in personal topics such as love is not a coincidence. In fact, the example is characteristic of the girls' way of talking about each other's romantic feelings without actually revealing too much. Unlike the other group of British working-class girls, Pat and her friends, these five British Bangladeshi girls tend to view the possible face threat involved in talk about love (or sex) as too high a risk to choose mutual self-disclosure as a means of mitigation. I therefore believe that in this instance the teasing serves as a type of 'politeness strategy' which helps them to signal respect for their own and each other's face needs when engaging in highly romantic/personal talk. Brown and Levinson (1987: 66–7) list 'irreverence, mention of taboo topics' and 'raising of [...] emotional or divisive topics' as examples of threats to the positive face. For Ardiana, Dilshana, Rahima, Varda and Hennah personal topics such as love or sex would fall into these two categories. The girls clearly show their awareness of each other's feelings of apprehension about these topics by choosing a strategy which allows them to remain ambiguous about their position. The teasing makes it possible for the girls to engage in highly sensitive topics in a playful frame, whose advantage lies in signalling that they are only joking.

Staves 3–4 demonstrate the girls' preference for a playful frame when talking about personal feelings. After Ardiana dismisses Rahima's denial in a teasing voice ('yeah yeah'), she briefly adopts a serious tone when admitting that her own thoughts are with her boyfriend at present (staves 4–5). However, she does not even allow herself to finish the utterance before assuming a laughing voice. This switch clearly reframes her earlier self-disclosure as non-serious and thus functions as some form of mitigation. The mitigating effect of the playful frames lies in the possibility of denying the truth value of the proposition being made, which is exactly what Ardiana does in her following turn.

'As if' is uttered in a surprisingly serious voice, which is distinctly different from the one adopted to mitigate her self-disclosure. Thus the seriousness of the earlier self-disclosure is doubly called into question.

In the remainder of this section I shall establish a link between the face-saving function offered by the teasing in this extract, and aspects of the girls' negotiation of cultural, ethnic and religious norms. Again, the interview suggests that the reasons for this remarkable way of dealing with a highly sensitive topic such as love appears to be rooted in the discourses which the girls themselves associate with their Muslim Bangladeshi background. In my collaboration with Hennah, my in-group informant, she once explained the behaviour of one of her friends with the saying 'unspoken love is the strongest'. On probing Hennah about the origin or cultural associations of this saying, she first argued that it was 'universal', but then explained it in relation to a Muslim Bangladeshi norm which does not encourage the voicing of one's feeling of love. The following transcript contains evidence of this claim from one of my tape-recorded 'interview' sessions with Hennah.

Extract 12: Bengali people are religious

1)Hennah:	cause you know Bengali people yeah because most of them are
2)	religious yeah they {Pia: yeah} don't talk about love because some
3)	you know it's not (shown) in books yeah they haven't really
4)	{Pia: yeah} (completely) some people say that erm love is like
5)	dangerous thing and some people say erm (Allah gave you love)
6)	you're supposed to accept it wherever it is do you {Pia: yeah yeah} get
7)	me {Pia: yeah} so they're mixed up that's why they don't like to be in
8)	that situation so they don't even talk about it. (1) it is not
9)	[supposed to be xxxxxxxxxxxxx)]
10)Pia:	[what sorry they don't want to be] in what situation.
11)Hennah:	they don't want to able to talk about it do you {Pia: right} get me
12)	because like some people think it is dangerous some people think it's
13)	OK {P: yeah} s so they to avoid arguments and {Pia: yeah yeah}
14)	danger {Pia: yeah} they [don't talk about it]
15)Pia:	[you just don't talk about] it at all
16) Hennah:	or write about it do you get me {Pia: yeah yeah} that's why you don't
17)	see much of it but otherwise I think they would have said it if they

18)	were allowed to {Pia: yeah yeah} but religious wise they are not sure if
19)	they are supposed {Pia: yeah} to
20)Pia:	OK ...

The explanations of my in-group informant actually reveal two opposing discourses. Although both appear to justify themselves by their conformity with religious rules, the discourse which opposes (rather than justifies) love appears to constitute the dominant norm for Hennah. In this extract Hennah claims that whenever the two discourses come into conflict, the discourse that views love (and possibly love matches) positively is silenced and gives way to a feeling of unease about the topic, which results in an avoidance of the topic of love. This extract from our interviews therefore suggests that Hennah positions what she describes as religious discourses about the problematic status of love as a significant influence on her friendship group's discursive practices.

From a linguistic point of view it is interesting that the girls frequently resort to teasing as a strategy to negotiate a potentially complex topic such as dating and love in their spontaneous talk. Eder (1993: 27) found that American teenage girls in her study 'use teasing both to mock traditional female behaviour and to experiment with non-traditional gender role behaviour'. My data support Eder's findings to the extent that teasing allows the girls to experiment with unconventional or even new behaviours and discourses. However, for Ardiana, Dilshana, Varda, Hennah and Rahima the topic of romantic love per se is part of a discourse which offers alternative rather than traditional norms. By choosing to engage in the topic of love the girls are actually positioning themselves in opposition to what Hennah presents as a Muslim Bangladeshi discourse which discourages talk about love. Nevertheless, as they mostly do so in a playful frame such as teasing, which allows them to protect their own and each other's face, they are able to signal respect for this Bangladeshi discourse at the same time. The protection of face, which the teasing offers due to its playful frame, makes it a preferred strategy for the girls not only to present themselves as though, but also to reconcile, opposing culture-specific discourses of love, dating and sex (see Chapter 6).

Traditions of marriage

Whereas none of the other two groups ever speak about marriage, this topic was central to the spontaneous conversational talk of Ardiana,

Dilshana, Hennah, Varda and Rahima. However, differently from their talk about dating, boyfriends and love there is not much teasing in the girls' talk about marriage proposals, potential bridegrooms and their future as wives. The girls do not playfully experiment with a discourse of love marriage in their talk in the same way as with discourses of sexual experience and dating, but largely approach the topic of marriage from within a modified discourse of arranged marriage. This discourse, however, I shall argue, emerges itself as a hybrid in the course of the girls' complex negotiations of a range of cultural discourses with ethnic, gendered, classed and local inflections. Moreover, my interview data suggest that my own celebration of cultural hybridity with regard to the topic of (arranged) marriage is not always shared by the research participants themselves.

Before I turn to my data I would like to give a brief overview of the non-linguistic research that has been carried out on the topic of arranged marriage with regard to young British Asians. Fauzia Ahmad (2003: 44–5) is critical of what she feels to be an 'overemphasis' on arranged marriage in relation to South Asian women in academic work. My own study was not led by any a priori interest in the topic of marriage, but instead the topic was positioned as significant by Ardiana and her friends themselves. My exploration of these conversational data on marriage, however, benefits greatly from the wealth of previous research. Most of these scholarly investigations agree that 'arranged marriage' continues to be prominent among second and third generation Asians in the UK, but that it is also undergoing significant changes. However, research traditions and individual studies vary greatly in how they present this tradition. Thus, one of the issues investigated by large-scale studies such as Anwar (1998), Ghuman (1994, 2001), Modood et al. (1994) is the effect of and relationship between categories and factors such as ethnicity, religion, generation, gender and parental involvement in the choice of their children's spouses. Although some of these studies emphasise that there might not be any conflict with parents about the tradition of arranged marriage, they tend to take a more critical, or, at least non-celebratory stance to arranged marriage, arguing that there is 'reluctant obedience, especially among the young Muslims' (Modood et al. 1994: 79) and even describing it as 'most troublesome [custom]' (Ghuman 1994: 71). Anwar (1998: 111–3) presents ambivalent evidence about arranged marriage, arguing that (a decreasing) majority of young people still support the tradition, but that an even greater majority expects there to be more resistance to the custom in future.

On the other hand, recent long term and/or small-scale ethno-graphic, feminist studies provide evidence for Avtar Brah's (1996: 77) conceptualisation of marriage as a 'joint undertaking between parents and young people', which is also reflected in the terms 'assisted marriage' or even as 'arranged introduction' (Ahmad et al. 2003: 36). Thus, Catherine Gavron's (1997) and Chris Phillipson, Nilufar Ahmed, and Joanna Latimer's (2003) work in the Bangladeshi community in the London district of Tower Hamlets report a general contentment with the prospect of arranged marriage among young women. Both Gavron's (1997) and Tehmina Basit's (1997) East England work with young Pakistani Muslims highlights that there is a good degree of agreement between parents and young people that love/romance or personal happiness are not sufficient for a successful marriage. Whereas both of these studies approach their data largely on a content level, Farzana Shain (2003) presents an in-depth critical analysis of the different and frequently opposing discourses and subject positions adopted by the 44 girls in her study. Shain confirms that most girls are happy to have 'arranged marriages', but also shows that the girls' expectations in relation to marriage (as well as schooling) can differ considerably. Shain argues that these differences cannot always be explained by macro-categories such as ethnicity and religion, but need to be seen in relation to the girls' 'subjective experiences in their local situations' (Shain 2003: 55). The heterogeneity of the strategies and positions adopted by Shain's girls in relation to marriage is also evident in my own data, albeit on an intra- rather than an inter-group level. The following discourse analytic discussion will focus on the girls' negotiations of consensus on the topic of marriage (Eckert 1993) within their friendship group.

The wedding proposal

The following discussion is divided into three subsections which capture the negotiations and contestations of discourses and positions that are central to the development of the group's positioning in relation to the topic of marriage. The first section focuses on the girls' accommodation strategies to the discourse of arranged marriage, the second on the girls' resistance to this discourse, and the third and longest section on the evolvement of what I define as a modified discourse of arranged marriage.

Discourse of arranged marriage: accommodation

The story of the wedding proposal reveals a discourse which positions parental choice of children's future spouses as the appropriate form of marriage arrangement (staves 1–9).

Extract 13: the wedding proposal

(1)
Ardiana   .hh >did I tell you something< er [thingie] my brother
Dilshana   [what]

(2)
Ardiana   came from Bangladesh innit like   (.) a wedding proposal
Dilshana   \huh

(3)
Ardiana   (-) f[or me] for me (.) and I was so: shocked they wrote
Dilshana   (-) [WHA::T]

(4)
Ardiana   a letter to my s- my mum and dad right saying that .hh

(5)
Ardiana   {drawling}"she's really ni::ce she s- talks politely"

(6)
Ardiana   and everything {swallows} and I was shocked my brother

(7)
Ardiana   (>was like<) my sister was like reading it to me yeah and

(8)
Ardiana   she goes "<they want me to be their bride>" and everything

(9)
Ardiana   and I was like saying (.)   ["EXCUSE ME-"]
Dilshana   wh[o are they]   related to you

(10)
Ardiana   =they just live next door to m[y h]ouse in
Dilshana   (.) cousins=   [ah]

(11)
Ardiana   Bangladesh (.) and they just want **me** (.) as their

(12)
Ardiana   son's bride
Hennah   oh [my God]
Varda   [(Ardiana)] did you see the photo (.)

(13)
Ardiana   {swallows} I've seen the guy when I went to
Varda   (that-){swallowing}

(14)
Ardiana   Bangladesh [(he is alright)] looking he's alright
?Dilshana   [is he nice]
?   (xxx)

(15)
Ardiana   looking   [but he's::-] the same height as me EXCUSE ME
Hennah   {- laughs -}
?Varda   {amused}[(yeah:::)]

This extract shows the group's familiarity with and acceptance of a discourse of arranged marriage which allocates a significant role to the two families of the couple to be. The girls have no difficulties in understanding the referent of the third person personal pronoun 'they' (staves 3, 8, 9, 10, 11), showing no sign of surprise that the authors of the letter turn out to be the parents of the suitor, rather than the young man himself (staves 9–12). Similarly, they do not question the fact that the proposal is not addressed to the bride-to-be but instead to Ardiana's parents (stave 4). Dilshana's assumption that the family of the suitor is in fact related to Ardiana (staves 9–10) signals her knowledge of the surviving cultural practice of consanguineous marriage (Basit 1997; Dwyer 2000; Gavron 1997; Phillipson et al. 2003). The enquiries and reactions of Ardiana's friends show that their aim is to find out the particulars of the wedding proposal, but it does not suggests that the girls question the practice of arranged marriage itself. It seems that the girls do not expect to choose their future spouse on their own; instead they align themselves with a discourse where the role of active matchmaking is assumed by the families of the young couple.

Ardiana's acceptance of her family's matchmaking is reflected on a micro-linguistic level. Whereas she creates a distance between herself and the groom's parents by subverting their voice when reporting details of the wedding proposal in stave 5, Ardiana does not change the quality of her voice when she reports what her sister said in stave 8, thereby refraining from signalling a detachment from the voice that she is reproducing (Bakhtin 1986; Coates 1999; Maybin 2003, 2007 – see also Chapter 3). Whereas in stave 5 Ardiana reports the groom's parents' voice in direct speech (despite introducing it with 'saying that'), when she reproduces her sister's voice in stave 8 she slides from direct reporting, 'she goes', to indirect reported speech, 'they want me to be their bride' (rather than 'they want you...'). Although these grammatical cues suggest more ambivalence about Ardiana's identification with her sister than the paralinguistic cues, the reporting here captures a mingling of Ardiana's voice with that of her sister.

Thus, overall the first 15 staves position the discourse of arranged marriage firmly in the repertoire of the group. Although there are also some expressions of surprise and 'shock' in this part of the extract, these are not used by the girls to signal their resistance to the tradition of arranged marriage. Dilshana and Hennahy articulate their surprise in stave 3: 'WHAT' and stave 12: 'oh my God' respectively. However, the remainder of the extract suggests that the girls' surprise is directed at the news and details of Ardiana's marriage proposal, rather than at the procedure adopted by the two families. Moreover, Ardiana frames her story in a way to maximise its potential news worthiness and thereby encourages her friends' display of surprise: her introduction of the wedding proposal in stave 2 is abrupt and is followed by a deliberate pause in stave 3, which invites her listeners to produce an appropriate acknowledgement (of surprise). Ardiana's own affirmations of being shocked in staves 3 and 6, uttered in an entirely unmarked voice, also serve to position her story as newsworthy rather than to signal a resistant stance to the discourse of arranged marriage.

However, the above extract does contain some first signs of resistance. In stave 9 Ardiana raises her volume to protest: 'EXCUSE ME' but is prevented from voicing her objections by her friends' eager questions about the proposal and the suitor. Ardiana finally manages to complete this utterance a few staves below.

Discourse of arranged marriage: resistance

In staves 15–17 Ardiana then vehemently airs her opposition to the proposed marriage when she switches into a discourse which appears to value love-marriages:

Extract 14: the wedding proposal – continued

(15)
Ardiana   [but he's::-] the same height as me EXCUSE ME I LOVE
Hennah
?Varda   [(yeah:::)]

(16)
Ardiana   MY BOYFRIEND here right I don't wanna get married to

(17)
Ardiana   somebody else I don't /**know**
Hennah   (-)   [(inn]it) (.)
Rahima   (-) innit ma[n]
?Varda   (-) {- - - *laughs* - - -}

(18)
Ardiana   [but then
Hennah   {*amused*}he may be gorgeous but then again he mig[ht have a

(19)
Ardiana   again (a] ha-)
Hennah   (a)]   personality like a (.) **ape** or **some**thing=

Ardiana here introduces a discourse of romantic love in relation to
marriage, which constitutes the popular norm in a large majority of
today's western communities. Initially, it seems as if the other girls
were following Ardiana's lead and accepted her switch into a discourse of romantic love (stave 17 'innit man'; 'innit'). Following
Ardiana's criticism of marrying a young man she does not know,
Hennah provides the reasons for their reservations in staves 18–19: if
a girl does not know her future husband before getting married, she
runs the risk of ending up with a husband who may be good looking,
but has a flawed personality. Hennah's joke and the girls' agreement
with Ardiana appear to signal the group's unanimous alignment with
the tradition of love marriage, and consequently their rejection of
arranged marriages. However, previous extracts show that alignment
with a discourse of romantic love is frequently problematic in this
group (Extracts 11, 12). Moreover, the girls' interactive negotiations
in this instance suggest a much more complex process of positioning

within the group. On a sequential, micro-linguistic level, the presence of a hesitation in the form of pause after Ardiana's utterance signals that the group's acceptance of Ardiana's switch into a discourse of romantic love is not entirely smooth (see conversation analytic work, e.g. Pomerantz 1984, Levinson 1983: 334 on the significance of pauses as markers of dispreferred seconds). Moreover, the remainder of the conversation does not provide any further evidence of the group's unanimous resistance to the tradition of arranged marriage per se, but instead suggests that the girls only resist a very specific version of it.

Modified discourse of arranged marriage

Ardiana's protest is expressed in her utterance 'EXCUSE ME I LOVE MY BOYFRIEND here right I don't wanna get married to somebody else I don't **know**' (Extract 14, staves 15–16). Whereas the first part of the utterance in this instance clearly aligns Ardiana with a (western) discourse of romantic love, I argue that the second can be interpreted as positioning Ardiana in a modified discourse of arranged marriage, emphasising solely her resistance to getting married to somebody she does not know.

I argue that the other girls align themselves only with the latter part of Ardiana's proposition. The third extract from 'the wedding proposal' provides evidence for this claim, showing that the girls do in fact align themselves with a modified form of arranged marriage.

Extract 15: the wedding proposal – continued

(20)
Ardiana   =YEAH:: [that's] true (.)
Dilshana   [yeah]   (.) yeah when they come to England

(21)
Ardiana   they just wanna get
Hennah   [(they just]xxx-)
Dilshana   yeah they just lea[ve you man]

(22)
Ardiana   married to girls from London [because like they are
Varda   [yeah because of the

(23)

Ardiana	Londoni] (.) **yeah**	[they are from London they are
Varda	passport] (.)	[they want their passport
Dilshana		(ah[::)*{agreeing}*

(24)

Ardiana	British] they are British and they wanna come to this
Varda	inn]it

(25)

Ardiana	country as well
Varda	(-) *{swallows}* they want the

(26)

Ardiana	
?Varda	passports (the British) passport
?	*{dental click}*

What the girls *do* challenge in this extract is the tradition of being married to men from Bangladesh. The interactive manner in which the girls formulate this challenge is highly collaborative, mirroring and building on each others' contributions in a way that Coates (1996, 1999) found to be characteristic of the friendship talk of white adult middle-class women. Thus, the girls use many thematic repetitions ('Londoni – British') and lexical repetitions ('passport'), supportive minimal agreements such as 'yeah' and 'joint constructions involving simultaneous speech' (Coates 1996: 121) as in staves 22 to 24. One explanation for their objection to men from Bangladesh is based on the girls' view that Bangladeshi men are only interested in British citizenship and that they leave their wives once they have established themselves in Britain. All the girls reject their role in this alleged pursuit: Ardiana and Varda collaboratively and simultaneously express their condemnation of the men's motivation to get married to girls from Britain because of their British passport; Dilshana voices her agreement in stave 23.

It is hard to imagine that the girls' concern about their role as potential gateway to British citizenship has not been affected by a widespread popular anti-immigration discourse in the UK (see also Ahmad 2003: 48–9). However, this anti-immigration discourse appears to overlap with a trend among many young British Asians and a substantial number of their parents to object to marriages of British girls being arranged with suitors from the Indian subcontinent (Anwar 1998: 112; see also Gardner and Shukur 1994; Ghuman 1994; Shain 2003: 90; but for conflicting evidence see Gavron 1997: 124). On the other hand, connections with Britain are still valued highly by Bangladeshi families, as the term 'Londoni', which tends to be applied to people, houses and entire villages that have connections to Britain (Gardner and Shukur 1994: 147) shows. In stave 23 it is used by Ardiana to signal her understanding of the value attributed by many Bangladeshis to a potential link with Britain and therefore with girls like themselves.

One motive for the girls' rejection of Bangladeshi men could be that it is obviously much less likely for the girls to get to 'know' their future husbands to some extent if they are from the Indian subcontinent. However, the data allow for another explanation of the girls' bias against husbands from Bangladesh. When Hennah says that a Bengali groom might have 'a personality like an ape' (Extract 14, stave 19), the connotation of the word 'ape' suggests that Hennah expects the men's behaviour to be ill-mannered or even uncivilised. By referring to Bangladeshi men in these derogatory terms Hennah's utterance also reveals an influence of a discourse of imperial Darwinism, which allows the girls to establish their own superiority. At the same time the girls reveal their anxiety about feeling alienated from their future husbands' (Sylheti village) background, which they appear to contrast negatively with their own (urban British Bangladeshi) background.

Hennah's own interpretation of this extract, which she revealed to me in our interview sessions, also aligns itself with mine. As I did not tape-record our session on that day I can only sum up her comments from my notes. Hennah stated that the girls' comments were directed against marrying boys from Bangladesh rather than against arranged marriage. She then explained that one reason for the group's stance was their knowledge of the difficulty and long-windedness of the process of obtaining visas for their future husbands. However, Hennah also repeatedly argued that the reason for any girl's aversion to men from Bangladesh was that these men would have, as she put it, 'no education'. When I tried to investigate the meaning of this claim further, she explained that as a consequence of having 'no education', men from Bangladesh did not know how to treat women correctly. Hennah claimed that Bengali husbands treat their wives in Britain badly (e.g. beat them) because in Bangladesh they are allowed to do so. Although this view clearly draws on a negative stereotype it also provides further evidence of the dominant influence of a discourse of cultural incompatibility which caused the girls in the group to feel anxious.

This discourse of cultural incompatibility between British Asian girls and grooms from the Indian subcontinent due to cultural and educational differences appears to have established itself recently in many parts of the British Bangladeshi and other British Asian 'communities' (Anwar 1998: 112; Basit 1997: 81–4; Gardner and Shukur 1994: 156; Phillipson et al. 2003: 51; but see also Gavron 1997 for counter-arguments). However, I would argue that by engaging in this (essentialist) discourse and by orienting to their own 'Londoni' or 'British' identities, the girls in this group in fact acknowledge their own hybrid identities, which they position in opposition to the identities of their Bangladeshi suitors.

Although the girls' spontaneous talk about Ardiana's wedding proposal reveals a range of different discourses, including a discourse of romantic love and a discourse of cultural incompatibility, the group negotiates a consensus (Eckert 1993) in the form of a modified discourse of arranged marriage. In this discourse the girls' wish to get married to men they 'know' does not constitute an expectation or even a wish to marry their boyfriends. Although several girls in the group actually date, choosing a boyfriend without the knowledge of their parents is positioned as slightly more acceptable (albeit not to all the girls) in the group's talk than choosing a husband without the knowledge and help of their families. Rather than aligning themselves fully with a discourse of love marriage, it seems that the group's consensus is to favour grooms they consider compatible with their 'British' or 'Londoni' Bangladeshi identities, without challenging the discourse of arranged marriage per se.

The compromise that the group achieves in this modified discourse of arranged marriage allows the girls to demand some agency (in wanting to meet their future husbands and/or be compatible with them) and even, in Ardiana's case, to adopt a resistant position (in her alignment with a discourse of romantic love). At the same time the girls do not position themselves in opposition to their parents. Significantly, even Ardiana's resistance to the wedding proposal does not appear to go hand in hand with a critical position towards the role of her own family in the match-making (see Extract 13). There are other examples in my spontaneous conversational data from this group which support this interpretation, providing further evidence that good family relations are very important to the girls, and that

Asian families are not prone to greater inter-generational conflict than non-Asians in the UK (see also. Ahmad, Modood and Lissenburgh 2003; Brah 1996; Shain 2003).

Torn between cultures?

In the girls' spontaneous group talk about Ardiana's wedding proposal popular 'culture clash' discourses therefore serve more to explain the girls' rejection of grooms from Bangladesh, than the girls' relationship with their parents or their position to (a modified version of) the tradition of arranged marriage. However, my interview data present a different perspective. I had originally planned these ethnographic-style interviews with my in-group informant, Hennah, as a means to collect additional information about individual girls, their friendship group, families and wider community. However, in the course of these 'interview sessions', which took place a year after the recordings, I was also able to give Hennah feedback on my progressing analysis of the girls' talk, as, for example on my interest in the girls' bicultural or hybrid identities.[5] At times Hennah accepted my interpretation by highlighting the girls' agency in choosing their husband (Extract 9) and by acknowledging her own ability to, as she said, 'do both', that is, to align herself with what she perceived to be as English and as Bangladeshi discourses and practices. However, she also spoke about hardship in relation to coping with different sets of norms. The following example will show an instance in which she goes very far in distancing herself from a celebration of 'hybrid identities'.

Extract 16: torn between two cultures

1)Pia:	the thing is I I do not you know from from like
2)	looking at **this** {Hennah: yeah} I do not think that it's:
3)	like true: .hhh ah: how a lot of like sociologists[6]
4)	have said *[slightly mock dramatic]*'oh you know like
5)	.hh erm: .hh it's so: difficult and people:
6)	and and (.) you know like (.) girls .hh they are
7)	completely torn between the two cultures'
8)	{Hennah: *[outbreath?]*} *I* think that you lot are doing
9)Pia:	really **well** *you know with the two* {Hennah: *[laughs]*}
10)	with the two (-) I mean *don't you /think* {Hennah: no nono}
11)Hennah:	nonono .hh you know this yeah {Pia: yeah} this i- we'r (-)

12)	there's so much teasing there yeah {Pia: yeah yeah}
13)	that it makes it look like but it it isn't honest to God
14)	*[almost staccato]*it is not **like** cause if you look {Pia: yeah}
15)	at Dilshana Ardiana yeah {Pia: yeah} look at the mess they're in
16)	(-) and look at Rahima {Pia: yeah} .hhh if it was erm: (-)
17)	if it was OK they wouldn't be torn now (-) do you get me
18)	because .hhh {Pia: yeah} %her parents are really (angry)%
19)	they **know** that she's going out with someone .hh but
20)	she won't tell them .hh w*ho it* {Pia: yeah} is or who erm when
21)	he's gonna come for her (like) for good and stuff like that
22)	and they aks her *[authoritarian]* '**tell** <u>him to come to you</u>
23)	<u>for good</u> cause (-) I don't like what people are saying to me'
24)	(-) {Pia: yeah *yeah*} *d'you* get me {Pia: yeah} and erm:
25)	*[laughing]*<u>Ardiana she's in aboard</u> (sic) {Pia ye*ah*} *and*
26)	Shashima she's already **married**

In this extract Hennah objects to my assessment of the girls as 'doing well' (lines 8–9) and my challenge of the 'torn between cultures' discourse (line 7). Hennah points out that (at the time of this interview more than ever) several of her friends in the group, including Dilshana, were 'in a mess' (line 15); Ardiana abroad (in Bangladesh amongst speculations that she would be married off) and another friend, Shashima, already having been married off (after her parents' discovery that she was dating), see lines 25–26. Interestingly, Hennah also challenges my interpretation of the relevance of teasing for the group (which I had told her about previously), positioning it as a strategy to cover up difficulties (line 12), rather than as a strategy to resolve difficulties and synthesise different cultural discourses and norms, as I had suggested on the basis of the girls' spontaneous talk. Thus, in the extract above Hennah argues that some of the girls in the group are in fact torn 'between two cultures' (Watson 1977), rather than stressing their hybrid identities, clearly positioning the different norms on dating and marriage as incompatible and adopting a rather essentialist definition of culture.

My analysis of the interview data elsewhere (Pichler 2008a) takes into consideration that interviews, just like conversations, are co-constructed events, in which subjects take on a range of frequently conflicting discourses and subject positions. It is also essential to acknowledge that Hennah's views and stances may or may not be representative of the entire group. However, I felt that this extract also requires me to ask whether Hennah's voicing of this discourse of 'being trapped between two cultures' reveals an experience of another 'reality' of the girls' heterosexual relationships outside the context of conversational interaction, which is more difficult to manage than what my spontaneous talk suggests. In connection with this I felt it was necessary to consider whether a focus on conversational micro-phenomena can attribute too much emphasis on participant agency. Critiques of extreme constructionist approaches to language and (gender) identity highlight the relevance of this question (Rampton et al., 2004: 15; Sealey, 2005; McElhinny, 2003).

> It is worth considering why post-structuralist models of gender have been so readily embraced by sociolinguists and linguistic anthropologists working on gender. Our very subject matter – language – may lend itself to an ability to focus on gender and the social construction of 'sex'. People's ability to adapt language readily and rapidly from situation to situation, addressee to addressee, may accord people an unusual degree of agency and flexibility in their construction of themselves in a way that other forms of cultural and actual capital can and do not (e.g. body hexus, occupational opportunities). (McElhinny 2003: 26–7)

In the light of the above quote Hennah's claims about the girls' difficulties in balancing religious and other cultural norms in relation to marriage and dating could suggest that my conversational data do not sufficiently capture the girls' experience outside the context of their friendship talk (see also Hammersley 2006). It is possible that in the cultural field (Bourdieu 1991) of the girls' wider community (gender) norms about heterosexual relationships are much less flexible than the diverse and shifting discursive positions analysts might identify in the girls' spontaneous conversations.

Conclusion

The informal talk about the wedding proposal as well as the conversations about boyfriends, love and school show that the girls draw on and negotiate a wide range of discourses and cultural practices in their heterogeneous group. In their talk about truanting and about school as well as in their tough teasing ad verbal duelling the girls frequently adopt tough girl stances, aligning themselves with adolescent identities that appear influenced by ideologies and norms of British lad(ette)/working-class youth culture. Whereas these tough femininities position the girls in opposition to values like studiousness and quietness, stereotypes frequently associated with (young) Asian women, the girls' talk about topics such as dating and love shows that cultural concepts and religious discourses of shame, gender segregation and the policing of female virtue by parents and the community also influence the group's negotiations of practices and subject positions. Frequently the girls switch between different conversational frames in their talk, using teasing to move into a playful frame when talking about boyfriends and their emotions to, as I argue, present respectable femininities and save each other's face, or, quite the opposite, present themselves as tough and show off their competitive verbal skills. This switching between frames and cultural discourses allows the girls to position themselves both as British and as Muslim Bangladeshi girls, and therefore, to accomplish hybrid identities.

In the girls' talk about marriage there is less switching between conversational frames and between discourses of love marriage and arranged marriage. The girls do not ever align themselves with a discourse which positions marriage merely as a matter of individual choice, and the group's negotiations remain largely within the boundaries of a modified discourse of arranged marriage. However, even this discourse emerges as a hybrid in the girls' talk. On one hand, the topic of marriage is clearly positioned as very central to the adolescent femininities of Ardiana and her friends, whereas marriage was simply not a topic pursued in the other two non-Asian groups of adolescent girls I was working with at the time. On the other hand, in their spontaneous talk one of the girls briefly adopts a discourse of romantic love and all girls insist on 'knowing their partners', however without necessarily adopting a discourse of premarital dating. At the same time as positioning marriage arrangements as a family undertaking the girls also voice their opposition to marrying men from Bangladesh, by drawing on anti-immigration discourses as well as on discourses of cultural incompatibility and imperial Darwinism.

I would argue that in the girls' spontaneous conversations about marriage ethnic boundaries and cultural differences are frequently constructed interactively and locally (Brah 1996: 163); they mostly remain implicit, as, for example, when Ardiana objects to her marriage proposal on the grounds of loving her boyfriend. These ethnic and cultural boundaries are constantly de-constructed, re-negotiated and/or synthesised by the girls in their talk, allowing them to engage in 'identity formations which cut across and intersect [...] frontiers' (Hall 1992: 310), that is, in the construction of hybrid identities.

The significance of an essentialised and stereotypical notion of ethnic culture is also acknowledged explicitly on some occasions by the girls in the group talk, as when they position themselves as British and Londoni in opposition to Bangladeshi suitors, but much more frequently by Hennah in our interviews (Pichler 2008a). As Bauman (1997: 209) argues, dominant and essentialist notions of culture(s), equated with discrete and homogeneous ethnic groups, remain relevant aspects in a critical examination of culture as a process, as they 'form [...] part of the discursive competence of citizens from 'ethnic minorities' themselves, and continue [...] to function as one element in the negotiation of difference'. Whereas in some instances Hennah aligns herself with my own celebration of flexible, hybrid cultural practices and identities, in others she relies on much more essentialist discourses of culture and difference. These discourses can reveal cultural experiences and norms which are much less easily synthesised than the linguistic practices that can be identified in the group's conversational data.

I do not believe that my interview data invalidates my findings that spontaneous talk about marriage contributes to the local construction of hybrid identities in this group of five British Bangladeshi girls. As I argued above, one way to resolve what appears to be a discrepancy between my emphasis on cultural hybridity and Hennah's alignment with a discourse of culture clash is to acknowledge our different foci, my own, initially mostly on linguistic micro-phenomena, and Hennah's, on non-linguistic experiences. Another solution would be to refrain both from a re-alignment with the dominant popular discourse of 'being torn between cultures' *and* from an academic over-romantisation of hybridity (Puwar 2003).

Thus the comparison of my two sources of data suggests to me that the translation and negotiation between cultural practices and identities which Hall (1992: 310) deems essential for the formation of hybrid identities is not necessarily free of contradictions and conflict (see also Ballard 1994: 31). There is some evidence for this in the girls' spontaneous talk about dating and marriage, as the group needs to engage in complex negotiations of individual stances and cultural norms to achieve a consensus. These complex discursive negotiations that the girls carry out locally in their friendship talk may reflect some of the issues and difficulties which Hennah identifies in the interviews, in relation to cultural norms and practices surrounding love, dating and marriage outside their friendship group. At the same time, however, I would argue that their spontaneous talk offers the girls a platform to negotiate different cultural discourses, and therefore not only reflects but potentially also affects cultural practices and identities.

Part II

Sex Talk and the Construction of Young Femininities

In this part I shall investigate the three groups' talk (and silences) about a wide range of sexual experiences, norms, practices, orientations and desires. I shall demonstrate that each group's distinct approach to sex talk constitutes a rich resource for the local negotiation of discourses and identities that transcend sexuality and highlight the complex interplay between gender, ethnicity and social class.

My analysis of the girls' informal and spontaneous sex talk has a three-fold aim. Firstly, it examines the young women's construction of heterosexuality from a cross-cultural perspective, combining analytical foci on both local and extralocal dimensions of the cultural 'practices, ideologies and identities that make up sexuality' (Bucholtz and Hall 2004: 492) in the talk of the three groups. The significance of a socio-cultural contextualisation of sexuality is highlighted by Sauntson and Kyratizis (2007: 5–6); '[s]exuality, then, is not just psychological and physical, but is also social and cultural. It is not something which is experienced in a social or cultural vacuum, rather, our sociocultural experiences shape and influence our perceptions and constructions of sexuality'. The foregrounding of a discourse-centred approach to sexuality constitutes the second important basis for my exploration of the girls' sex talk. As Cameron and Kulick (2003a: 18) argue in line with Michel Foucault (1980), '[t]o say that sexuality is "discursively constructed" is to say that sex does not have meaning outside the discourses we use to make sense of it'. My analysis of the girls' talk will therefore focus on the (socio-cultural) discourses that frame the girls' local positioning in relation to a wide range of topics about sex and sexuality, including kissing and (hetero)sexual intercourse; bodies and sexual organs; reproduction and contraception; pornography and paedophilia in film and in literature; (loss of) virginity and 'the first time'; hetero- and homosexual practices and orientations. Thirdly, I seek to investigate sex and sexuality in relation to gender norms and identity performances and therefore show how the girls in my study use their sex talk not only to identify as heterosexual or to signal varying degrees of sexual experience, orientations and desires, but also to carry out important gender and other identity work.

In a critique of the 'unhappy fixation on identity' in established research on language and sexuality, Don Kulick (2000a: 272; 2000b) argues for a re-orientation of the field towards an inquiry of 'language and desire'. The challenge from this desire-oriented approach has led to a defence of identity-centred studies of language and sexuality, which argue that 'the social meanings of sexuality are not just restricted to desire' and highlight the importance of investigating even sexual desire in the context of ideologies, practices and identities (Bucholtz and Hall 2004; but see also Morrish and Leap 2007; Sauntson and Kyratizis 2007a, 2007b). Kulick (2000a: 270) also warns that research should not 'vaporize sexuality into gender', although Kulick's later collaboration with Deborah Cameron acknowledges the strong link between sexuality and gender, arguing that 'while gender does not subsume sexuality, it is clear that no absolute separation between them is possible. An investigation of either will involve the other as well. Whenever sexuality is at issue, gender is also at issue – and, importantly, vice versa' (Cameron and Kulick 2003a: 142). For the purpose of the following chapters in this section I will maintain a conceptual differentiation between sexuality and gender, however, my data strongly suggest that it is neither possible nor desirable to exclude gender and identity from a discussion of sex and (hetero) sexuality.

Before analysing several conversational extracts from the different groups of girls in the following three chapters, I shall give an overview of previous research on girls' sexuality, followed by a brief introduction to the different types of sex talk I found in the three friendship groups and an initial consideration of explanations for the different types of sex talk in relation to the girls' actual sexual experience and to the groups' different relationships with me. I finally propose that the different types of sex talk need to be approached from a discourse level, arguing that the girls use their sex talk as a resource to explore and to re-negotiate socio-cultural discourses which influence their local construction of (hetero)sexual, gender and other identities, and I illustrate and develop this argument in the next three chapters.

Researching girls' sexuality

Whereas research on language and sexuality has only recently attempted to balance its interest in same-sex identities, practices and desires with an exploration of heterosexualities (Sauntson and Kyratzsis 2007; Cameron and Kulick 2006), the exploration of young female heterosexuality has been considerably more established in non-linguistic research on adolescents. This cross-disciplinary research on adolescent female heterosexuality has frequently focused on girls' disempowerment or on the risks associated with young female sexuality (Holland 1993; Holland et al. 1998; Lees 1993; McRobbie 1978). Angela McRobbie's (1978) classic study of 14–16-year-old working-class girls found that the young women's loud classroom discussions about their boyfriends, marriage and family life (as well as their use of make-up and clothing) served to highlight their 'developing sexual identities'. This emphasis on sexuality and romance was central to the 'culture of femininity' which on one hand allowed the girls to resist the class based oppression they encountered at school, but, on the other hand, also disempowered the girls by locking them into very traditional femininities. Sue Lees' (1993) ethnographic study of 15–16-year old London girls in the 1980s also explores the relationship between sexuality and gender norms. Lees found that girls were concerned about preserving their sexual reputation, but also felt pressurised by their peers into finding a boyfriend. In her interviews, Lees discovered that the girls had adopted a discourse that stigmatises active female sexuality and were expressing concern about the preservation of their sexual reputation and of the risk of being perceived as 'slags' or 'sluts' (see also Holland 1993; Holland et al. 1998). Janet Holland's feminist sociological research from the Women, Risk and AIDS Project (WRAP) found that 62 per cent of the 148 young women had had sexual intercourse by the age of 16, rising to 96 per cent by the age of 21 (Holland 1993: 7). However, although this sample across different ethnic groups shows a relative high percentage of sexual experience (not restricted to intercourse), the young British women's view of active female sexuality was rarely positive. Holland et al. (1998) argue that young women's desire is both framed and silenced by the 'male in the head', that is, their own and societal foregrounding and naturalising of male sexual desire.

These findings from studies of girls' actual (hetero)sexuality appear to support Wendy Hollway's (1995: 87) feminist argument that 'there is no emancipatory discourse of women's heterosexual desire'. This quote sums up Hollway's earlier work (1983, 1984) based on (edited) interviews with women in which she discusses discourses of (hetero)sexuality in relation to gender roles and power asymmetry, focusing especially on the 'male sexual drive' discourse, which positions male (hetero)sexuality as a physical and natural need, and therefore allocates the subject position to men and the object position to women, and the female 'have/hold discourse', which frames female (hetero)sexuality in relation to romance, marriage and children and reverses the subject/object positions of the 'male sexual drive' discourse.

The presentation of young women as sexually repressed has been challenged to some extent in more recent research. Lynne Segal (1997: 81) admits that many young women still feel pressurised into having (heterosexual) sex, but opposes the equation of female sexuality with passivity, highlighting the 'diversity and fluidities of heterosexual experiences'. Deborah Tolman's (2005) psychological investigations of girls' stories about sexual desire, elicited by the researcher in interviews with about 31 adolescent girls aged 16–18 from urban and suburban US schools, present a more differentiated and complex picture of young female sexuality and sexual desire. Tolman confirms that young women tend to experience the task of balancing their sexual feelings and desires with their concern for their own safety as a (personal) dilemma. In some of the young women's stories she found a total absence or partial repression of female adolescent sexual desire, in others she found evidence of resistance to repressive discourses of female sexuality, of self-positioning as confident, active and entitled to desire.

Some recent linguistic/discourse analytic research also appears to have shifted its focus from the 'heterosexual marketplace', that is, the powerful 'means by which the social order comes to *presume* heterosexuality, marginalising and rendering deviant any who do not eventually participate' (Eckert 2003: 27) to a foregrounding of young women's agency in taking up different positions in relation to their heterosexuality. Evidence of young women's efforts to construct themselves as agents when talking about their heterosexual experiences can be found in studies by feminist psychologists Hannah Frith and Ceilia Kitzinger (1998), who take a conversation analytic stance to their data, and by Susan Jackson and Fiona Cram's (2003) discourse analytic exploration of agency and resistance in the sex talk of young women. Both studies acknowledge the importance of treating interview data not as 'a transparent window on to people's beliefs and behaviours' (Frith and Kitzinger, 1998: 317), but as a resource for the interviewees to construct their identities. Frith and Kitzinger (1998) demonstrate that a focus on participants' rather than analysts' categories in self-report data of young women can change our perception of young girls as victims of unwanted sex and male power abuse to young women as active agents who are powerful and in control of their sexual encounters. Although this shift of focus should not, I believe, replace the analyst's critical engagement with dominant discourses about heterosexual relationships which remain evident also in Frith and Kitzinger's data, it allows for a relevant exploration of the young women's own rejection of the 'victim label' (315). Jackson and Kram (2003) align themselves with Frith and Kitzinger's aims and methodology in many ways, but engage critically with both dominant and resistant discourses of young female (hetero)sexuality. Their interview study on the heterosexual dating relationships of several groups of 16–18-year old young women from New Zealand provides examples of 'how new meanings and new subject positions may be produced within dominant discourses', for example in talk which positions 'chicks' as 'active desiring agents' (118).

Like Frith and Kitzinger and Jackson and Cram my own study also views the sex talk of young women as a resource to construct identities (and express their sexual experiences, desires and anxieties), but my focus is on the girls' own interactions rather than on those of interviewer and interviewee (but see Chapter 6 for some interview data). Thus, in contrast to most studies on young women's sexuality, I do not elicit the girls' views on sex(uality) in interviews, but study extracts of predominantly spontaneous talk in which the girls address the topic themselves. Although I support the validity of interview studies on the subject, and indeed I also supplement my recordings of the girls' talk with some extracts from ethnographic-interviews in one of the following chapters, I believe that my spontaneous conversational data can offer some fresh insights. Firstly, it captures the varying significance that groups of adolescent girls do in fact attribute to the topics sex and sexuality in their same-age friendship group/talk. Sex talk is not equally important for all three groups I studied, and as I did not encourage the girls to engage in sex talk, or steer the girls' sex talk in any way, this difference has remained very clear in my data. The fact that the sex talk of the girls was not elicited by me also meant that there was no danger of the girls being embarrassed or even silenced by an adult researcher's questions about their sexuality. Contrary to Sue Lees' (1993: 115) experience I did not find that adolescent girls were 'either unaware or embarrassed to talk about sex openly'. The fact that I did not impose my own agenda on the girls' interaction allows me to explore the girls' different positioning of sexual experiences, identities and desires both in relation to the norms and practices of their own friendship groups, and in relation to a range of different discourses which index the girls' membership in contrasting socio-cultural groups.

As in the previous chapters my largely qualitative analysis of the talk on a discursive level in this section is supported by a micro-linguistic investigation. Thus, my exploration of the girls' positions in relation to specific discourses is based on an examination of the structure and organisation of talk, on lexical choices, paralinguistic and nonverbal cues and at times on phonetic and grammatical features. These analytic features were relevant both to my focus on discourses and to my exploration of conversational frames in the sex talk of the girls, allowing me to differentiate between sex talk which is characterised by intimate self-disclosure (Chapter 5), sex talk that has been framed as playful or as serious (Chapter 6), and sex talk which is staged more like an impersonal academic debate (Chapter 7).

Different types of sex talk

Although I take a predominantly qualitative approach to my analysis, the varying importance of the topic 'sex' for the three groups of girls is first evident on a quantitative level. The four East End girls, Pat, Susan, Natalie and Jenny, dedicate about 23 per cent of their total recording time to sex talk, whereas the Bangladeshi group of Ardiana, Dilshana, Rahima, Varda and Hennah spend approximately 6.4 per cent and the four private-school girls, Roberta, Elizabeth, Nicky and Jane, only 3.3 per cent of their time talking about sex and related issues.

The qualitative analysis of my data shows that the girls in the three groups cover different subtopics in their sex talk and, moreover, approach these subtopics in contrasting ways. Personal self-disclosure about penetrative sexual experience only features in the talk of Pat and her predominantly white working-class friends, who deal with this and other sex-related topics such as peer pressure to have sex, with an astounding openness and directness. The Bangladeshi girls' only explicit references to penetrative sex talk occurs in the context of porn movies, and personal sex talk centres on boys' nudity, kissing and even pregnancy although there are also some playful challenges about having or not having 'been through it'. This sex talk is characterised by the girls' frequent switches between serious conversational frames and teasing or boasting activities, which, as I will show, allows them to preserve face and to reconcile culturally opposing discourses. In the private school/upper-middle-class group, on the other hand, the topic of sex takes a significantly more marginal role than in the two working-class groups. When they do talk about sex-related topics, they do so freely, but without engaging in any personal self-disclosure.

It could be suggested that these differences are due to the fact that some of the girls have not had sex or do not even date. Although these factor are certainly not irrelevant, my data suggest that the correlation between actual sexual experience and quantity (and quality) of sex talk is not that straightforward. The number of girls that appeared to have boyfriends varied in each group (from one in the upper-middle-class group to three in both working-class groups) but it seems that in all three groups no more than one of the girls has had sexual intercourse. Moreover, my data will show that the girls' readiness to self-disclose or take up liberal positions in sex talk does not necessarily increase with their sexual experience.

I have also considered the question whether the upper-middle-class/ private-school girls might have refrained from engaging in (personal) talk about sex, because they were the only group who knew me not only as a researcher but also as a part-time member of staff at their school. Again, I feel that my status as a member of staff cannot be ignored, but I would not see this as the sole or even main reason for the girls' specific approach to sex talk. In fact, only one girl in the group had ever been taught by me, and most students who knew me perceived me as a 'lower status' member of staff who they were allowed to address by first name, as I had held the position of a language assistant in the first of my two years at their school. More importantly, several of my extracts from the tape-recorded material indicate that the girls' greatest concern was not the confidentiality of their own 'taboo' experiences, such as sex or drugs, but more the confidentiality of their 'gossip' about fellow students and their criticism of members of staff. I also consider it to be an advantage in this respect that this group was the only one that actually carried out all the recording at home as the girls had not found enough time to be undisturbed at school (see Chapter 1). I believe that this home environment as well as the fact that the speakers are friends who are used to conversing with each other could have largely offset any effects my status as a member of staff might have had on the girls' sex talk.

Thus, although I accept that the girls' contrasting 'real' experiences with boyfriends (and sex) or my status as a member of staff could have had some influence on the characteristics of each group's sex talk, I shall argue that their different approaches cannot fully be explained by these real circumstances. Instead, I suggest that it is rewarding to explore the different approaches to the topic of sex and sexuality in relation to socio-cultural discourses and their dialectic relationship with the local (identity) practices that emerge in the talk of the three groups. In the first of the following three chapters I first turn to Pat's group, whose talk most clearly establishes sexuality and sex as significant, in the following chapter I examine the playful sex talk of Ardiana and the other Bangladeshi girls, in the third and final chapter I explore the impersonal and frequently 'academic' sex talk amongst Roberta and her upper-middle-class private-school friends.

5
Self-disclosing Sex Talk: Self-determined Girls

My interest in comparing the 'sex talk' of the three friendship groups in my study first arose when I became aware that Pat and her white/mixed British working-class friends had dedicated almost a quarter of their total talking time to sex and sexuality-related topics. Working-class girls' sexuality has frequently been problematised; it is associated with stereotypes about 'hypersexual "bad" (poor, of colour) girls', as Tolman (2005) observes in relation to young urban women in the US, and with teenage pregnancy and a 'discourse of welfare scroungers' as Walkerdine et al. (2001: 188–9) note in Britain. Public discourses which position working-class sexuality as deviant are certainly not new. Indeed, Weeks (1981: 19–20) in Skeggs (1997: 42) speaks of 'an obsessive concern with the sexuality of the working-class' in Britain since the end of the eighteenth century, arguing that this allowed for a shift of focus from class conflict to morality. The historic and continuing dominance of classed (and racialised) discourses of (respectable) female sexuality are summed up by Skeggs (1997: 122) in the following quotation about nineteenth-century Britain. 'White middle-class women [...] were able to locate themselves within a pure and proper femininity, precisely because Black and White working-class women were designed and designated as unpure, dangerous and sexual [...]'. More recently, research on young women's sexuality has investigated working-class girls' alleged investment in romance, interpreting this romantic investment as a lack of agency and resistance to boyfriends' sexual desire (Martin 1996; Tolman 2005); as rooted in anti-school culture (McRobbie 1978); as revealing anxieties about the physical and material dangers of expressing girls' own sexual desire (Tolman 2005); and as indicative of the girls' striving for respectable heterosexual femininity (Skeggs 1997).

The following chapter provides a discourse-analytic exploration of the sex talk in a group of London working-class girls, who embarked on these conversations spontaneously rather than in reaction to a researcher's pre-established interest in classed sexuality. In this rich spontaneous data the girls talk about their (hetero)sexual experiences, expectations, desires and anxieties; the use of the morning-after pill and condoms; the significance of their virginity and decisions about when and where to have sex for the first time. I will examine the ways in which the girls approach these topics, focusing on their very personal, self-disclosing talk initially, then showing the girls' awareness of pressures from within their own peer group to become sexually experienced, and finally exploring a range of different discourses which the girls draw on to resist both these pro-sex pressures from their friends and other societal and parental pressures to protect the girls' sexual innocence.

Direct approach to sex talk

Pat and her friends approach the topic of sex predominantly from a serious conversational 'frame' (Bateson 1987/1972; Goffman 1974), in spite of self-disclosing very intimate details about themselves in their conversations. Whereas a question about personal sexual experience is dealt with mainly by a switch to a playful frame in the Bangladeshi group (Chapter 6), or is ignored entirely in the group of private-school girls (Chapter 7), it is answered fully and directly by Pat and her friends.

Extract 1: the first time

(1)
Natalie   %>did you \do*{high p.}* it with him (with Simon)<%

(2)
Pat   *{smiling}no:: I didn't* (.) I didn't do anything
Pat's voice suggests that she is smiling

(3)
Natalie   (1) *%(you never shagged him xxxxxxxxxx)%{smiling}*

(4)
Pat   *{smiling}I didn't I didn't do nothing I [promise you]*
Natalie   [(alright no]

(5)
Pat   [if I did] I would tell you
Susan   alright (-) /mm
Natalie   I'[m just saying)]

In the above example Natalie asks Pat whether she had sex with her former boyfriend. Although the reduced volume and the faster speed of utterance delivery signal Natalie's awareness that the topic is sensitive or even embarrassing, the question is surprisingly direct. There are no hedges or hesitation sounds nor any mitigating pre-sequences to counteract the potential face threat posed by Natalie's personal question. The same holds true for Pat's reply, in which she denies having had sex with her former boyfriend (stave 2). Natalie's disbelief manifests itself sequentially in the reformulation of her question after a 1-second-pause (stave 3). Pat's reply follows immediately, without any hesitation which would indicate her discomfort. The smiling voices and Natalie's reduced volume are the only cues suggesting that the girls are engaged in a potentially sensitive topic. However, Pat is clearly not outraged or offended by the question and her readiness to answer Natalie is reinforced by her (serious) reassurance 'if I did I would tell you'. Most importantly, Pat and her friends do not switch into a teasing or boasting frame in order to avoid a serious discussion about sex.

It is also interesting to note the girls' syntactic and lexical choices in this extract in relation to discourses about young gendered sexuality. Natalie's questions, 'did you do it with him', 'you never shagged him', and Pat's reply 'no I didn't' are in the active voice and thus highlight Pat's agency. Natalie and Pat therefore co-construct a girl's position in a first sexual encounter very much in opposition to the passive acquiescence that Tolman (2005) found in the 'it just happened' discourse of many young women she interviewed. In fact, provided my transcription of stave 3 is correct, Natalie's grammatical choice to ask Pat whether she has 'shagged him' not only signals her avoidance of reciprocal constructions which highlight the mutual desire of two people (Cameron and Kulick 2003a: 30), as in 'we shag' or 'I shagged with him', but also subverts the dominant representation of 'men [...] in the subject slot' and 'women in the object slot' (Cameron and Kulick 2003a: 30 referring to Manning 1997) in relation to verbs denoting sexual activity.[1] Natalie's use of the verb 'shag' is also worth considering. 'To shag' clearly positions sexual activity in a less romantic discourse than, for example, 'to make love'. It belongs to a range of verbs which are still considered taboo or at least derogatory by many (older) speakers of British English, although it is not en par with offensive terms such as 'fuck' or 'screw', and Cameron and Kulick even refer to it as 'an affectionate colloquialism for intercourse in British English' (2003a: 30). Thus this extract shows that Pat and her friends can approach sex talk directly, as agents, and sometimes even without linking it to romance, although the latter is more unusual, as I shall show further below.

Personal self-disclosure

The sex talk of Pat, Jenny, Susan and Natalie is very personal, containing many instances of self-disclosure, both about their sexual experience and about their lack of it. In all other extracts, sexual experience is seen as synonymous with sexual intercourse. In one instance Susan admits to wondering whether thicker (and therefore safer) condoms might constitute a problem in case 'your womb is tight'. In the subsequent discussion Natalie self-discloses about what appears to have been her own 'first time'. Another girl, Nix, is present during this exchange.

Extract 2: contraceptives

(1)
Pat   [so when the f]irst time you have sex you
?Susan   [I'm only like]

(2)
Pat   can't have some (-) **big fat** (-)%dick%

(3)
Pat   {laughs}
Susan   (xxxxxxxxxxxxxxxxxxxxxxxxxxxxxxxxx)
Natalie   yeah but remember the first time you have sex
Liz   (xxxxxxx)

(4)
Susan
Natalie   you [don't properly] have sex you don't properly
Liz   [{brief laugh}]

(5)
Pat   =yeah
Susan   (.) yea[h]
Natalie   you don't feel like   [(you)] just had sex=

(6)
Pat   because *{#####} {laughing}<u>yeah</u> (-) you(r thing)
Jenny   {high pitched}<u>I</u>
*tape recorder cuts out

Whereas Susan's earlier comments express concern about the thickness of condom material, Pat seems to suggest that the real problem is the thickness of the penis itself (staves 1–2). In both cases, however, the girls self-disclose about their anxieties regarding their first sexual intercourse. As the girls' later discussions show, this concern is linked to an apprehension about experiencing the first sexual intercourse as painful and leads to a later discussion about the breakage of the hymen (stave 6: 'your thing' and following staves). Pat's laughter in stave 3 (which renders Susan's utterance indecipherable), her hesitations in stave 2 and finally the reduced volume in which she utters 'dick' signal her embarrassment. However, again Pat's embarrassment does not lead to a topic change, as with Ardiana and her Bangladeshi friends (Chapter 6). On the contrary, after the girls have relieved their feeling of unease about the topic, the discussion is resumed on a more serious level again.

In staves 3–4 Natalie positions herself as an expert when she asks the others to 'remember' that first time sex is not and does not feel like proper sex. This expert-stance goes hand in hand with a self-disclosure, as Natalie's utterance indicates that her first time was not and did not feel like 'proper' sex. The reasons for these claims are only implied here, but are revealed in the following staves; they concern the girls' anxieties about not feeling relaxed in front of their partners, about experiencing pain and bleeding. Natalie receives support from (sexually inexperienced) Susan and Pat in staves 5 and 6. Pat immediately signals that she also shares this expert-knowledge by latching onto Natalie's utterance, showing her agreement with and understanding of Natalie's implicature, and introducing a gender-related discourse of virginity which centres on the material loss of their hymen (Holland et al. 1998). Thus, my data confirm Holland et al.'s (1998) findings that girls do not expect their first sexual intercourse to be an entirely positive experience.

However, this extract also confirms that the girls tend to feel at ease when talking about sex, signalled by their laughter and lack of awkward silences. The personal and direct approach of Pat and her friends towards the topic of sex is very evident. The girls (and in particular Jenny) do show embarrassment of varying degrees when they self-disclose, but the group never refrains from pursuing the topic further. Although even displays about a lack of sexual knowledge are encouraged by the group,

Natalie's self-disclosure shows that girls with personal sexual experience (of intercourse) do not need to be afraid of being stigmatised but instead can adopt an expert stance and therefore claim status within the group.

Pro-sex discourse

The girls' talk about heterosexual activity is not framed as playful teasing, nor is it balanced by a discourse that establishes sexual innocence as the norm. Pat and her friends construct a display of and/or interest in active heterosexuality as appropriate and even desirable gendered behaviour for adolescent girls. However, Pat, Susan, Jenny and Natalie are actually conscious of this 'pro-sex' discourse and at times appear to experience it as a pressure. The following extract captures the continuation of Extract 1.

Extract 3: the first time – continued

(6)
Susan   it is- it is a big pressure (when) when you're (with

(7)
Pat   [yeah of course .hh]   {clicks tongue}
Susan   someone in a) [relationship=]   =but~

(8)
Pat   look right (.) as soon er cause we're fifth- like (all)

(9)
Pat   older than fifteen this sex thing is such a big issue now

In stave 6, Susan first reveals that she, and presumably other adoles-cents, can feel pressurised into having sex. Whereas Susan, who is dating a sexually experienced young man several years older than herself (see also note 1), appears to be referring to pressures within a heterosexual relationship, Pat interprets Susan's utterance as a description of peer pressure. Pat's interpretation becomes evident in staves 8–9, when she suggests that sex has become a big issue for herself and others from the age of fifteen onwards. Her use of the first person plural pronoun 'we' indicates that she is referring to a group that she is part of, and the following staves confirm that she is referring to her peer group.

Susan Moore and Doreen Rosenthal (1993: 69) highlight the significance of the peer group for shaping adolescent attitudes to and experiences of sexuality, but they also argue that youth culture constitutes a more distal but equally significant social influence on adolescent sexuality (ibid.: 70).

In our highly sexualised society, many of the values and norms of the youth culture concern sexual behaviour. Consequently this subculture probably has more influence on young people's sexual activity than it does on, say, their career choices. Thornburg (1975) suggests that the pressures inherent in the adolescent subculture may thrust young people into heterosexual involvement before they are physically and emotionally ready to deal with it, almost bullying them into premature sexual activity.

Like Moore and Rosenthal my data identify youth culture filtered through the adolescent peer group as a significant source and site for pressures on young people to have sexual intercourse (see also Holland et al. 1998 on 'social pressure'; Martin 1996: 16 on 'classed' peer pressure). Interestingly, my own data only provides evidence for the dominant role of this pro-sex discourse in the two groups of girls from a London East End/working-class background and not in the same-age group of London private-school girls. In the three groups I studied the discourse which encourages and even rewards sexual experience with status therefore appears to be particularly prominent among adolescents with specific socio-cultural (working-class) affiliations. However, my data also show that these (working-class) adolescents either balance this discourse with a discourse of pre-marital chastity, as in the case of my Bangladeshi group, or challenge it overtly, as in the case of Pat and her friends. By signalling her awareness of this discourse Pat already hints at her critical position towards it. As the conversation continues there is more evidence of the girls' awareness of and resistance to this dominant pro-sex discourse within their peer group.

Extract 4: the first time – continued

(13)
Susan *{eating noise}* you don't you don't [necess- you
Jenny   [(xxxxxxxxxx

(14)
Pat   [no but y-
Susan   don't necessarily have] to have [sex in a
Jenny   xxxxxxxxxxxxxxxxxxxxxxxx)]

(15)
Pat   everyone's tal]king about it and they're like
Susan   relationship]

(16)
Pat   *{raucous voice}*"<u>oh have you done</u> anything yet"
Natalie   [in this day (day and age)
?Jenny   I don'[t

Again, it becomes clear that Susan is speaking about the pressures of having sex within a (heterosexual) relationship whereas Pat is describing peer pressure. This slight misunderstanding is clarified in staves 14–15 when Pat confirms that it is possible to be in a relationship without having sex ('no but') and then explains that what she means is that 'everyone's talking about it'. Again, Pat's peer group is likely to be the referent of 'everyone'. In stave 16 it seems that Pat is mocking a teenage-like enquiry about the sexual experience of another teenager. This mock enquiry provides further evidence for the existence and significance of a dominant pro-sex discourse in the girls' same-age peer group. At the same time the sexual overtone of the raucous voice signals Pat's subversion of the voice and discourse she invokes. A few staves below Susan aligns herself with Pat.

Extract 5: the first time – continued

(21)
Pat   *{laughs}* yeah
?Susan   or like it's a *<u>fashion</u> (xxxxxxxxxxxx)
Jenny   *{loud laughter}*
{mock effusive}

By using the word 'fashion' Susan signals that she, too, is aware of this pro-sex discourse which is so powerful that many adolescents around Susan and Pat follow it like a 'fashion'. Likening sex to a fashion suggests that it is not only perceived as a dominant norm but that it is also valued positively by the majority of adolescents. However, Susan's comparison also suggests that she positions this 'fashion' critically, and considers alternatives for herself. Moreover, just like Pat Susan uses a paralinguistic sign, her exaggerated, 'effusive' tone of voice, to signal that she distances herself from this powerful discourse.

In his study of Glaswegian working-class boys, Wight (1994: 721) confirms public belief that male adolescents do not like to admit to 'being virgins'. Wight explains this by pointing to male peers and family members as well as to the media that 'construct vaginal sexual intercourse as a normal, and essential, element of masculinity, as highly pleasurable, legitimate and something that many boys of their age are probably engaged in' (Wight, 1994: 721). My own data suggest that although a discourse of virginity is still evaluated more positively by some girls than boys (see below), 'having done it' is also constructed as the norm for many adolescent working-class girls in their peer group. However, unlike Wight's working-class boys, Pat and some of the other girls in the group try to distance themselves from this dominant pro-sex discourse, marking their opposition both on a content level and by paralinguistic cues such as their changed voice.

Discourses of morality, romance, pleasure, resistance and self-determination

The remainder of this chapter will be dedicated to the range of frequently conflicting discourses which the girls draw on to balance the strong pro-sex discourse they experience in their peer group with discourses and positions which foreground their own needs, anxieties/concerns and pleasures in relation to sexual intercourse. In these discussions Pat, Susan, Natalie and Jenny switch between different discourses, constructing themselves alternately as moralistic, romantic, sexually experienced, resistant or liberal, and, above all, self-determined girls.

Discourse of sexual morality

The girls' resistance to being pressured into their first sexual experience is not rooted in a discourse of pre-marital chastity, which constitutes an important influence on the sex talk of the Bangladeshi girls and goes some way to explain their playful framing of this talk (see Chapter 6). However, the repertoire of Pat and her friends also contains a discourse of sexual morality, usually voiced by Jenny.

Extract 6: in the back of a car

(1)
Pat   you know his ex-[girlfriend]
Jenny   d'you know Joanne   [she lost] her

(2)
Jenny   virginity to him in the back of his (own) car (-)
?Natalie   (xxxxxxxxxx)

(3)
Pat   blatantly [after about] two months
Susan   [it's cool]
?Beth   in the back

(4)
Pat   [yeah
Jenny   *(amused)*.hh (exactly cause)
Susan   [yeah it's cool man
?Beth   of a **car**

Jenny clearly expects her friends to morally judge the behaviour of
Joanne, the ex-girlfriend of Jenny's boyfriend. Jenny's expectation is
signalled by the pause in stave 2 but at the same time the pause and
delayed reactions of the others show an initial lack of support for
Jenny and her evaluation of Joanne. Only Pat, who knew about this
story, signals her support for Jenny by providing some further information about Joanne's improper sexual behaviour ('blatantly after about
two months') with the intention to obtain the desired shock effect.
The partial success of this strategy can be seen in stave 4. Beth,
another student who joined the group for this discussion, signals her
understanding of Jenny's and Pat's indignation by mirroring Jenny's
utterance and putting contrastive stress on the word 'car'. On the other
hand Susan appears to challenge the other girls' moral judgement by
positively evaluating Joanne's actions as 'cool', and therefore adopting
a resistant and liberal stance (see Extracts 12, 13).

   Jenny's celebration of sexual morality goes hand in hand with a
discourse of virginity. This discourse positions virginity as something
(precious) that Joanne 'lost ... to her boyfriend' (stave 1) and therefore
appears to uphold the 'cultural symbolism of the sex act: masculinity as
activity, femininity as passivity' (Segal 1997). Jenny, however, also voices
a discourse of virginity in relation to boys, saying that her boyfriends
'lost his at fourteen'. However, the girls' virginity talk still remains
gendered, as their concerns regarding the breakage of the hymen and
their lack of sexual pleasure they expect for their first time indicate
(see Extract 2). Moreover Jenny still attributes blame only to the
young woman for consenting to sexual intercourse, reflecting the double

standard of sexual reputation that young women have frequently been found to have appropriated (Holland et al. 1998; Lees 1993; Tolman 2005). About one minute later Jenny explicitly orients to a discourse of sexual morality.[2]

Extract 7: in the back of a car – continued

(35)
Jenny   the second girls she was the second girl he slept with

(36)
Jenny   (-) and I guarantee that I'm not gonna be the third

(37)
Jenny   (2)   [I have morals]   I'm mo- {mocking}**I** have
?   how?
?Beth   [you don't have to be] (xxxxxxxxxxxxxxxxxx)

(38)
Jenny   morals me   in the back of a car **man**{disgusted}
?   yeah (xxxxxxxxxxxxxxxxxxxxxxx)
?Beth   (did you

(39)
Jenny   {high pitch}I **know** man in the back of the car (.) how tacky
?Beth   speak to her)

This is the most straightforward example of a member of this group voicing a discourse of sexual morality to position herself as a 'good girl' concerned about her 'respectability' (Skeggs 1997). Although Jenny refrains from using derogatory labels like 'slut' or 'slag' whose significance for girls' sexual reputation has been established in several interview studies (Lees 1993; Holland 1993; Holland et al. 1998; Tolman 2005), she still passes moral judgement, first in relation to active young female sexuality itself 'I'm not gonna be the third' (stave 36), and then in relation to its location, 'how tacky' (stave 39). However, even at its most extreme, differences between Jenny's discourse of sexual morality and the Bangladeshi girls' positioning as 'good girls' are evident (see Chapter 6). Firstly, Jenny does not specify for how long she intends to remain celibate. This contrasts with the other group's discourse of premarital chastity (see Dilshana's 'I would never do it until I get married then').

Although Jenny's moralistic position shows that she is worried about her reputation, there is no sign that sleeping with a boy would shame her to the extent of not being able to find a husband or partner (compare Rahima: 'let's say your boyfriend left you and you've done it with him'). It seems to me that this difference is due to the fact that for Jenny, unlike for the Bangladeshi group, a girl's personal chastity is not a matter of family honour or *izzat*.[3] Moreover, whereas most girls in the Bangladeshi group are experimenting with discourses that challenge the ideology of premarital chastity only playfully, the sex talk in the white/mixed group draws on a variety of resistant discourses in a serious frame. Jenny also signals that she is aware of potential opposition to her stance in the group, when she assumes a self-mocking voice in staves 37–8 'I have morals me'. I believe that this playful subversion of her own moralising needs to be seen in reaction to Susan's earlier challenges, including one that ridicules Jenny by addressing her as 'Virgin Mary'.

Romantic discourse

Some of the support that Jenny receives in the above extracts from friends like Pat and Beth appears to be linked less to their aim to preserve their virginity per se than to the girls' wish to determine the right time (not as soon as after two months) and place (not in the back of a car) for their 'first time'. These wishes can be seen as expressions of a desire to experience their first sexual intercourse as 'special', and are indicative of a romantic discourse.

Extract 8: the first time – continued

(26)
Pat   =yeah but you get some girls who just do it

(27)
Pat   and they regret i::t and (.) they just wann[a get
Susan   [yeah

(28)
Pat   it over and done with]   [lose (the)
Susan   I know (a) few people] who's done it an[d regret it
?Natalie   (xxxxxxxxxxxxxxxxxxxxxxx sex)

(29)
Pat   virginity innit (.) I'm sorry but .hh for my first

(30)
Pat   time I'm not gonna just (.) do it % (I'm [gonna
Susan   [yeah

(31)
Pat   love them)%]
Susan   but then again-] (.) that's what I I I was thinking

This extracts captures Pat's reaction to one of Susan's resistant/liberal positions in relation to virginity and first-time sex (see Extracts 12, 13). In stave 26 Pat signals her lack of alignment with Susan, following her token agreement 'yeah' with a connector which announces a contradiction ('but …'). She clearly distances herself from girls who have sex for the first time only to 'get it over and done with' (stave 27–28). Her utterance highlights once more her opposition to being pressured into her first experience of penetrative sex. Pat also positions herself in opposition to the 'it-just-happened-discourse' (Tolman 2005; but see also Holland et al. 1998; Martin 1996), emphasising her own agency. Moreover, she does not appear to position herself in a discourse which views the premarital loss of a girl's virginity as degradation for the girl herself (or even a shame for her entire family – see Chapter 6). When she talks about the girls regretting their first sexual experience in stave 27 or when she imagines her own 'first time' in stave 30 Pat voices a discourse which links sex to romantic love. This romantic discourse is explicit in stave 31 when Pat produces an utterance which appears to ends in the words 'love them'. Pat thus indicates that for her first-time-sex without any romantic feelings is undesirable.

The following extract provides further evidence for this 'romantic discourse' and its position between liberalism and morality.

Extract 9: the first time – continued

(52)
Pat   (saying) for (like [inci]dent) if you did (lose
Susan   [yeah]

(53)
Pat   vigi-) virginity with John you can say .hh "I lost

(54)
Pat   with- my virginity to someone I was with for a

(55)

Pat   long time and I loved him" .hhh yo[u can't] just
Susan   [yeah]

In this extract Pat disagrees with Susan's earlier dismissal of first-time
sex (see Extracts 12, 13) indirectly when she talks to Susan about the
advantages of 'losing her virginity' with her long-term boyfriend. Not
only does Pat think that it is better to be in love with the first boy a
girl sleeps with but she also makes a point about being in a long-term
relationship. Thus, she voices a discourse which does not only
contain (traditional) values about virginity and romantic love but
also advocates getting to know one's boyfriend well before having sex
with him. Wendy Hollway (1983, 1984) argues that women tend to
position themselves as subjects (and men as objects) in a discourse
that views sex as being linked to love and commitment, offered by a
long-term relationship. Hollway (1984: 65) highlights the Christian
connotations of this 'have/hold discourse' by framing it as 'a loving
commitment between a man and a woman [which] should lead to
bringing up a family'. Although connotations of marriage and
reproduction apply much less to Pat's romantic discourse than to the
discourse of premarital chastity voiced in the Bangladeshi group
(Chapter 6), it is clear that the girls position sex firmly within a
loving relationship. A wide range of research found that (young)
female sexuality and especially the experience of sexual intercourse is
often framed by a dominant discourse of romance (Wetherell 1995;
Hollway 1983, 1984; Holland et al. 1998; Segal 1997; Jackson and
Cram 2003; Tolman 2005). Feminist scholarship has frequently
argued that this focus on love and romance can have both a legitimis-
ing and a silencing effect on girls' expression of physical sexual desire
(Holland et al. 1998: 100; Tolman 2005; Jackson and Cram 2003).

My data confirm the lack of a discourse which is the equivalent
of the biological and natural 'male sexual drive' (Hollway 1983, 1984).
However, I align myself with Jackson and Cram (2003: 124) who argue
that '[i]f we accept that the biological imperative is an undesirable
construction of sexuality for young men, as many do, then perhaps we
must also question whether it is desirable for young women.' My data
suggest that the link that Pat and her friends establish between sex and
love/romance does not necessarily go hand in hand with a repression of
female sexual desire. I interpret the girls' wish to experience their
first sexual intercourse within a long-term relationship as indication
of some individual agency. Rather than worrying about losing their

reputation if they have sex before marriage, Pat and her friends appear to be concerned about the right time and place and the right partner for sex. It is undeniable that Pat suggests that girls should preserve their virginity until they meet somebody who is 'worthy'. However, it seems to me that this suggestion is at least equally founded in Pat's concern about her own enjoyment and well-being as in an effort to preserve a good-girl reputation (although there clearly is a dialectical relationship between the two). Pat does not allow her peers to push her into having sex just for the sake of being 'experienced' but neither does she bend to the pressures exerted by moralistic discourses which view the 'loss of her virginity' as a loss of a good-girl identity. Instead it seems to me that Pat positions herself midway in a romantic discourse, which advocates first time sex with a loving/loved partner as a special and worthwhile event.

I argue that the romantic discourse in Pat's group balances (social) sexual morality with a fulfilment of individual (romantic) needs and desires.

Extract 10: the first time – continued

(57)
Pat   you can't be one of the girls that say I don't even

(58)
Pat   remember when I lost it [(you have to)] grow up
Susan   [oh yeah]

(59)
Pat   say to your kids like-
?Jenny   "oh yeah that was e:r

(60)
Pat   {laughing} [yeah] {laughs}
Jenny   was {singsong}<u>worth having oh [don't] be scared</u>"

(61)
Pat   {laughter}   but you
Susan   <u>yeah</u>{laughing}
Jenny   {laughter} (you) know what I mean {laughs}

(62)
Pat   can't you don't wanna be one of them like "oh yeah

(63)
Pat   it just happened and that"=
Natalie   ="(yeah) it happened

(64)
Pat   [ye]ah*{laughing}* in the
Natalie   in the back of a stree[t]"
Jenny   *{laughs}*

(65)
Pat   pu[b toilet] *{laughter - - - - - - -}*
Susan   [right]
?Jenny   in the back seat*{squeaky voice}*

(66)
Pat   .hhhh [hhhh]*{laughing, high}*wha::t *{laughs}*
Susan   [*{unconvinced laugh}*]   true true

In the above exchange the girls distance themselves collaboratively from
casual or non-romantic first-time 'sex' and from (real and fictitious) girls
who do engage in casual sex. In staves 59–60 Jenny gives the first example
of the conditions that she (and the group) consider to be important for
having a first-time-sex experience which is 'worth it', that is, presumably,
positive and special (stave 60). In staves 62 and 63 Pat produces a new
variation of the 'you-can't-be-one-of-the-girls'-theme which she had
voiced earlier. Subsequently the other girls build on Pat's utterance,
mirroring and elaborating it. Natalie starts by giving a (hypothetical)
example of a context in which the girls would not want to have sex
for the first time and in the following two staves the girls collaboratively
produce a three-part list (staves 64–65).

   This extract makes a significant contribution to the girls' bonding, both
through its jocular, light-hearted tone and through its joint development
of a moralistic stance, which allows the girls to construct their own and
the group's behaviour as superior to that of the girls they are joking about.
However, I would claim that the undeniable influence of a discourse of
sexual morality in the extract is balanced by the girls' desire to fulfil their
own personal needs and romantic expectations about sleeping with a boy
for the first time. They do not want to experience their first intercourse as
something that 'just happened' *to* them (stave 63). Thus, Pat and her
friends oppose the 'it just happened' discourse, which Tolman (2005)
found to stifle both agency and the sexual desire of young women. I argue

that this romantic discourse does not actually position the girls as passive and selfless, awaiting the arrival of their prince like the heroines of girls' comics described by Valerie Walkerdine (1984). Instead it signals a degree of agency, as the girls want to determine with whom, where and when they will have sex for the first time to guarantee that it will be an enjoyable, worthwhile experience for them.

Discourse of sexual pleasure

Positive stories and discourses of sexual pleasure and bodily desire are frequently found to be missing, partially covered or deferred in many interview studies with young women (Burns and Torre 2004; Holland et al. 1998; Martin 1996; Jackson and Cram 2003; Tolman 2005; West 1999). In my own spontaneous conversational data from the three groups of girls, there is also very little evidence of talk about sexual pleasure and desire. However, the next extract indicates that this lack of explicit talk about these aspects of sex and sexuality does not necessarily mean that the girls do not *expect* to experience pleasure and desire. The extract comes from a lengthy conversation about contraceptives amongst Pat, Jenny, Susan and Natalie and a couple of other girls. The girls' conversation has turned from the morning-after pill to condoms. Just before this extract some of the girls have been explaining the benefits of a very thin condom called 'Fetherlite' to the others. The conversation could therefore be said to be framed by the 'reproductive paradigm' (West 1999: 534), with its focus on (unwanted) pregnancy, periods as well as contraception, which is not only central to many young women's talk about sex/uality, but also dominates interactions between adults and young people, both at home and at school in sex education (West 1999: 534; see also Holland 1993: 14). This reproductive talk, which, as Bucholtz and Hall (2004: 479) argue, has been ignored by recent desire-based approaches to language and sexuality, is central to the sex talk of the girls in this group. Interestingly, my data show that even within this reproductive frame young women can find space to engage in talk about sexual pleasure.

Extract 11: in the back of a car – continued

(1)
Natalie   (.) it's yeah but it's obvious though

(2)
Natalie   cause they're so thin Susan (.)

(3)
Natalie   the thinner they are the more pleas]ure you're
?   (xxxxxxxxxxxxxxxxxxxxxxxxxx)]

(4)
Natalie   supposed to get [that's what it is /right]
?Liz   [(it's like a balloon)]   d'you

(5)
Natalie   d'you know you know (-) most
?Liz   know if you (.)

(6)
Susan   y[eah]
Natalie   boys say condoms are passion killers   tr-
?   [yeah]

(7)
Pat   {mock boy}it's like SWIMMING WITH YOUR
Natalie   true or false (xxxxxxxxxxxxxxxxxxxx right)

(8)
Pat   BOOT[S ON] {laughs}
Natalie   [because-] (-) w- we (.) like girls may

(9)
Pat   {peal of laughter}
Natalie   get the pleasure (-) **bu:t** boys don't because

(10)
Natalie   they have to wear the condom the they still
?   {quiet laughter}

(11)
Natalie   get the pleasure but not (.) >as [much as]
?Beth   [so much]

(12)
Susan   =yeah
Natalie   (that) what they want=   [so tha]t's why
?Beth   (poor [xxxxx)] {quiet

(13)
Natalie   (they've) Fetherlite they're so thin they give
?Beth   *laugh}*

(14)
Susan   [yeah]
Natalie   a boy **more** (.) like they feel more pleasure

(15)
Natalie   but they're not that safe
?   (right)
??   (but-)

In staves 3–4 Natalie begins to show off her expert knowledge about (Fetherlite) condoms and the effect of their thinness. Natalie does not approach the topic from a purely pseudo-scientific (Coates 1999) angle about condom-use, as she also introduces the issue of sexual pleasure into the conversation. This extract could be interpreted as an example of young women's 'male in the head' (Holland et al. 1998), that is, of 'the subordination of female desire to male' (ibid. 121). Indeed the talk appears to centre on how to increase male sexual pleasure 'give a boy more like they feel more pleasure' (staves 13–14), and their perceived dislike of condoms ('passion killers' stave 6; and 'swimming with their boots on', stave 7–8). However, I believe that this interpretation is too restrictive, as it would gloss over clear signs of the young women's sexual agency and desire. An in-depth focus on (para)linguistic signs helps to identify the girls' agency. Whereas Natalie's unchanged voice in stave 6 suggests she has appropriated the boys' view and this dominant discourse of condoms as 'killers' of male passion (see also Holland 1993: 29), Pat subverts this discourse and shows her disapproval of the boys' stance in staves 7–8 by assuming a loud, mock-laddish voice when imitating a sexist utterance which likens safe sex to swimming in boots. Moreover, Natalie's sympathy with the boys' view does not imply that she accepts the repressive discourse that views contraception as being a girl's responsibility. She does not argue that girls should take the pill but suggests that the use of a thinner condom would allow boys to gain the *same* (!) amount of pleasure as girls (staves 8–15). Thus, despite her undeniable concern about male sexual pleasure, I would argue that Natalie actually normalises the fulfilment of sexual desires for both girls and boys (staves 8–12). This also supports my earlier argument that the girls are more worried about rendering sex a worthwhile experience for themselves (and their partners) than preserving a 'good-girl reputation'. The fact that Natalie presupposes that girls can expect even more sexual satisfaction than boys shows that she has moved far beyond a traditional, repressive discourse which positions women as mere objects to men's sexual needs. Instead Natalie constructs herself as a progressive and emancipated girl who considers sexual fulfilment as essential for both women and men.

Resistant discourses

Although the extracts I have discussed so far have already provided some evidence for the girls' alignment with resistant stances in their talk about peer pressure, romance and virginity, I would like to look at two resistant discourse in more detail.

Susan: resistance to the celebration of virginity

This extract follows a discussion of the girls which I explored in relation to their alignment with a discourse of romance in relation to their 'first time' (see Extracts 8–10). It shows how Susan challenges both moralistic and romantic discourses about female virginity, thereby adopting a resistant position.

Extract 12: the first time – continued

(32)
Pat   [**love** them]{mocking?}
Susan   {clicks tongue} [not that] I've had sex but obviously

(33)
Pat   gotta [talk] Jenny (ain't) said (nothing)]{laughing}
Susan   but~   [I was-]
Jenny   (I xxxxxx)]

(34)
Susan   I was thinking that {slightly worried}"oh no .hh erm it's

(35)
Susan   a big thing" but if you think about it ain't really a

(36)
Pat   (.) it's just **that** (.) [s- stuff]
Susan   big thing   [your] virginity

(37)
Susan   (ai-) ain't a big thing at all (-) [when when
?Jenny   (-) [(if you see-]

(38)
Susan   if no but WHEN YOU THINK OF IT]   PEOPLE SAY
Jenny   it depends how you're thinking about it]

(39)
Susan   .hh (THEY ALL GO ON LIKE) like people go on like it's

(40)
Pat   *{laughs}*
Susan   (.) .hh li::ke a million Dollars that you're throwing away

In staves 35–36 and then again in staves 36–37 Susan argues that 'your virginity ain't a big thing at all'. By refusing to view first-time-sex as a significant experience Susan also challenges the significance of a differentiation between a 'virgin' and a sexually-experienced girl. Thus, Susan openly challenges both moralistic and romantic discourses about first-time-sex, constructing herself clearly as liberal and emancipated. It is interesting to note that in the preceding stave (32) Susan emphasises that she has not yet had sexual intercourse, highlighting that she does not adopt a resistant stance because she is sexually experienced herself. Paralinguistic cues help Susan to subvert this celebratory discourse of virginity. When she reports that in the past she also thought that having sexual intercourse for the first time is a 'big thing' Susan changes her voice to capture her former anxieties about losing her virginity at the same time as distancing herself from her former anxieties, as well as of the discourse which shapes them.

The reactions of the other girls show some re-positioning as well as the careful negotiation of a compromise. Pat initially sides with Susan, challenging her own earlier alignment with a romantic discourse about virginity by opposing the value that is attributed to the hymen in celebratory and moralising discourses of virginity with the help of dismissive comments such as 'just that' and 'stuff' (stave 36). Jenny, however, signals her disagreement with Susan's assessment in stave 38. After a pause and a false start in stave 37 Jenny produces her counter assessment, which she phrases as a compromise 'it depends how you're thinking about it'. Although Jenny does not disagree with Susan directly or emphatically her utterance implies that she would be defensive of a more moralistic or romantic discourse which positions virginity as a valuable good. On this occasion, however, Jenny negotiates a consensus (Eckert 1993) in stave 38 by positioning virginity as a matter of personal rather than social morality (Coleman 1980).

In the final staves (39–41) Susan ridicules people who view the loss of a girl's virginity in similar terms to the loss of an enormous amount of money to reinforce her criticism of a discourse that celebrates virginity. However, positioning herself in opposition to her friends is a delicate task even for a confident speaker such as Susan, as the next extract shows.

Extract 13: the first time – continued

(69)
Susan   yeah but (I) true it ain't (.) I don't
Natalie   *[laughs]*

(70)
Susan   think- (.) I don't think it's a big thing as people

(71)
Pat   [it's not   [like-]
Susan   make it out to b[e honest=
?Natalie   =[yeah] (-) cause I'm

Susan produces two false starts 'yeah but I' and 'true it ain't' and one more repetition 'I don't think-' in staves 69 and 70, which indicate her conversational effort and difficulty in opposing her friends without alienating them (see Coates 1996 on women friends' ways of mitigating opposition). In this way she manages to make it clear that she does not agree with any moralistic or even romantic notions about virginity and, as the remainder of this extract shows, she also causes a shift in the positions of two of the other girls.

Natalie and Pat: resistance to the celebration of first time sex

At first sight it appears that Natalie and Pat now mirror Susan in adopting a resistant/liberal discourse in relation to virginity. However, Natalie's and Pat's resistance is directed at a slightly different subject matter from Susan's.

Extract 14: the first time – continued

(72)
Natalie   I'm not being funny everyone says (.) "<u>oh:: it</u>

(73)
Natalie   <u>oh:: it oh:: it you got y-</u>*{raucous voice}*

(74)
Natalie   you do it this (.) you do it like tha::t"

(75)
Natalie   .hh and then when it comes down to it you think

(76)
Pat   [it's] nothing   ∨ bi::g i[t's noth]ing like
Natalie   it's erm (.) [erm]   [(no::]

(77)
Pat   ["is that it" *{laughing}*/<u>yeah</u>] <u>like [two minutes lat]er like</u>~
Jenny   [(it is \big)]
Natalie   [it ain't that (xxxxxxx)]

Natalie and Pat interpret Susan's claim that losing one's virginity is 'not a big thing as people make it out to be' in the light of their own and other girls' nervousness and anxiety about the sexual act itself rather than in relation to dominant norms about virginity and young female sexuality. In staves 73–74 Natalie explains that girls are offered a vast amount of advice on how to go about their 'first time'. Natalie immediately shows her disalignment with this wealth of advice by adopting a raucous and almost seedy voice. Nevertheless, her utterances indicate that there is an exchange of sexual advice seeking and giving in her peer group. On the one hand this shows again, that rather than just being driven by bodily desire 'young women construct [...] sexuality as a cognitive process' (Jackson and Cram 2003: 123). However, young women's need to acquire knowledge about what to expect does not only reveal that they are anxious about the first time, but also that they do not want to present themselves as naïve and inexperienced. Although this 'knowing' position is potentially very empowering, Natalie's utterance about the excessive amount of sexual information indicates once more that the girls feel a performance-related pressure, similarly to young men (Holland et al. 1998).

When Pat finishes off Natalie's incomplete utterance in staves 76–77 with 'it's nothing big' she mirrors Susan's earlier wording but signals alignment with Natalie's stance by ridiculing the shattered expectations of first-time sex and subverting a discourse of (male) sexual performance. This jocular subversion continues in the next staves.

Extract 15: the first time – continued

```
(78)
Pat                          yeah but [(xxxxxxx-)]
Natalie                               [yeah it's]
Jenny      %it's a big thing%
                        {sharp bang}


(79)
Natalie    a big thing (.) right (OK) but when it comes down to


(80)
Natalie    i::t .hh y- when you've done i::t you think to yourself


(81)
Natalie              when you've- (.) you think to yourself
Jenny      {laughter}


(82)
?Pat                              {laughs}
Susan                            yeah
Natalie    I got all worked u:p over that        (.) and I worried
?Jenny                            {laughs}        (.) {laughs}
?          {snorts}


(83)
Pat                                   {laughter-}
Susan                        =Miss Experience eh{amused}
Natalie    myself sick over that=
```

In stave 79 and 80 Natalie seeks a compromise by agreeing with Jenny that 'it's a big thing' but then immediately adds that it is not worth worrying about it beforehand. The reason for this 'contradiction' lies in the two different sub-topics that are being pursued. Whereas Natalie agrees to some extent with Jenny's continuing defence of the significance of virginity, she is actually making the point that after the first experience of sexual intercourse, girls, including herself, realise that there was no need to be anxious about 'that' beforehand (staves 82–83). Thus she dismisses all the girls' worries about first-time sex, implying that it is in fact not as distressing or even memorable an experience as one might think. Natalie does not only indicate that she is speaking from experience but, similarly to Pat in staves 77 and 78, also conjures an overtone of ridicule about the quality (and duration) of first time sex. Natalie does not explicitly agree with Susan that the 'loss of virginity' is not significant for a girl. Nevertheless, by ridiculing the act itself she signals some resistance to attributing too much relevance to 'the first time', thereby constructing herself as an unprudish and emancipated young women who does not fear to be perceived as 'Miss Experience' (stave 83) in the sex talk with her friends.

Discourse of self-determination

The above extracts show how the girls negotiate a range of discourses and norms regarding young female sexuality, resisting pressures to have sexual intercourse prematurely at the same time as displaying both experience and interest in active young female hetero-sexuality. The girls' sex talk is characterised by their efforts to balance discourses of sexual morality with their wish to fulfil what they see as their own romantic and sexual desires. This desire to prioritise their own wishes and determine their own private lives rather than comply with the expectations of either their peer group, their family or even the wider public is evident throughout the talk of Pat and her friends.

Extract 16: the first time – continued

(42)
Natalie   [but it is for you]   [(but
Jenny   =it's just something [personal to you=]=it dep[ends

(43)
Pat   yeah it's [PERSONAL]
Natalie   it's a thing that~]   [once it's] gone you
Jenny   what you (think)]

(44)
Pat   [yeah] (.) i[t's pe]rsonal it's like
Susan   [yeah] (.) [I know]
Natalie   can't get it back

(45)
Pat   .hh it's:: like (.)   [special (do you get xxxx)
?Jenny   (.) %your[s%

This extract shows how the girls balance dominant discourses which
celebrate virginity with stances which highlight the girls' agency and
personal choice. In reaction to Susan's preceding challenge of 'people's'
notion of virginity as 'a big thing' or 'a million Dollars that you're throwing away', Jenny offers a compromise by voicing a discourse which
moves the discussion of virginity from public morality or (peer) group
pressure to a private, personal, individual realm. The meaning of the
word 'personal' is explained by Jenny as 'it depends on what you think'
(42) and then later as 'yours' (stave 45). The other girls collaborate with
Jenny in her emphasis on 'virginity as a personal choice', Natalie by arguing that 'it's for you' (stave 42), and Pat by repeating the word 'personal'
in staves 43 and 44. It is very clear in the above extract that many of the
girls continue to align themselves with a discourse that romanticises
virginity 'once it's gone you can't get it back' (staves 43–44), 'it's special'
(stave 45), but it seems that their compromise between these and more
liberal/resistant stances is to highlight their agency by presenting it as a
personal choice.

In addition to showing some resistance to public morality and even
more to their peer group, the girls' also oppose the interference of their
families. The following extract captures the group's reaction to one of
Jenny's comments about the influence of her watchful and moralising
mother on her decisions to have sexual intercourse. (But see Chapter 3
for the girls' acceptance of their mothers' authority in other realms.)

Extract 17: the first time – continued

(90)
Pat   [I wouldn't **tell** my mum]
Susan   [yeah but then again (now)] but then again if you

(91)
Natalie   yeah but it's up
Susan   think about it it's like~ (-)

(92)
Natalie   to **you** it's not what [your mum says]
Susan   [it's **you** at the] end of the

(93)
Natalie   it's what you wanna [do d'you
Susan   day it's you   [and your mum

(94)
Natalie   know what I mean]
Pat   >unless
Susan   ain't gonna know]
Jenny   (.) %yeah I know but (xxxxxxx)%

(95)
Pat   [you have] it written [all over your face<]
Susan   [(if-)]   [if you're close-]

Although Pat has a very close relationship with her mother (see Chapter
3) she states that she would not tell her mother about having sex for the
first time (stave 90). Natalie then builds on Pat's contribution, arguing that
Jenny's or anyone else's decision to have sex or not is a personal one in
which not even mothers have the right to interfere (staves 91 and 92). After
receiving support from Susan in stave 92 Natalie reinforces her stance by
telling Jenny that the real issue is what she herself wants to do rather than
what she is told to do (stave 93). Thus Natalie emphasises her own and
even Jenny's (potential) agency. I argue that this notion of individual
choice and self-determination, which can be highly problematic in post-
modern discourses of personal autonomy and classnessness (Reay 1998;
Walkerdine 2003), here actually offers the girls some scope for agency. It
not only informs Natalie's stance in relation to Jenny's mother's objection
to her daughter's sexual activity but also shapes Susan's resistance to her
peer group's exaggerated encouragement of adolescent sexual activity.

Extract 18: the first time – continued

(22)
Pat   but I'm in no hurry [to lose my virginity]
Susan   [I won't I won't be] I'm

(23)
Susan   not pressured in- (.) if if peo- do people do

(24)
Susan what they wanna wa- erm do like .hh their

(25)
Susan relationships's (.) theirs innit >see what I mean<

This extract builds on an earlier exchange which captured the girls' awareness of and resistance to pressures to have sex from within their own peer
group (see Extracts 3–5). Pat's utterance in stave 23 is one of the many
examples in which a member of the group establishes her resistance to
this pro-sex pressure. Although Pat's utterance could be interpreted as
her compliance with an equally dominant, but even larger-scale, social
pressure to preserve young women's virginity and sexual morality, Susan's
following utterance is informed by a discourse of self-determination,
indicating that a couple's decisions whether and when to have sex must
not be governed by (public, family or peer-related) social norms but
instead should remain an individual, personal choice. Thus Susan emphasises the girls' right to self-determination and fulfilment of personal needs
in relation to their sexuality.

Conclusion

The topic of sex is clearly of great importance to the talk and identity
work of Susan, Pat, Natalie and Jenny in their friendship group. Their
sex talk is extensive, direct and characterised by personal self-disclosure.
Unlike in Ardiana's Bangladeshi group the girls in Pat's group do not
feel it necessary to switch to a playful frame to make the topic and its
implications more acceptable for each other. Whether the girls speak
about their own or their peers' sexual experience, or the lack of it, an
interest in active young female (hetero)sexuality is positioned as the
norm in this group and as central to the girls' construction of adolescent femininities. However, the girls also show their awareness of and
resistance to the 'pro-sex discourse' that dominates their peer group.
Although this resistance appears influenced by traditional discourses of
virginity and morality, these tend to be balanced by discourses which
allow the girls to foreground the fulfilment of their personal romantic
and even sexual desires about 'the first time'. Thus the girls do not
position sex as something that 'just happens' to them (Tolman 2005)
but instead highlight their own agency. Differently from the two other
groups, John Coleman's (1980) observations about adolescent sexuality
still resonate with the data I obtained from Pat and her friends.

Firstly, young people today are more open about sexual matters, secondly, they see sexual behaviour as more a matter of private rather than public morality, and thirdly, there appears to be a growing sense of the importance of sex being associated with stable, long-term relationships. (Coleman 1980: 122)

The analysis of spontaneous conversational extracts in this chapter revealed that the group's open, self-disclosing sex talk is characterised by complex negotiations of a wide range of discourses, which allow the girls to position themselves alternatively as moralistic, resistant/liberal, romantic, sexually desiring and self-determined in relation to the (hetero)sexual experiences, practices, norms, desires and anxieties that they discuss.

6
Playful Sex Talk: 'Good Girls' and 'Bad Girls'

There is a dearth of research exploring young British Asian women's discursive positioning in relation to sexual identities, experiences, desires and anxieties. Moreover, ethnographic studies of British girls (Griffiths 1995; Hey 1997; Lees 1993) and sociological and psychological explorations of young sexuality (Holland 1993; Holland et al. 1998) tend to provide very limited data on Asian girls' 'actual' sexual experiences. This may partly be due to (what the researchers perceive as) Asian girls' reluctance to talking about sexual intercourse and to the girls feeling less pressure to find a boyfriend (Lees 1993; Griffiths 1995). Indeed the interview and questionnaire data from the Women's Risk and AIDS Project (WRAP) in Britain show that whereas 66 per cent of white adolescents aged 16–17 admitted to having had sexual intercourse, only 14 per cent of the comparatively smaller sample of Asian girls in the corresponding age group said that they were sexually active (Holland 1993). Hennink, Diamond and Cooper (1999: 879) also refer to Raleigh et al.'s (1997) findings based on the 1991–95 General Household Survey data which reports that 42 per cent of '16–29-year old women from Indian, Pakistani and Bangladeshi backgrounds were not in a sexual relationship compared with 22 percent of their white peers'. The scarce research on Asian girls' sexual practices and experiences tends to focus on arranged marriage and its strong moral code about pre-martial chastity, a perspective which has been supported by evidence from studies of British adolescent sexuality like Holland (1993) as well as by sociological, psychological and anthropological studies of young British Asians. Earlier studies by Wilson (1978) and Jamdagni (1980) argue that Asian girls refrain from talking about sex, as this is taboo by their religious and cultural standards. More recently, Hennink, Diamond and Cooper's rare (1999) interview study on young British Asian women's sexual relationships did manage to get young women to talk about sex and male–female relationships but also shows that although some of the 36 young women in the study may have been involved in pre-marital dating, this was without their parents' knowledge (see also Shain 2003). Moreover, even for the few girls who admitted to having experienced some kissing and light petting 'relationships did not involve any further sexual activity' (Hennink et al. 1999: 880). Like Wilson and Jamdagni, Hennink et al. refer to the religious-cultural concept of 'izzat' or family honour to capture the significance of the young women's reputation as sexually inexperienced before marriage. That the policing of an Asian 'good girl' reputation goes beyond what is usually experienced by young Anglo women has been suggested by several studies, most explicitly by Louise Archer (2002b: 116), who argues that her British Pakistani teenagers define 'respectable femininity' by a distinctly Muslim gendered context. Further evidence for the policing of young female sexuality in British Asian communities has been found in interview data from young Asian men (Archer 2001), as well as in the interview and conversational data of young Asian girls themselves (Shain 2003; Henink et al. 1999; Barker 1997, 1998).

This chapter is not concerned with Asian girls' actual sexual activity. Instead I am interested in how the five young Bangladeshi women position themselves interactively and discursively in relation to sex and sexuality in their spontaneous talk within their friendship group. The group's self-recorded interactions show that Dilshana, Ardiana, Hennah, Rahima and Varda do engage in some personal sex talk, about kissing, (male) nudity, heterosexual and lesbian sexual practices. However, as in their conversations about love and dating (Chapter 4), most of the sex talk in this group is contained in a playful conversational activity or 'frame' (Bateson 1987/1972; Goffman 1974; Gumperz 1982; Tannen 1993) such as teasing or boasting. This suggests that although the girls do not always present themselves as sexually inexperienced, the sex talk is in many ways more problematic than in Pat's group from the same London East End school (see Chapter 5). The girls' spontaneous conversations as well as the interviews I carried out with one of the girls (see Chapters 1, 4) contain evidence to suggest that this difference is at least partially due to specific cultural discourses of young female sexuality and gender identity which exert an influence on the discursive practices and subject positions negotiated by Ardiana and her friends in their talk.

Strategies to prevent serious sex talk

Whereas Pat and her friends (Chapter 5) conduct their sex talk in a serious frame despite its very personal and self-disclosing content there are only a few occasions in Ardiana's group which feature 'serious' sex talk. Moreover, on the rare occasions that Ardiana, Dilshana, Hennah, Rahima and Varda engage in non-playful sex talk they tend to oppose premarital sex and present themselves as sexually inexperienced. The rare challenges to this discourse of premarital chastity in a serious conversational frame are not only exclusively initiated by the same speaker, Rahima, but are also thwarted by the other members of the group. Thus the dispreferred status of serious sex talk in this group is usually signalled by a switch of frame, a switch of topic, or by open condemnation.

Condemnation and silencing of intimate sex talk

The boundaries of what is and what is not an acceptable topic and an appropriate femininity are constantly being negotiated in the group's sex talk, as the following two extracts about snogging and male nudity show.

Extract 1: snogging and naked boyfriends

(1)
Hennah   =I amo::r [Sharukh Khan]
Ardiana   [uhhhh]*(impatient)*
Rahima   =Dil[shana]=   [Dilshana did] (.) did you s- snog

(2)
Hennah   [(I just said)] that I I amor Sharukh Khan
Rahima   Ran   did you sn-
?Dilshana   [(hi Helen)]
Helen, a girl from a different group, has come into the room

(3)
Rahima   (.) did you snog Ran
Dilshana   =yeah
?Varda   (xxxxxxxxxxxxx)
?Helen   so hot in here man (xxxxx

(4)
Rahima   =e:r
Dilshana   you snogged erm xx-=
?   xxxxxxxxxxx)

{tape recorder is switched off}

Rahima has to repeat her question a couple of times (staves 1, 2, 3) to get an answer from Dilshana about whether or not she has 'snogged' her boyfriend. After Dilshana answers the question in the affirmative in stave 3, she returns the same question to Rahima in stave 4. Despite Dilshana's repetitions and what seems like Rahima's hesitation (in stave 4) the extract suggests that the topic of 'kissing boyfriends' seems to be positioned within the realms of acceptability within the group. The fact that the tape recorder is switched off briefly in stave 4 before Rahima can provide her own answer, seems due to the arrival of Helen, a girl from a different group, rather than Rahima's reluctance to talking about kissing boys.

The rest of the conversation, however, shows clearly that Rahima's efforts to discuss anything 'beyond' kissing are either condemned in a serious conversational frame or dealt with by a switch into a teasing frame. The collaborative effort to negotiate and reinforce these boundaries within the group is evident in the following extract which captures the development of this conversation a couple of minutes later.

Extract 2: snogging and naked boyfriends – continued

(18)
Ardiana   yeah yeah what[ever]
Rahima   (Dilshana did you see Ran naked)   [>(have you ever)<]
?Helen   (XXXXXXXXXXXXXXXXXX)

(19)
Ardiana   GET LO[ST MAN]
Rahima   seen Ran naked (.) ever=
Dilshana   =NO
Hennah   [she's so] si[:ck
?   [I can't
??   [(xxxxxx

(20)
Ardiana   YOU] ARE SICK [I swear she is
Rahima   [no topless did

```
?          xxxxxxxxxxxxxxxxxxxxxxxxx)]
??         xxxxxxxxxxxxxxxxxxxxxxxxx)]
```

(21)

Rahima	you see his muscle or anything (xxxxxxxxxxxx)
Hennah	(she's saying
Dilshana	yeah yeah

{pips indicates end of break}

(22)

Ardiana	PIPS GO:: BYE
Hennah	xxxxxxxxxxxxxxxxxxxxxx)
?Varda	PIPS GO (XXX) *{tape recorder switched off}*

Rahima's daring question in stave 18–19 may have to be seen in the context of a preceding verbal duel of sexual teases and boasts, which took place between the girls and Helen shortly after Extract 1 above (see Extract 6: 'your man' in Chapter 4). In addition, it has to be noted that Rahima also frequents the group which Helen belongs to. It is therefore possible that Rahima is trying to match Helen's notorious bad/tough girl image in what appears to be her attempt to test the boundaries of acceptable sex talk in this group. However, Rahima does not proceed carefully by framing her question as play; her tone of voice suggests that she is being serious when asking Dilshana whether she has ever seen her boyfriend naked. Dilshana's loud and unmitigated 'NO' is followed by an equally forceful 'GET LOST MAN' by Ardiana. It is clear that the other girls feel that Rahima has transgressed the boundaries of what is acceptable here. 'Get lost man' functions both as an expression of indignation and as a request to stop Rahima from pursuing her line of questioning further. Moreover, both Hennah and Ardiana express their condemnation by referring to Rahima as 'sick' (staves 19 and 20), which is the same label the girls use in relation to sexual practices shown in a porn movie in a different conversation (see below). It is only by justifying herself and rephrasing 'naked' as 'topless' that Rahima manages to return within the boundaries of permissible sex talk as defined by the group. Differently from the other group of girls from their school, the sex talk of Ardiana and her friends stops well short of anatomical details of male (and female) bodies. At the same time this group's negotiation of what does or what does not constitute permissible sex talk also constitutes a negotiation of norms about acceptable sexual experience (heterosexual kissing) and unacceptable sexual experience (male nudity). The positions the girls' take up in relation to these norms are significant in relation to their accomplishment of identities with gendered and, as I will argue below, ethnic and even religious inflections.

Topic change

Some of the extracts suggest that Rahima, who is responsible for most challenges to the group's norms about sex talk and young female sexuality, may have some sexual experience beyond kissing. My data also show, however, that an individual member's personal norms tend to be adapted to those of the group. Thus, differently from Natalie in Group 2, Rahima never admits to her (alleged) sexual experience. This reluctance to position herself as sexually experienced is certainly encouraged by the other girls' collaborative effort to prevent each other from engaging in serious sex talk.

Another strategy employed by the girls to this purpose is to perform an abrupt topic change. The following extract is part of a longer conversation which was triggered by the girls' singing a song with the lyrics 'sex on the beach'. There is a lot of singing and teasing in this conversation, but it also contains some instances of serious sex talk.

Extract 3: sex on the beach

(1)
Ardiana   no::: the only person I would [have sex with i:s
Rahima   [(no ha-)

(2)
Ardiana   my boyfriend
Rahima   (if I am xxxxxxxxxxxxxxxxxxxxxxxxxxxxxxxxxxxxxx
Varda   (xxxxxxxxxxxxxxxxxxxxxxxxxxxxxxxxxxxxxxxxxx

(3)
Ardiana   no <u>one else</u>]*{laughing}* (1)
Rahima   xxxxxxxx]xxxxxxxxx) (1)   (let's >say xxxxx<)
Varda   this thing] man Go::d) (1)
                                                (1)*(whistling and other noises}*

(4)
Rahima   your boyfriend left you and you've done it with him and

(5)
Ardiana   you mean pregnant
Rahima   (.) he left you /yeah and (xxxxxxx)   no >no not<

(6)
Rahima   pregnant but e:r you know you've done it and everything

(7)
Ardiana   [but if he DID] leave me I wanna him to make me pregnant
Hennah   [(xx xxxxxxx)]

(8)
Ardiana   before he leaves me (.)   (.) my <u>boyfriend</u>*[laughing]*
Hennah   (.) WHO

(9)
Ardiana   [oh d'you like] my flowers=
Hennah   [you're such a]
Dilshana   =oh where did you get it from

Ardiana's utterance in stave 1 follows on from an episode of sexual teasing. When Ardiana then thinks out aloud about 'the only person [she] would have sex with' this seems to be the ideal lead back into a serious discussion about pre- or post-marital sex and/or sexual desire. However, the laughing voice in which she utters 'no one else' (stave 3) renders her hypothetical statement slightly ambiguous. The laughter could function both as an indicator of embarrassment and as a strategy to signal that she is only joking and that she is not seriously thinking about having (pre-marital) sex. Clearly most of the other speakers are not comfortable with the turn the conversation has taken, which is indicated by the significant pause after Ardiana's hypothesising about her future sexual activities in stave 3. However, Rahima ignores her friends' hesitation in relation to the topic. Her (equally hypothetical) question in staves 3–5 appears to aim at eliciting some serious sex talk from her friends, by asking them what they would do if they were left by a boyfriend who they had slept with. Rather than wanting to speak about the risk of pregnancies (as Ardiana suspects) it seems that Rahima wants to discuss the implications of being sexually experienced. The implication of a question like this is that not being a virgin is considered to be problematic by the girls. However, Rahima's attempt at initiating a serious discussion about sexual experience and virginity fails yet again.

Ardiana does not engage with Rahima's question in her reply, moreover, she appears to turn the whole issue into a laughing matter. It seems to me that her reply cannot be taken seriously, but instead constitutes a boasting activity which is inherently ambiguous (see also 'kissing in the street', Extracts 16, 17). By expressing her wish to be an unmarried single mother Ardiana challenges traditional values about respectable young (Asian) femininity and thus presents herself both as resistant and as a sexually desiring 'bad girl'. Significantly, this 'bad girl' identity is not set in a serious frame, which is highlighted by Ardiana's laughing reply 'my boyfriend' to Hennah's scandalised request for clarification 'WHO' in stave 8, followed by an incomplete accusation or criticism in stave 9 'you're such a ...'. After that Ardiana abruptly changes the topic and starts talking about the flowers she received from her best (female) friend. It is possible to interpret Ardiana's abrupt topic change either as a sign of her having got bored with her playful challenges or as a conscious effort to avoid a sensitive topic. In both cases, however, this sudden change of topic in combination with Ardiana's exaggerated earlier claim and her laughter, signal that Ardiana does not wish to pursue the topic or her sexualised 'bad girl' identity in a serious discussion.

Sex talk in a playful frame

Differently from Pat's group (Chapter 5), most of Ardiana and her friends' sex talk is set in a playful frame. Evidence of metamessages which signal that an activity is framed as 'play' or else as 'nonplay' was first highlighted by Bateson (1987/1972: 179) and has since then informed a number of studies on dispute strategies and conversational humour (Alberts 1992; Drew 1987; Eder 1990; Goodwin 1990; Straehle 1993). I shall define playful frames as speech activities which signal ambiguity about the truth-value of the propositions being made. The two playful frames that I shall focus on in this chapter are a teasing frame and a boasting frame, which are both seen in opposition to more serious conversational frames. This section builds on my exploration of the girls' frame-switching in their talk about dating and romantic love in Chapter 4. It shows how Ardiana and her friends also explore each other's positioning and experience in relation to sex predominantly in their teasing and in their boasting. By switching between serious and playful frames the girls are able to present themselves alternately as sexually innocent and as sexually experienced, thereby moving in between what has frequently been described as 'good girl' and 'bad girl' positions (Cameron and Kulick 2003a; Orellana 1999; Tolman 2005).

TV soaps and pornography

In the following extract from a conversation about TV soaps the girls
first approach the topic of sex in relation to a scene in the Australian
soap *Neighbours* which featured a lesbian relationship. Like the British
Asian girls who Chris Barker (1998) encouraged to talk about soap
operas, the 'soap talk' of Ardiana and her friends soon leads to a discussion about what can or cannot be considered as 'normal' sexual behaviour or orientation. A little later the girls' talk turns to sexual practices
portrayed in pornographic films, which are positioned as deviant by
the girls in their talk.

Dominant and resistant discourses: the serious frame

The first part of this longer conversation shows how the girls engage in
competing discourses: a dominant heterocentric discourse is challenged
by a liberal discourse. By expressing her disgust about the scene with
two lesbian lovers in staves 4–5 Ardiana signals her detachment from
lesbian orientations and thus positions herself within the discourse of
'compulsory heterosexuality' (Rich 1983; but see also Tolman 2005;
Cameron and Kulick 2003a).

Extract 4: blue films

(1)
Rahima   you know in Neighbours you know Ra- Rachel (when that

(2)
Ardiana   mm:*[crumples up paper]*
Rahima   girl got together)   yeah *[higher pitch]*<u>I find it's so</u>

(3)
Ardiana   *[continues to crumple up paper]*   /why (.)
Rahima   <u>weird something</u> about (her) I dunno why

(4)
Ardiana   I feel weird when an a girl is on top of a girl (.)

(5)
Ardiana   [it's **disgusting** to] watch it (.)   [I swear it] is
Rahima   [no it's not that]   (.) no [it's not that]
Dilshana   (.)   [innit innit]

(6)
Ardiana   (.) (it looks-) (.) *{disgusted}*<u>ugh::</u> it's r-

(7)
Ardiana   *{disgusted sound}* (*kobe so la [kana)]
Rahima   no-   [no it's] not that it's
**Bengali: 'in a disgusting way'*

(8)
Rahima   not that (.) I fi- [I find I find Rachel weird hers]elf
Dilshana   *{laughs}*   [<u>you watched some BLUE FILMS</u>]*{amused}*

Ardiana reinforces her heterosexual identity several times in the following staves: stave 4: 'I feel weird when ...'; stave 5: 'it's disgusting...' and
'I swear it is...'; stave 6: 'it looks (.) ugh...'; stave 7: (Bengali) 'in a disgusting way'. In stave 5 one of the other girls, Dilshana, aligns herself
with Ardiana by supporting her with the tag 'innit innit'. Rahima, on
the other hand, is positioning herself in opposition to Ardiana's negative
assessment of lesbian relationships. She repeatedly denies that her dislike of the female soap character Rachel is related to her sexuality (cf. her
repetitions of 'no it's not that' in staves 5, 7–8). Thus Rahima does not
align herself with the dominant heterocentric discourse voiced by
Ardiana, positioning herself as a young liberal and showing a degree of
resistance against the conventionally accepted link between femininity
and heterosexuality (Cameron and Kulick 2003a: 47).

    This extract demonstrates how the five Bangladeshi girls voice and resist
dominant notions of sexuality and femininity. There is a discourse of heterosexuality, which constitutes the dominant norm for young women in
the Bangladeshi as much as in the white British community (see also
Chapter 7, Extracts 9–11). However, Rahima's contributions reveal an
alternative to normative practices and identities of gender and sexuality.
Interestingly, Rahima's challenge of this dominant discourse of compulsory female heterosexuality is expressed overtly and is framed as serious
disagreement. This contrasts with all the following extracts of talk, where
the girls employ altogether different strategies to deal with conflicting
cultural norms about their personal (hetero)sexual experiences.

'Good girls' and 'bad girls': alternating playful and serious frames
After the initial exchange about lesbianism, there is a switch of frame
from serious to teasing, and at the same time a shift to more personal
'sex talk'.

Extract 5: blue films – continued

(8)
Rahima   I fi- [I find I find Rachel weird hers]elf
Dilshana   [you watched some BLUE FILMS]*{amused}*

(9)
Ardiana   [oh shut up]   I d-*{laughing}* .hh *{amused}*I watched
Rahima   [(that's all xxx)]

(10)
Ardiana   it ages ago it was **so** disgusting (I xx[xxxxxxxx)]
Dilshana   [I watched] it

Dilshana interrupts Rahima in stave 8 and playfully accuses her of having watched some 'blue', that is, pornographic films. Her switch of
frame is signalled by a change of voice quality, indicated as 'amused' in
parenthesis. This tone of voice suggests that the speaker is smiling and
conveys the playful nature of the challenge. As appropriate in a teasing
sequence, Ardiana replies laughingly with a rebuttal, 'oh shut up', but
then admits that she has watched some pornographic films a long time
ago (staves 9–10). Although Ardiana does not counter Dilshana with
another tease, she accepts the topic introduced by Dilshana: pornography. Thus Dilshana's tease successfully steers the topic development
into a new direction, thereby preventing it from turning into a serious
discussion about sexual orientations.

   This is one of the many examples which shows how the girls position
themselves and one another in opposition to what I call a 'good girl'
identity. With Tolman (2005: 12) and Orellana (1999: 72) I equate a
'good girl' identity with a respectable femininity based on a denial of
sexual experience, knowledge and desires. Thus, rather than presenting
themselves as shy and sexually inexperienced 'good girls', Ardiana and
Dilshana reveal their familiarity with pornographic films in this extract.
Notably the 'bad girl' identities that Dilshana constructs for herself and
for Ardiana are set in a playful, a teasing frame.

   In the following staves the girls switch between serious and more playful frames as well as 'good girl' and 'bad girl' identities. On one level
they collaboratively present themselves as 'good girls' by establishing
their opposition to the pornographic films. The following staves illustrate this 'good girl' position as Ardiana expresses her disgust about the
sexual practices portrayed in the film.

Extract 6: blue films – continued

(11)
Ardiana   you know them (.) %blue /films% {eats}   =it was [**so**
Dilshana   [blue
?   /hm=

(12)
Ardiana   H O]R R I B[L E]   so dis**gust**[ing]
Dilshana   films]   {triumphant}[I] <u>watched it</u>=
Varda   {amused}[<u>do</u>] <u>you watch i::t</u> {laughs}

'Good girls' are not only repulsed by pornography (and, by extension, by their pornography-watching experiences) but they also signal that they find it embarrassing to talk about pornography. This becomes evident when Ardiana first utters the word 'blue films' in a notably reduced volume, followed immediately by a strongly emphasised expression of her disgust about these films which is repeated several times later on. Other girls align themselves with Ardiana's 'good girl' position.

Extract 7: blue films – continued

(22)
Ardiana   that [**is** si]ck (-) a man's putting
Rahima   **that is** sick yeah
Varda   [(xxx)]

(23)
Ardiana   his %dick% inside a {laughing}<u>woman's bum</u>
Varda?   (sounds

(24)
Ardiana   [**that**] <u>is sick</u> (.)   = (yeah it) was so- ugh
Dilshana   I know=
?Varda   qu[ite~)]

Differently from her earlier resistance to Ardiana's derogatory remarks about lesbian sex, Rahima now expresses her agreement with Ardiana openly in stave 22. Varda supports Ardiana in staves 23–24 with her unfinished utterance 'sounds quite', which is likely to mean 'sounds quite sick'. Hennah signals her reluctance to participate in a discussion of this topic and thus her alignment with the 'good girl' identity by her silence.

On the other hand Dilshana and Ardiana frequently present themselves as 'bad girls' in their sexual teasing or, like in the next example, in their sexual boasting about having watched blue films.

Extract 8: blue films – continued

(13)
Ardiana   so dis**gust**[ing]   =I watched it **last** (time)
Dilshana   [I] watched it=*{triumphant}*
Varda   *{laughs}*

(14)
Ardiana   (-) when I came back from [Bangladesh]
Dilshana   [I watched it] twice

(15)
Ardiana   (-) I watched it once in Bangladesh (-)
Dilshana   (**man**)*{cool}*
?   %(xxx)%

(16)
Ardiana   on[ce before I went]   (-) and once when I came back
Varda   [*Bangladesh (kanya)]
*Bengali: 'why in Bangladesh?'

Crucially, the pornography watching and therefore sexually knowing 'bad girl' identity is set in a playful frame. Dilshana clearly engages in a boasting activity here and she is soon joined by Ardiana. The girls are trying to outdo each other by each claiming that she has watched porn films more often than the other. Dilshana speaks in a different, more daring, or 'cool' voice from her usual, supported by what appears to be the equally cool and streetwise vocative 'man' (stave 15). I interpret this as a further indication of Dilshana having adopted the different subject position or identity of the 'bad girl' which is supported by verbal competition and cool slang. Dilshana's voice quality and lexical choice in staves 14–15 are also contextualisation cues which indicate her switch of frame from serious talk to playful boasting. It is mainly in playful frames such as this that Ardiana and Dilshana position themselves in opposition to a good girl identity.

The boasting allows the girls to present themselves as sexually experienced (in terms of being consumers of pornographic films) without losing face and without risking alienation of and from other members of the group who uphold much more stringent cultural codes of sexual morality.

Who's been through it?

Although the girls' talk about pornography contains some degree of personal self-disclosure (about watching blue films) it is far from the intimate, personal sex talk of Pat and her friends, who are also from the same school. However, this changes when the girls shift their conversational topic from porn films to one another.

Bad girls' tease

In Group 2 the girls' interest in each other's sexual experience (e.g. Natalie to Pat 'did you do it with him', Extract 1, stave 1) does not steer the conversation away from a serious frame. The opposite is the case in Ardiana's group. The remainder of the conversation shows how the girls skilfully exploit a teasing frame to shift their sex talk onto a more personal level without losing face.

Extract 9: blue films/who's been through it

(24)
Ardinana   =(yeah it) was so- ugh it was disgusting
Rahima   =[(but you
Dilshana   I know=   =[(xxxxxxx

(25)
Ardiana   {amused}oh: yeah
Rahima   don't know you might enjoy it if you were there]
Dilshana xxxxxxxxxxxxxxxxxxxxxxxxxxxxx UGH:::::::::::)]

(26)
Ardiana   Rahima we know you've been through it [we know you've
Rahima   {laughing}[no I don't think

(27)
Ardiana   done it].hhh   {- laughs -}
Rahima   so I] don't think so I don't think so (-) but still

(28)
Rahima   (.) it's **their** man [(they're doing it innit >it's them
Dilshana   *{slow tease}*[someone's been through it

(29)
Ardiana   [someone']s been
Rahima   the ones who xxxxxxx<)]
Dilshana   over]=   =here some[one ha:s]*{slow tease}*

(30)
Ardiana   through it *{teasing}*haven't they:: (-) [it] is
Rahima   [what]

(31)
Ardiana   Rahi:::ma:*{mock childish}*
Dilshana   (.) what was it=*{staccato}*ip dip

The playful tone of the girls' voices and several other contextualisation
cues suggest that they interpret this sequence as an episode of teasing
rather than as a serious dispute. In staves 24–25 Rahima challenges
Ardiana by teasing her 'but you don't know you might enjoy it if you
were there'. Ardiana counters the teasing in an amused voice and thus
signals her acceptance of the switch of frame. Rahima, too, expresses her
denial laughingly, thereby confirming the non-serious nature of the
accusations. Rahima asserts her liberal position once more after having
laughed off Ardiana's mock accusation, 'but still it's their man ...' (staves
27–28), drawing on a discourse of self-determination which, similarly to
Pat and her friends in Group 2, positions (sexual) choices as a matter of
personal rather than social morality (Chapter 5). However, at the same
time Ardiana and Dilshana collaborate to keep the conversation on a
playful key. They do not really ask Rahima about her sexual experience,
but instead cheerfully accuse Rahima of 'having been through it' or in
other words, of having had sexual intercourse (staves 25–30). The girls
mark their teasing by assuming a mock-childish voice. This child-like
effect is emphasised by their slow, drawling voice in staves 28–29: 'someone has been through it' and the lengthened vowels in stave 30: 'it is
Rahi:::ma'. The fact that the girls simply repeat their accusations and
denials instead of giving explanations for their claims is also reminiscent
of child-like teasing; see Rahima in staves 26–27: 'I don't think so';
Dilshana and Ardiana in staves 28–30: 'someone has been through it ...'.
Goodwin (1990: 158–63) found that children 'recycle positions', that is,

repeat their challenges rather than offer an explaining account, in order to sustain their playful disputes. The repetitions of specific utterances in this sequence support the interpretation that the girls do not want to resolve this dispute, because they are actually enjoying it. Thus, the teasing allows three of the girls to position themselves as sexually experienced. Although this friendship group of Bangladeshi girls does engage in some talk about personal sexual experience, the problematic status of this talk is indicated not only by Hennah and Varda, who do not participate in this talk but instead pursue another topic (which has not been transcribed here), but it is emphasised also by the fact that this more personal sex talk is almost exclusively framed as playful.

Good girls' premarital chastity

When the girls switch from their playful teasing to a more serious key, they also distance themselves very clearly from any sexual experience. This becomes evident during the last couple of minutes of this long conversation, which are dominated by Dilshana's playground rhyme, the culmination of the previous teasing.

Extract 10: blue films/who's been through it – continued

(31)
Dilshana   *{staccato}* = ip dip dog shit fucking (bastard silly git)

(32)
Ardiana   *{amused}*it's **you** .hh [it's **you**] it's you it's you
Dilshana   you are not IT *{laughing}*no [no no] .hhhh

(33)
Ardiana   [Dils]hana it's you Dilshana   =yes it is (-) yes it is=
Dilshana   [no no]*{laughing}*   (-) nn*{negating}*

(34)
Dilshana   =I know I haven't been through it I would never do it

(35)
Ardiana   (1) when do you wanna get married
Dilshana   until I get married then~

This playground rhyme serves a dual purpose. On one hand, the use of expletives adds toughness to the sexual 'bad girl' identity Dilshana has been constructing for herself and for some of the others. On the other hand the rhyme also takes the focus off Rahima as the main target of the playful accusations. Thus, Dilshana defends Rahima's innocence, but at the same time she implies that somebody else might have had sex. Ardiana's reaction acknowledges this dual function of the rhyme. She ceases to tease Rahima and redirects her mock accusations at Dilshana, thus orienting to the bad/tough girl identity displayed by Dilshana. The end of the teasing frame is signalled by Dilshana in stave 34, when she switches from her laughing voice into a serious voice to reaffirm her denial of having had sex, thus adopting a 'good girl' position 'I know I haven't been through it I would never do it until I get married'. Once this teasing episode is concluded, the conversation turns to the topic of marriage.

Sex talk, cultural discourses and identities

I suggest that the switching between teasing and serious frames allows the girls to perform both sexual 'bad' and non-sexual 'good' girl identities. These opposing adolescent identities are to a significant extent informed by two very different discourses, which are not only gendered, but also influenced by cultural norms. The norms regarding young women's sexual behaviour in these two discourses contrast sharply with each other. One is a discourse which positions dating and sexual experience as an essential part of adolescence. As I argued in Chapter 5, I view this discourse as central to British youth culture, and the evidence I collected from my three groups of British girls suggests that it is particularly prevalent in the adolescent working-class peer group (see Extracts 3–5, Chapter 5). The other discourse upholds traditional norms linked to the girls' ethnic (Bangladeshi) or, as Hennah would claim, religious (Muslim) background, presenting young female experience of dating and sexual intercourse as a serious threat to an unmarried girl's reputation. Positioning themselves as sexually experienced therefore helps Ardiana and her friends to align themselves with a normative femininity in their adolescent British (working-class) peer group. The other discourse, however, which allows the girls to adopt 'good girl' positions, celebrates the conservative value of sexual innocence in young girls.

A discourse of sexual morality constitutes the dominant norm for respectable young femininity in many cultural groups with different ethnic and religious inflections, as my own data show (see Chapter 5, Extracts 6–7). However, the version of this discourse of sexual morality which is invoked here is one of pre-martial chastity, as Dilshana's utterance in staves 34–35 shows, rather than a discourse which sanctions pre-marital sex in a committed (romantic) relationship (see Chapter 5, Extracts 8–10). Whereas Pat and her friends want to make sure they can determine with whom, where and when they will have sex for the first time to guarantee that it will be an enjoyable, worthwhile experience for them, these are no real concerns for Ardiana and her friends. Moreover, this pre-marital chastity is of even higher importance in the group as it affects not only the girls' own but also their entire family's reputation and honour. As I argue in the introduction to Part II and in Chapter 4 in relation to the girls' dating, my data suggest that the concepts of a woman's *sharam* (shame, modesty, shyness) and the family *izzat* (honour) remain significant in understanding the discursive negotiating and positioning that dominates Ardiana and her friends' (frequently playful) talk about boyfriends and love as well as kissing and other sexual experience. Much non-linguistic research on Asian femininity has explicitly drawn on *izzat* and/or *sharam* (Ballard 1994; Bhopal 1999; Dwyer 2000; Ghuman 1994; Hennink, Diamond, Cooper 1999; Jamdagni 1980; Wilson 1978). Although I agree with Ahmad (2003) that frequently there may have been on overemphasis on 'izzat', I note that both researchers and researched in recent feminist studies continue to link the significance of British Asian girls' sexual innocence to cultural norms with ethnic and religious inflections (Shain 2003; Archer 2001). The same goes for my own research.

In the following extract from the girls' spontaneous talk about Rahima's boyfriend, Ardiana engages in some sexual teasing, which implicitly establishes a link between the girls' Bangladeshi (Muslim) background and the policing of young female sexuality.

Extract 11: Rahima's boyfriend

(1)
Rahima   I see him on Saturday and on Sunday as well

(2)
Ardiana   ["oh:: what] do you get up to*{teasing}* (-)
Dilshana   ah th[at's nice]

(3)
Ardiana   [very NI::CE]"*{mock Bangladeshi voice}*   *{laughs}* (.)
Rahima   (nothing)] nothing for your nose*{amused}* (.)
Dilshana   [tell us (xxxx)]*{mock tough}*

(4)
Ardiana   >they get
Rahima   *{swallows}* (.) (definitely)
Dilshana   *{faint laugh}*

(5)
Ardiana   [up to< something] **really really** nice*{teasing}*
Dilshana   [GUESS WHAT HELEN-]   guess what Helen got

Ardiana's teasing follows her earlier serious enquiry about the state of Rahima's relationship with her boyfriend. However, neither Ardiana nor Dilshana really seem to want to discuss Rahima's relationship (problems) seriously. In stave 2, finally, Ardiana first reacts to Rahima's lengthy reply to the earlier enquiry, but only by shifting into a playful frame. Ardiana's tease in stave 2 playfully accuses Rahima of having a sexual relationship with her boyfriend, stave 3 captures how both Dilshana and Rahima play along with the tease. Interestingly, when uttering the words 'very nice' (stave 3) Ardiana adopts what Hennah, my in-group informant, later confirmed to be a mock Bangladeshi accent associated with the adult generation. Changes of voice such as this can constitute a strategy to subvert adult or dominant voices/discourses for younger adolescent girls (Coates 1999; Maybin 2007). Ardiana's subversion of the adult Bangladeshi voice in the context of an episode of sexual teasing supports my hypothesis that the girls associate the 'good girl' identity, which is opposed to girls' sexual activity or even the topic of sex itself, with a Bangladeshi norm. When Ardiana wants to continue the teasing, it is cut short by Dilshana's topic change. This strategy of switching to another, less 'sensitive' topic thus abruptly could be seen as serving a similar purpose as the teasing. The topic switch, too, functions as a distraction from the potential face-threat of discussing sex in a serious frame.

An even clearer link between the girls' Muslim Bangladeshi background and the policing of young girls' pre-marital chastity and reputation is established by Hennah. In one of our interviews/conversations it transpired that she was not herself familiar with the (originally Persian/Urdu) term *izzat*, but very much so with the concept. For example she explained to me that girls are not supposed to be dating and that if their parents find out about it, the girl in question would either be married to the boy she has been with or get taken abroad to get married as the parents 'don't wanna face the shame' (see Chapter 4, Extract 9). Hennah even goes as far as claiming that a mere association with boys or men in public would be problematic for adolescent girls due to religious norms.

Extract 12: our religion is really strict (interview[1])

61)Hennah: because like you (know >when I) say<
62) like (.) I wanna go out something like *that*
63) {Pia: yeah} and I can't **do** it because (.) (obviously)
64) I have to wear a scarf and then I have to (.) think
65) about erm cause when I- in *our* {Pia: mm}
66) religion yeah you are supposed to be really
67) strict yeah you are not supposed to go next to
68) your (.) even your **dad** when you're (not) **older**
69) th- erm about the age of fifteen or stuff like
70) *that* {Pia: right} (>you're not supposed to go<)
71) next to your dad or your brother .hh and when
72) I go outside there's loads of guys {Pia: there's loads
73) of guys} yeah (.) and even in college you know
74) *(xxxxxx)*
75)Pia: [and even] if you don't go look*ing* {Hennah: yeah}
76) for them they are still ***there*** {Hennah: yeah}
77)Hennah: {amused/embarrassed}they're still the*re* {Pia: yeah}
78) and sometimes if there is a religious person
79) around you they assume that you're
80) {amused/embarrassed} looking for it {Pia: yeah yeah}
81) *d'you* get me {Pia: yeah} and it's really hard

As in many other instances of our interview-encounters Hennah identifies religion as a central normative influence on the girls' gendered and sexual practices and identities. Here Hennah explains what she views as strict gender segregation for girls who reach mid/late adolescence by religious norms, and also emphasises the difficulty of coping with a situation like this in line 81: 'it's really hard'. The explanation Hennah offers in her interview therefore provides insight into a significant cultural discourse, that is, cultural knowledge which speakers draw on to make sense of their experience. In this discourse 'good girl' identities are policed by religious members of the Bangladeshi community, which suggests a link between female pre-marital chastity and cultural-religious norms.

Kissing in public

In this section I will discuss how another sexual activity, kissing, is approached by the girls from alternating cultural positions in their talk. Whereas at the beginning of the chapter I showed that some of the girls admit to 'snogging', the following extracts capture the girls' awareness that a *public display* of kissing can be far from unproblematic in their Bangladeshi community. However, the discourse which asserts that kissing a boy in public is not appropriate for a girl is alternated with a discourse which values public displays of non-conformist behaviour and views dating as an integral part of adolescence. Whereas I view the former as rooted in British youth culture (see Chapter 5), the girls link the latter discourse to their (Muslim-) Bangladeshi community, as the following extracts will show.

Kissing in the street is 'weird': good girls

All of the girls distance themselves from public kissing to some degree during this long conversation. In the first five staves Hennah, Dilshana, and interestingly, Rahima, voice their unease about it explicitly.

Extract 13: kissing in the street

(1)
Rahima   (xxx) listen (-) {embarrassed}do you find it **weird**

(2)
Rahima   %(it's like) when you're kissing someone in the street%

(3)
Ardiana   {grabs microphone[2]} SAY THAT AGAIN
Rahima   do you find that weird

(4)
Rahima   {amused}do you find that weird {laughs}{laughing}kissing

(5)
Ardiana   I don['t
Hennah   [oh my] God it **is** weird
Rahima   someone in the street
Dilshana   [yeah::]

In this extract Rahima introduces the question whether it is 'weird' to kiss someone in the street. The implication here is clearly heterosexual kissing, as the remainder of the conversation shows. Dilshana's and Hennah's partially simultaneous replies in stave 5 confirm that the girls do indeed find kissing in public 'weird', whereas Ardiana foreshadows her opposition to this stance. Extract 15 will show that Dilshana's answer in stave 5 above reflects, at least to some extent, her personal sense of unease about her own kissing experiences, but Hennah's anti-dating position suggests that for her 'weird' also connotes a sense of moral inappropriateness. Rahima's slightly embarrassed and lowered tone of voice when she asks her initial question (staves 1–3) hints at her detachment from such 'weird' behaviour, and she expresses this detachment even more clearly later in the conversation.

Extract 14: kissing in the street – continued

(24)
Rahima   oh Go:d <u>I just get so</u> **embarrassed**{*amused/embarrassed*}

By positioning kissing in public as 'weird' and presenting themselves as embarrassed Rahima and Hennah and Dilshana negotiate 'good girl' identities for themselves. Again, I argue that this embarrassed 'good girl' identity is strongly influenced by a traditional discourse from the girls' Muslim Bangladeshi community. In my interview data Hennah explicitly attributes what she perceives as restrictions on adolescent girls' socialising or even being associated with boys or men to 'religious' norms: 'if there's a religious person around you they presume you're looking for it' (see Extract 12, above). Although Hennah also argued in this interview that a girl has to decide for herself what is right and what is not, her explanations serve as evidence for her sense of a dominant Muslim discourse which holds that it is not appropriate for a girl to be seen with a boy in public, let alone to be kissing him in the street.

'When everybody is staring at you that is weird': the compromise
Dilshana modifies her 'good girl' position a little later, suggesting that she only feels weird kissing her boyfriend in public if somebody is staring at her.

Extract 15: kissing in the street – continued

(6)
Dilshana   (no I find- when) everybody is staring at you that

(7)
Dilshana   that is (.) that is horrible yeah but th- I don't want

(8)
Hennah   [(y]eah)
Rahima   [(**see**)]   [yeah]
Dilshana   anybody to [stare] at me when I'[m kiss]ing my **ma[n]**

In this extract Dilshana attempts a compromise between her earlier 'good
girl' position that kissing in public is not appropriate, and Ardiana's challenge of the norm. Although such compromises are central to the talk of
English-speaking white middle-class girls (Coates 1999; Eckert 1993), the
Bangladeshi girls in this group frequently prefer different conversational
strategies, such as a switch into teasing, thereby attempting to achieve a
consensus by juxtaposing opposing discourses and positions. In this
example, however, Dilshana opts for a compromise solution by admitting
that she does kiss her man in public, but not without feeling 'horrible'
when being watched, or 'stared at'. Dilshana is thus the first member of
the group to link her unease and concern about kissing in public to being
watched. Just like my data from the ethnographic-style interviews with
Hennah (see Extract 12), the group's spontaneous talk contains evidence
for the influence of the watchful eyes of the Bangladeshi community on
the girls' heterosexual practices and ('good girl') identities. Several of the
teenage Hindu, Sikh and Muslim girls interviewed by Hennink et al.
(1999: 877) also express a concern about being seen by members of their
own community, summing up the normative influence of the collective
on the behaviour and reputation of an individual as the 'culture of the
community'. The following staves provide further evidence for this policing of 'good girl' behaviour, but it also shows that there is vehement and
angry resistance to it within the group.

'I make everybody come and kiss': bad/tough girl
In the following staves Ardianas reverse the direction of the moral gaze.

Extract 16: kissing in the street – continued

(9)
Ardiana   [this is them (xxxx) they stare] with their big eyes
Hennah   [(xxxxxxxxxxxxxxxxxxxxxxxxxxxxxx)]

(10)
Ardiana   like [(and it's like)] they haven't seen this n::
Dilshana   [**innit**]

(11)
Ardiana   (in the whole) **world**]
Dilshana   innit they're watching] <u>free cinema you /**know**</u>*{mock Bangladeshi adult}*

In staves 9–11 Ardiana criticises the adult onlookers for their staring,
and thus defines *their* rather than *her* own behaviour as inappropriate.
Dilshana supports Ardiana's opposition by mocking the voice of the
community elders in stave 11 'they are watching free cinema you
know'. Referring to kissing in the park as a public display comparable
to 'free cinema' identifies this utterance as part of the discursive repertoire of the Bangladeshi adult generation who view this open display
of affection with its sexual connotations as something that should be
reserved to the fictional/cinematic realm. By changing her voice quality to a higher pitch when adopting the adult voice Dilshana expresses
her detachment from it. Dilshana and Ardiana thus collaboratively
challenge the dominant discourse about the inappropriateness of kissing in the street.

Ardiana's resistance is expressed even more clearly in her story about
kissing her own boyfriend in public. The story gives a concrete example
of the staring behaviour which Ardiana associates with other (adult)
members from her community.

Extract 17: kissing in the street – continued

(12)
Ardiana   Shashima's siste:r what's her name Naime   last time
Rahima   =yeah
Dilshana   mm=

(13)
Ardiana   (yeah I) we went to the park Spiderpark with (-) my guy

(14)
Ardiana   yeah = we are like kissing (right) .hh **[this]**   is her sister
?Hennah   [%mm%]

(15)
Ardiana   she's *{amused}***staring** like this   [(and) the guy-]
Rahima   (OH GOSH [man not]

(16)
Ardiana   [(I was like)] you know her I [I]   didn't
Rahima   in front of her [xxx sta::re)]
?   [mm]

(17)
Ardiana   see her stare and everything and her she goes to Shashima

(18)
Ardiana   that she's (.) watching free cinema .hh she would love to

(19)
Ardiana   see that again (.)   =and I was like saying to
Dilshana   (.) oh Go:d=

(20)
Ardiana   Shashima .hh tell her sister to come on **that** day to see

(21)
Ardiana   **me** kissing him **again** (.) that's free I've g- I make

(22)
Ardiana   everybody come and kiss (-) {laughs}]
?Dilshana   {faint laugh}]

(23)
Ardiana   <u>yeah as though she would</u>{laughing} (.)

Ardiana's story captures this traditional discourse in the Bangladeshi
community which positions kissing in public as inappropriate. This discourse is invoked by one of the characters in the story, the sister of
Ardiana's friend, when expressing her disregard for Ardiana's behaviour
both verbally (staves 17–19) and nonverbally by her staring (stave 15).
At the same time Ardiana distances herself from the discourse expressed
by the sister of her friend by marking it with a different voice (stave 15)
and finally challenging it in a boasting frame at the end of the story
(staves 19–22). The boasting about repeating her public kissing performance for an audience and about encouraging others to do the same
allows Ardiana to position herself even more clearly in opposition to
the dominant discourse of her own community. She constructs a bad
(sexual) and tough (daring) young femininity for herself, challenging

the dominant behavioural norms for good Asian girls. At the same time she acknowledges the playful character of this claim by her laughter and the disclaimer 'as though she would' (stave 23).

'Good girl' and 'bad girl' positions: alternating frames and cultural discourses
Similarly to the girls' teasing in their conversation about pornography and 'having been through it', the alternating of playful boasting with serious conversational frames allows the girls to switch between different cultural discourses and between 'good girl' and 'bad girl' positions in the girls talk about kissing in public.

Extract 18: kissing in the park – continued

(23)
Ardiana <u>she would</u> (.)
Rahima   (but-) oh Go:d *<u>I just get so</u> **embarrassed**=
*{embarrassed/amused voice}

(24)
Ardiana =**that** is fu[nny] though kissing somebody on the
Rahima? *amused}* [(I really-)]

(25)
Ardiana street everyone [watching] you
Rahima   *{disgusted}*<u>ugh</u> that is so (-) %stupid
Dilshana   [innit]

(26)
Ardiana   (-) it's ALRIGHT [if you're] kissing someone
Rahima I find it% (-)   [(yeah but-)]

(27)
Ardiana in front of a **white** person right

Rahima reacts to Ardiana's earlier boasting by reasserting her 'good girl' position (stave 23). As a consequence, Ardiana herself displays her opposition to Rahima and reinforces her tough/bad girl identity in another boasting challenge to the established norm (staves 24 and 25). Dilshana's support for Ardiana in stave 25 ('innit') also indicates that the girls are aware of the playful key of their dispute at this stage, as earlier on Dilshana had expressed a similarly negative opinion about kissing in public as Rahima (see Extract 13, stave 5). Rahima, however, does not want to accept the playful frame of the exchange and emphasises her 'good girl' identity once more (staves 25–26). Interestingly, in her concluding utterance (staves 26–27) Ardiana adopts the serious frame defended by Rahima and also positions herself to some extent within the dominant 'good girl' discourse which is enforced by what Hennink et al.'s (1999) research on Asian girls terms the 'culture of the community'. By explaining that she does not feel inhibited to kiss (her boyfriend) in public as long as the onlooker is a 'white person' Ardiana implies that she would feel differently if she was being watched by a Bangladeshi person instead. This revelation indicates that Ardiana, too, is affected by the (moral) expectations of the Muslim Bangladeshi community and its alignment with a discourse that positions kissing in the street as inappropriate behaviour for 'good girls'.

This final extract makes explicit Ardiana's awareness of two discourses in relation to public kissing which purport different cultural norms with ethnic and religious as well as gendered inflections. Whereas some of the girls in the group speak about kissing their boyfriends in private (Extract 1) they are all aware that a public display of kissing (and, of course, dating and love, see Chapter 4) is much more problematic as it is not condoned by a large (adult) part of the Bangladeshi community. Ardiana's resistance to this dominant Muslim Bangladeshi discourse is clearly informed by her knowledge of a discourse rooted in British culture. Pre-marital dating and kissing in public is not considered to cause offence by the majority of today's white British population. Spending free time with and dating the opposite sex constitutes the norm in British youth culture, as Pat's talk indicates (Chapter 5, Extracts 3–5). By contrast, kissing and cuddling in public is positioned as incompatible with the 'culture of the community' (Hennink et al. 1999: 877) which Ardiana and her friends make responsible for the guarding of their 'good girl' behaviour and identities. In spite of opposing the dominant Bangladeshi norms about dating and kissing in public both in real life and in her talk, even Ardiana eventually acknowledges the importance of her 'good girl' reputation within the Bangladeshi community in her final utterance (staves 26–27).

Conclusion

My data demonstrate that the Bangladeshi girls in this group do in fact talk about sexual experience and knowledge, but it also shows that not all of them enjoy this type of talk. In some of the above extracts from the girls' spontaneous talk Hennah and Varda hardly participate in the sexual teasing and boasting. Hennah's and Varda's silence can be interpreted as an alignment with the sexually inexperienced 'good girl' identities which are also foregrounded in the group's serious talk. These performances of chaste femininities are challenged by the sexually experienced 'bad girl' identities which dominate the playful teasing and boasting of Ardiana, Dilshana and at times Rahima. However, by tackling the issue of sex in playful conversational frames the three 'bad girl' protagonists protect their own face as well as that of Hennah and Varda. It allows them to reduce the risk of offending others in the group and of being stigmatised as 'bad' girls, as the truth value of any of the propositions made in the teasing and boasting can easily be denied. At the same time this strategy confirms the girls' awareness of cultural norms that restrain both their sexual and gender practices and identities. The norms that influence the policing and protecting of their sexual innocence and reputation as 'good girls' are linked by the girls themselves to their Bangladeshi community and to their religion. On the other hand their 'bad girl' identities appear to be influenced by a discourse which positions pre-marital heterosexual relationships as the norm and which dominates their non-Asian British working-class peer group. This discourse, as Pat's group talk in Chapter 5 shows, exerts pressure on adolescents to become sexually experienced. By switching between these discourses Ardiana and her friends have found an (interactive) strategy which allows them to balance culturally different norms of young female sexuality and gender identity, and, ultimately, to position themselves as both British and Bangladeshi adolescent girls.

7
Impersonal Sex Talk: Knowing Girls

In contrast to the two working-class groups the topic of sex only plays a minor role in the talk of the four white private-school/upper-middle-class girls who took part in my study. In only 3 per cent of their self-recorded talk do Roberta, Nicky, Jane and Elizabeth address subjects related to sex and sexuality. The corresponding figure for Pat and her friends is 23 per cent and for Ardiana and her friendship group 6 per cent. Moreover, the limited sex talk of Roberta and her friends is strikingly impersonal; differently from the other two groups, the girls' own sexual experiences, anxieties or desires are largely left untouched. In the introduction to Part II of this book I considered some preliminary explanations for these differences in the sex talk of the three groups, including the girls' relationship with me as well as their actual sexual experience. Indeed, quantitative data on female sexuality from 148 young British women interviewed by Holland (1993: 8) suggests that middle-class girls experience a later onset of first sexual activity, with 'the average age of first sex[ual intercourse] being 14.5 years [for working-class girls] as opposed to 16.3 for middle-class girls'. This difference in the onset of actual sexual activity of their peers (which levels out shortly afterwards) may therefore shed some light on why the sex talk in Roberta's group is both limited and impersonal, whereas that of Pat's same age group is not only extensive but also characterised by personal self-disclosure. However, as I argue in the introduction to Part II, the quantitative and the qualitative characteristics of 'sex talk' should not be interpreted exclusively or even predominantly in the light of the girls' (lack of) actual sexual experience. The previous chapters showed that Pat, who has not had any previous experience of sexual intercourse, is both very interested in and open about sex talk, and the same goes for Susan, who takes up the most liberal stance in the group despite her lack of sexual experience. As in my previous chapters I therefore wish to investigate the sex talk, or lack of it, in the private-school girl group from a discourse analytic perspective. I shall demonstrate that the few instances of what I interpret as the knowledgeable but impersonal sex talk of Roberta, Elizabeth, Nicky and Jane are affected by and affect norms and practices which can be linked to the girls' private-school middle-class background, and which play a significant role in the girls' discursive construction of femininities.

Academic sex talk

Nicky, Roberta, Jane and Elizabeth frequently engage in what I would define as 'academic' debates and discussions about topics such as society, science and art, especially literature (see also Chapter 2). These debates in many ways reflect the academic ethos of their exclusive school and allow the girls to highlight their general knowledge and 'distinction' (Bourdieu 1984), that is, their prestigious and classed taste and understanding of high art and culture. Thus the girls tend to foreground their educated and academic selves, similarly to the British (upper) middle-class girls studied by Walkerdine et al. (2001) and Hey (1997) and the middle-class 'nerds' in a California highschool in Bucholtz (1999). It should perhaps not have come as a surprise to me then that the rare attempts at approaching sex-related topics in this group are also frequently set within such academic 'frames' (Goffman 1974; see also Chapters 4 and 6). The girls discuss male promiscuity as a subtopic in their lengthy 'scientific' debate about human nature, they talk about paedophilia on the basis of the book/film *Lolita* and read out quasi-pornographic material from a book by the Marquis de Sade.

Human nature

The first extract I discuss is part of a 7-minute-long debate about the topic of 'human nature'. In this debate the girls contemplate different arguments in relation to the question whether human behaviour can be explained by theories of evolution and genetics. The conversation then turns to the question whether or not human nature should serve as an excuse for 'problematic' behavioural patterns, such as sexual promiscuity. Thus sex is treated as a subtopic in a 'scientific' or 'academic' debate about human nature.

Extract 1: human nature

(1)
Roberta   yeah I guess to a certain extent >I just don't like it<

(2)
Roberta   when people use it as a sort of pretext for people

(3)
Nicky   =yeah I think=   like yeah
Jane   =yeah
Roberta   with like shit behaviour=

(4)
Nicky   [I was] watching *Kil/roy and there was this guy who says
?Roberta   [%(xxx)%]
*TV chat show

(5)
Nicky   like he sleeps with [(five other-)]
Roberta   {amused}[can we learn] from Kilroy (.)

(6)
Nicky   [(I think] it is [a-)]   [yeah]
Jane   [oh yeah]   [like] Kilroy [some]one's saying like
?Elizabeth   {laughs}

(7)
Nicky   * [he sleeps he said like]   [he's got a g- he's yeah
Jane   I [think it's human nature] to [want to have loads of sex
{*swallows}

(8)
Nicky   he has got a girlfriend]   yeah and he makes {amused}
Jane   with loads of different women]

(9)
Nicky   love to his girlfriend .hh but he has got **five** lovers

(10)
Nicky   at the same time he has **sex** with yeah .hh and he can't

(11)
Nicky   understand it when his girlfriends leave him because

(12)
Nicky   he says [it's in his genes]   .hh [he says it's
Jane   [yeah he'll say you know] obviou[sly everyone

(13)
Nicky   [natural for him to be] unfaithful [why should]   .hh
Jane   [wants to **do** that]
Roberta   [**bull**]shit

(14)
Nicky   [and he says why should he be] conditioned by socie[ty]
Jane   [yeah]
Roberta   [(that's all) bullshit]

(15)
Nicky   why shouldn't he do what he naturally wants to do .hh=but

(16)
Nicky   he's got a point though (i-) that's what (.) like (.) he

(17)
Nicky   treats them like shite though (there) no excuse for **that**

(18)
Nicky   but (1.5) {*high pitch/mocking*}it's (an) interesting topic

The bulk of the exchange is dedicated to Nicky's story based on a recent episode of a TV chat show, initiated in stave 4. In staves 6–8 Jane picks up Nicky's narrative thread about a particular episode of the talk show *Kilroy* and introduces the question whether promiscuity can be regarded as natural human behaviour, which constitutes a lead into the subtopic of sex. From staves 8–15 Nicky reports the arguments of one of the talk show guests who explains his promiscuity as 'natural' behaviour, caused by genetic imprint (presumably in males only). The chat show guest's arguments clearly play on what Hollway (1984: 63) defines as the 'male sexual drive discourse', which views male heterosexual promiscuity not only as natural but also as a 'biological necessity' for humankind and allows individual men like the chat show guest to position himself as a victim of his biological urges.

The most explicit resistance to the misuse of the concept of human nature and, at the same time, to the male sexual drive discourse comes from Roberta. Already in staves 1–3 she explains her reservations about the concept of 'human nature', arguing that people at times use it as a feeble excuse for their 'shit behaviour'. Her rhetorical question which interrupts Nicky in stave 5 allows Roberta to assume the position of a critical viewer, ready to engage in an 'oppositional reading' (Hall 1980: 138) or 'resistant reading' (Mills 1995: 75–6) of the content of the talk show. After Nicky finishes narrating, and Jane produces another non-disruptive stretch of simultaneous talk, Roberta delivers a vehement dismissal of the arguments of the talk show guest in staves 13 and 14.

The most ambivalent and therefore particularly interesting stance in this exchange is Nicky's. Initially she does not hesitate to pronounce her agreement with Roberta (stave 3) and the fact that she then proceeds with her story appears to suggest that she is about to present an example illustrating Roberta's point. However, Nicky evaluates the guest's arguments positively in stave 16 and also does not use any (para)linguistic cues, like a change of voice quality, to signal her detachment from the arguments she is reporting in staves 6–15, although her use of indirect speech 'he says why should he ...' foregrounds her own perspective more than that of the chat show guest (Leech and Short 1981; Maybin 2007; see also Chapter 3 on 'voice'). This suggests that Nicky positions herself in partial agreement with the voice of the male talk show guest. However, Nicky then changes her stance in stave 17 again, now clearly distancing herself from the man's behaviour. It seems to me that this apparent 'change' in Nicky's assessment is really a change of conversational activity or 'frame'. The conversational extract about 'human nature' is here set in the frame of an academic debate (see also Bucholtz 1999: 216). When Nicky says 'he's got a point though' in stave 16, she still operates within this debating frame, in which opposing views and behaviours are balanced off against each other on an argumentative level without being morally judged (stave 13). In stave 17 she then switches out of this frame and voices her own moral rather than academic assessment of the talk show guest's behaviour. In an utterance which mirrors Roberta's labelling of such behaviour as 'shit/e' (stave 17) Nicky opposes the 'male sexual drive discourse' (Hollway 1984) with a 'discourse of victimisation' (Moore and Rosenthal 1993: 80) which positions men as 'ready to exploit women in the service of their sexual urges'. Thus Nicky's switch of frame here allows her to alternately foreground her academic self; interested in a 'scientific' argument about male sexual urges and human nature, and her personal self; morally appalled by male promiscuity and resistant to the victimisation of women. Nicky's final utterance in stave 18 leaves no doubt about her awareness of the markedness of the academic debating frame: she comments on and mocks their debate of this 'interesting topic', adopting a voice that appears to mimic an intellectual person such as an academic or a teacher. This utterance and her changed/ mocking tone of voice show that Nicky recognises that what she has been engaged in for part of this exchange is 'doing an academic debate' (of an interesting topic).

Lolita

Nicky's academic self takes a very liberal stance to promiscuity and to sex talk in general. Academic liberalism is also displayed in the following stretch of talk, which provides further evidence that the girls enjoy discussing even problematic aspects of sexual practices in relation to a work of art. This time Jane dominates the floor after having just read a review of a new film version of *Lolita*. (In the following transcript some of the utterances from a simultaneous but separate conversation about Alexander Technique have been omitted.)

Extract 2: Lolita

(1)
Jane   they released the book yeah (.)   it's about
?Nicky   mm

(2)
Jane   Humbert Humbert who's this like (-) thirty year old=

(3)
Nicky   =(good name) (-) {chuckle}
Jane   thirty- year old bloke yeah
?   {laughter}

(4)
Jane   or maybe he's older actually and he's a paedo/phile .hh

(5)
Jane   and erm (.) he basically enslaves his twelve-year-old

(6)
Jane   .hh step daughter and rapes her repeatedly (1)

(7)
Jane   e::rm not so much enslaves but just basically re-

(8)
Jane   rapes her (a lot) .hh and sexually >abuses her<

(9)
Jane   .hh and erm that's [basically >the story<]
Roberta   [I've read i::t]

It is interesting to observe how Jane's summary of Lolita is not met by any comments, let alone expressions of indignation, from the other girls for more than 6 staves (staves 3–9). This is all the more surprising as Jane's description of the plot appears to aim at provoking moral judgements from the others. She frames the sexual relations as an act of paedophilia (stave 4), stresses the incestuous relationship (stave 6), and contrasts the under-age status of the girl (stave 5) with the mature age of the man (staves 2, 3, 4). Jane leaves no doubt about the nature of the relationship between the man and the girl by using verbs from the lexical field of sexual abuse, including 'enslaves' (stave 5), 'rapes' (staves 6, 8) and 'sexually abuses' (stave 8). She also positions Humbert grammatically as the agent, that is, the person who carries out the action, and Lolita as the affected, that is, the person who is acted upon (Mills 1995: 143; Halliday 1985), in constructions like 'he enslaves /rapes/ sexually abuses her', foregrounding his agency and responsibility rather than depicting Lolita as active/sexually provocative.[1] This suggests that Jane is positioning herself in opposition to a sexist discourse which reverses the relationship between agent/perpetrator and affected/victim with regard to an act of sexual abuse, as evidenced in feminist linguistic research of rape trials (Ehrlich 1998).

Despite this explicit and critical portrayal of sexual abuse (which, it has to be noted, could substantially reflect the voice of Jane's only source, the film critic) Jane does not show any signs of hesitation or embarrassment, which indicates that she is comfortable to talk about a highly problematic sexual relationship in relation to a book or film. The other girls also refrain from presenting themselves as shocked about Jane's summary of the book. On the contrary, the first reactions appear to suggest the opposite.

Extract 3: Lolita – continued

(10)
Jane   have you **read** it *[excited]*is it any **good**
Roberta   (.) yeah   (xxxx) it's (.)

(11)
Elizabeth   Sam read it she
Roberta   **w:icked** I mean it's really (bits xxxxxxxxxxxx)

(12)
Jane   [**yeah**
Elizabeth   liked it =
Roberta   = it's re- yeah it's really goo[d

By praising a book such as Lolita as 'wicked' and 'really good' (Roberta:
staves 11–12) and reporting a mutual friend's acclaim of it (Elizabeth:
stave 12) the girls emphasise their knowledge and appreciation of art, as
well as their open-mindedness about taboo subjects. However the
liberal positions they thus adopt have to be seen in the context of an
(academic) discussion about literature. It cannot, therefore, be assumed
that the girls would take up an equally liberal stance if the focus of the
discussion were to shift from the literary work to a personal and moral
assessment of paedophilia. The remainder of this extract illustrates my
argument.

Extract 4: Lolita – continued

(13)
Nicky   (who's xxxxxx it)
Jane   Jo said it's really good]
Roberta   it's really disturbing]   (xxxxxxxxxxxxxx)

(14)
Nicky   who wrote it I mean
?Jane   Nabok/ov
Elizabeth   is there loads

(15)
Elizabeth   of y- yukky sex scenes she said there weren't

(16)
| Roberta | (1) yes there $\vee$ **are** | (-) %it's |
| ? | | (1) *{breathy laugh}* |

(17)
Nicky		(1.5) so what they made a film
Roberta	quite **explicit**%=	
Elizabeth		=really

In stave 13 Roberta completes her utterance from stave 12, showing that her prior positive judgement of the book is not in spite but because of the 'disturbing' nature of its content. She thus confirms her academic liberalism, which values art that is intellectually and morally challenging rather than aesthetically pleasing. Elizabeth's utterance in staves 14 and 15 moves the discussion onto a more personal level. She reveals her personal feelings of disgust about the sex scenes she expects to be in this film. Now Roberta's judgement of the film as 'disturbing' is interpreted by Elizabeth on a much more personal level as 'yucky'. This switch of frame from the academic discussion around a book or film to the personal and moral discussion about paedophilia goes hand in hand with a switch of register from a more formal style, 'disturbing', to a more informal one, 'yucky'. Roberta's confirmation in stave 16 suggests that on a personal level she agrees with Elizabeth's assessment of the sex scenes as 'yucky', that is, disgusting. The girls' personal disgust is also evident when, after Roberta briefly switches back to a less emotive and more impersonal assessment of the sex scenes as 'quite explicit', there is no further request for any more details from the rest of the group (stave 17). Rather, after a significant 1.5 second pause Nicky moves the discussion onto safer grounds by turning away from the sex scenes to the larger debate surrounding the new film version of the book. Thus, the extract contains traces of both moralistic and liberal discourses, informing either a personal positioning in relation to paedophilia or an academic assessment of a work of literature.

Boundaries of academic sex talk: pornography

The above examples illustrate that the girls do not hesitate to speak about promiscuous or even incestuous sexual behaviour, but that these conversations are mostly framed as academic debates or discussions about science and literature. The next extract will provide a final example of this 'academic' sex talk, but also illustrate the borders of acceptability of this type of sex talk for the group. This extract is part of a longer stretch of talk about literature in which the girls exchange recommendations on which books to read. In the course of this discussion Elizabeth begins to explore the bookshelf in Roberta's brother's room (where the girls are doing their recordings) and comes across a book by the Marquis de Sade. After Jane explains to the others about the Marquis' work and its connection to the word 'sadist', Elizabeth starts leafing through the book.

Extract 5: Marquis de Sade

(1)
Elizabeth   =(.) well it can't be that old because it's got (3)
            {turns pages}

(2)
Nicky   (-) read a bit
Jane   (*{laughs}*)
Elizabeth   it' s got very rude **words** in it
            {continues to turn pages}

(3)
Nicky   /out
Elizabeth   (.) erm: *{reading}*"(then) horrors you shall have
                   {continues to turn pages}

(4)
Elizabeth   my friend (-) horrors you shall have said I consoling

(5)
Jane   *{high laugh}*
Elizabeth   his prick by mouthing it by squeezing it and by carefully

(6)
Elizabeth   (ejaculating) the last <*<u>drop of</u> (.) %**f::uck**%*{low pitch}*>
            slightly amused tone of voice from * to *

(7)
Jane   (-)*{disgusted}*<u>lovely</u>   l l lovely*{mocking}*
Elizabeth   <u>(from) it*"</u> (-)   ∧<u>mm</u>*{slightly amused}*

(8)
Nicky   [yeah (xxx)it's] (.)
Jane   are you still making Scooby Doos [or Loopy Loos]

In staves 3–7 Elizabeth complies with Nicky's wish and reads out some of the 'very rude words' in the book. The passage that Elizabeth recites contains a description of sexual acts whose explicitness is at times pornographic. After initially having identified the writing as 'rude' and thereby assuming a moralistic position, Elizabeth then detaches herself from her own personal judgement of the book when she reads out the passage. Again it seems that this switch from a more personal to a more distanced perspective allows one of the girls to manage very explicit sexual references. Unlike in the Bangladeshi group there is no laughter or a switch into a playful frame to save the face of the speaker or of the other girls. Instead Elizabeth's reading voice remains surprisingly unchanged when uttering the actual words in staves 3–5 and she does not interrupt her reading or show many signs of hesitancy. Thus for a few staves Elizabeth presents herself as largely unaffected by the sexual explicitness of the book, thereby emphasising her academic liberalism. However, the group has clearly reached the boundaries of permissible sex talk even in the frame of (academic) discussions about literature. Firstly, Jane marks these boundaries by a high pitched laugh in stave 5, which is followed by Elizabeth's slightly amused tone of voice (stave 6) and marginally reduced speed of utterance delivery 3 words later. Then Elizabeth lowers her pitch and volume when uttering the word 'fuck' (stave 6). On completion of Elizabeth's reading Jane finally distances herself from the paragraph in a clear but ironic way by commenting on it with the word 'lovely' (stave 7) and then changing the topic by asking Nicky about her Scooby Doo stencils. Nicky also signals her discomfort by her silence. Thus, in spite of managing to recite pornographic material without losing their cool or without switching into sexual boasting or teasing (like Ardiana and her friends), the private-school girls also clearly express some degree of discomfort about the sexually explicit topic. This indicates that even within the context of their longer discussion about literature, a conversation about explicitly pornographic material constitutes a challenge to the group's academic liberalism.

The academic sex talk contained in their discussions about 'human nature', 'Lolita', and the 'Marquis the Sade' allows the girls to construct themselves as knowledgeable and as uninhibited in relation to sex, without presenting themselves as sexually active. This type of sex talk accomplishes identity work that goes far beyond sexuality. It allows Roberta and her friends to position themselves as academic liberals and cool connoisseurs of literature and art, highlighting the symbolic capital (Bourdieu 1991, 1984) of knowledge and academic success in their group, which both reflects and shapes the girls' private-school upper-middle-class background. At the same time, however, the appropriation of these 'knowing' stances in their academic sex talk allows the girls to position themselves in opposition to the stereotype of the sheltered middle-class girl (see also Chapter 2) or the display of sexual naivety of the highschool 'nerds' in Bucholtz (1999), with whom they share their emphasis on knowledge.

Sex talk about others

The girls also construct themselves as (sexually) uninhibited in the few instances of their non-academic sex talk. However, this 'sex talk' does not contain any self-disclosure about the girls' own sexual relationships or desires. Instead, it frequently focuses on other people's sexual practices and orientations as the next examples will show.

Extract 6: that's quite surprising

(1)
Elizabeth   (1) they **didn't**
Roberta   no they d- didn't have sex (1)   no:

(2)
Elizabeth   that's quite sur[prising]
Roberta   [cause she] wouldn't (.) or something

Elizabeth expresses her surprise about the fact that one of their fellow students (who is depicted in a very positive light before and after the above extract) has not had sex with her boyfriend. This shows that rather than taking a moralistic stance or mourning the loss of sexual innocence like the nerd girls in Bucholtz (1996 in Bucholtz and Hall 2004), Elizabeth positions active heterosexuality as the norm for adolescent girls who are in relationships with boys. In addition, it signals that the girls in this group do not feel uncomfortable talking about the active sex life of their peers. This is also evident in the next extract from Roberta and her friends' longest conversation about their first theoretical sexual knowledge as children. The first stave is marked as stave '80' to indicate that this stretch occurs well into the conversation. Earlier parts of the conversation are included further below.

Extract 7: I don't know how I learned about it

(80)
Nicky   my mum had trust[ed us
Roberta   [my brother on- only started to

(81)
Nicky   [(not alone)-]
Roberta   [tell me about] his sex life like (-) this gap year

(82)
Nicky   (1) did he (tell you xxxxxx)
Elizabeth *(1) (xxxx) what time did he have like how old was
sucking noise - eating mints

(83)
Elizabeth he when he first did it
Roberta   like (-) fifteen or something

(84)
Elizabeth *{sucking noise}*]
Roberta   (or)]   (.) something like that

Roberta's revelation in staves 80–81 that her (slightly older) brother
has recently started to talk to her about his personal sex life suggests
that her brother is now also sharing the most intimate details of his
private life with Roberta. As in many other instances of the conversational data from this group Roberta thus highlights the closeness
between herself and her sibling (see Chapter 2). After an initial hesitation both Nicky and Elizabeth seem to express some interest in
learning more about Roberta's brother's sex life (stave 82). Elizabeth
asks a direct question about the age of the brother's 'first time',
which is met with a prompt and unmitigated answer from Roberta.
This brief extract serves as a further example of the group's readiness
to engage in talk about the heterosexual experiences of others
openly and without passing moral judgement. However, the following extracts will show that similarly to their 'academic' sex talk, the
group establishes certain boundaries in their conversations about the
sex life of others.

Boundaries of sex talk about others: derogatory remarks about teachers

The following extract shows that Roberta's derogatory remarks about a
teacher's lack of active sex life are not sanctioned by the group. This
extracts constitutes the final part of the girls' long discussion about
human nature, which has moved on to the question whether 'people
would naturally harm each other'.

Extract 8: getting no play

(1)
Nicky yeah like Miss [Stuart thinks that all] men are
Jane [ah yeah I think it's]

(2)
Nicky ev/il [and it's like] [she]'s [going]
Jane [I think it's] total[ly]
Roberta [she's just]

(3)
Jane {amused}.*hhh*
Roberta **bitter** because she is just getting no play {laughs}

(4)
Nicky (-) <u>oh:</u> **Roberta**{accusing + amused}
Elizabeth (-) <u>Roberta stop (it)</u>{accusing +amused}

(5)
Nicky you don't have to be **so** {amused}**crude** {laughs} (-)
Roberta {raised pitch}it's **true**

(6)
Nicky she's (.) having a really tough time apparently
Elizabeth (.) why

In staves 1–2 Nicky suggests that one of their teachers believes in the dark side of 'human nature', revealing that the teacher 'thinks that all men are evil'. Although immediately prior to Nicky's question the focus was on 'people' rather than 'men', Nicky herself had suggested a link between masculinity and violence by stating that 'blokes are just so aggressive' a couple of minutes earlier. It is therefore likely that 'men' in stave 1 does not generically refer to 'people' and that Nicky attributes a 'men-hating' stance to her teacher. This appears to be how Roberta interprets Nicky's utterance, as becomes evident in staves 2–3 when Roberta ridicules the teacher, invoking a sexist discourse which suggests that sexually unsatisfied women are emotionally frustrated. Although the other girls' reactions carry an overtone of amusement, they clearly distance themselves from Roberta's comment. This opposition, however, is not rooted in a feminist but instead in a moralistic discourse, which signals that most group members do not want to align themselves with 'crude', that is vulgar and therefore non-respectable femininities (Skeggs 1997). To most of the girls in the group Roberta has transgressed the boundaries of acceptable sex talk, their non-conformity or coolness (see Chapter 2) does not extend to derogatory marks about the (lack of) sex life of a teacher.

It is possible that the outspoken opposition Roberta meets with after her comment in staves 2–3 is not only caused by the 'crudeness' of her comments but also by her reference to a teacher, rather than one of their peers. This could also be explained by the girls' perception that they are speaking about a colleague of mine, but also by the loyalty and respect for their teachers which Nicky and Jane express throughout (whereas Roberta is often much more critical about her teachers). In fact after stave 6 Nicky proceeds to defend her teacher at length, describing her as 'super-intelligent' but currently suffering from 'low self esteem' due to a 'bitter divorce'.

Boundaries of sex talk about others: 'deviant' sexuality

Derogatory comments about their teacher's sex life do not constitute the only boundary of permissible sex talk about others in this group of private-school girls. Although two of the previous extracts show that the girls tend to talk about the sexual experience of their peers openly and without assuming a moralistic or prudish stance, this is not always the case. The following example shows that in spite of presenting active (hetero)sexuality in their peers as the norm, the group also distances itself from what they appear to regard as deviant sexual practices and orientation.

Extract 9: the strangest girl

(1)
Jane   (2.5) the strangest girl in the entire (year xxx **that**)

(2)
Jane   is Linda (1)   she is (-)
?Nicky   Lin[da's a] freak (1)
Roberta   [(Linda)]

(3)
Jane   [%(xxxx)%]
Elizabeth   [she said] she (-) first had sex when she was like

(4)
Jane   [she] **did** and she kissed me on the lips once
Elizabeth   twel[ve]

(5)
Nicky   >she kissed me on the lips<
Elizabeth   hhhhh*{amused}*

Linda's positioning as 'strange'; and as a 'freak' is – at least partly – due to her sexual deviance. One of Linda's 'transgressions' appears to be that she had sexual intercourse at the comparatively young age of twelve. Elizabeth's indirect speech '… she said she …' in stave 3 emphasises her disbelief as well as the strangeness of this alleged behaviour. Another type of sexual 'transgression' seems to be what Jane interprets as Linda's lesbian approaches. Here the focus briefly shifts from sex talk about others to personal sex talk. Staves 4 and 5 contain Jane's reasons for considering Linda to be strange. A girl kissing another girl on the lips is interpreted as a sign of (non-normative) sexual interest. It turns out that Jane is not the only member of the group who has been kissed on the lips by Linda (see stave 5). This initially leads to a mock competition between the two recipients of the kisses.

Extract 10: the strangest girl – continued

(6)
Jane   she kissed (xxxxxxxxxxx)*{laughing, laughs}*
Elizabeth   hhhhh*{amused}*
?Roberta   *{laughs}*   *{laughing}*when

(7)
Nicky   (Jane)
Jane   she was after your **arse***{laughing, laughs}*

(8)
Nicky   (she was after)] your arse she kissed Jane first
Jane   (xxxxxxxx)
Roberta   when]*{laughing}*

(9)
Nicky   yeah   (xxxxxxxxxx)
Jane   after [(you left)]*{laughing, laughs}*
Roberta   [when *{laughing}*]

When she accuses Nicky of being the object of Linda's sexual desire in stave 7 Jane changes her stance slightly, signalled by her laughing voice and use of a slang phrase 'she was after your arse', which clearly attributes (lesbian) sexual desire to Linda's advances. This utterance is reminiscent of the Bangladeshi girls' sexual teasing. As I showed in Chapter 6, Ardiana and her friends use a switch into teasing to present themselves as hetero-sexually experienced 'bad girls'. Whereas Roberta and her friends do not use this strategy when engaging in talk about heterosexual relations and practices, they do frame their accusations about same-sex encounters as teasing. This could suggest that to be associated with a lesbian identity is equally threatening to the display of 'respectable femininity' (Skeggs 1997) in Roberta's group as it is to admit to heterosexual experiences in Ardiana's. The risk of being associated with different types of active sexuality, one resulting in a heterosexual the other in a lesbian 'bad girl' identity, is miti-gated by the underlying ambiguity of the teasing in both groups. At the same time, however, the teasing frame allows Jane and her friends (who express amusement and interest in the incident from staves 6–9) to signal lack of inhibition rather than indignation about the 'lesbian' kisses.

Nevertheless, this uninhibited stance is abandoned by Jane in the following staves when she returns to a serious frame, re-establishing her clear opposition to Linda's advances. Interestingly, these final staves allow for a reinterpretation of Linda's deviance with regard to gender rather than sexual norms.

Extract 11: the strangest girl – continued

(13)
Jane   she like **hates** me yeah she **really** hates me .hh but
?Elizabeth   {laughs}

(14)
Nicky   [{laughs}]   ({giggles})
Jane   she comes up [to me yeah] (.) she like (-) like

(15)
Jane   comes up to me yeah .hhh and like goes like this=

(16)
Jane   =so I moved my head yeah so that she'd kiss me

(17)
Jane   on the cheek and she (xxxxxxxx) {kissing noise}

(18)
Nicky   (-) [(so then)]
Jane   .hh (-)*{disgusted}*UGH::::::::::: (-) [and she's]
?   (-) *{weak laugh}*

(19)
Nicky   [she's going out with
Jane   (going out with quite cool bl[okes)

(20)
Nicky   Pete who's a dude but she's got really nice trainers

In the serious frame Jane makes sure that the kissing incident cannot be
(mis)interpreted as a demonstration of mutual lesbian attraction. She even
goes so far as to assert that Linda hates her, a claim which could either serve
the purpose of highlighting that Linda's kissing came as a complete surprise
to Jane, or position the kissing as an act of defiance rather than sexual attraction. Jane then proceeds to express her disgust about being kissed on the lips
explicitly (stave 18) making sure that in case Linda's kissing should be interpreted as lesbian advance, it is understood that she herself neither invited
nor enjoyed it. Most importantly, in stave 19 Jane then reveals Linda's active
heterosexuality. As Bucholtz and Hall (2004: 483) argue in their discussion
of Cameron's 1997 data, a revelation like this in the context of othering
homosexuality also does important gender work. In the case of Linda it suggests that same-sex kissing, whether caused by lesbian sexual desire or not, is
perceived as a threat to a respectable and normative femininity.

Childhood sex talk

The only stretch of data in which the girls deal with a sex-related topic
from an exclusively personal perspective is a 3 minute 30 seconds long
conversation during which Roberta and her friends reminisce about
when and how each of them first learned about sex. Although this
'childhood sex talk' does not contain or even lead to any revelations
about the girls' current sexual experiences or desires, it allows them
to negotiate group norms and identity practices related but not limited to sex.

Knowledge about sex

Similarly to their academic debates about sex, this type of sex talk
shows the girls' efforts to highlight their theoretical knowledge about
sex and other subjects.

Extract 12: I don't know how I learned about sex

(9)
Roberta   (-) (it's funny xxxxxxxxx) I don't remember **ever**

(10)
Roberta   being told about sex so I don't know how I learned

(11)
Nicky   [I] (.) I read it .hh (in a) (.) children's
Elizabeth   (many) children are
Roberta   about [it]

(12)
Nicky   encyclopaedia
Elizabeth   very (xxxxxx)
Roberta   = I **know** I think I just sort of **knew**=

It is particularly characteristic of Roberta, Jane, Elizabeth and Nicky to present themselves as knowledgeable or enlightened about sex, even at an early age. Roberta's knowledge about sex appears to be innate ('I just sort of knew', stave 12). By arguing that she did not need to be informed about 'the facts of life' as a child, Roberta not only indicates that she was wise and mature beyond her years, but also that not even as a child did she consider sex to be a scandalous or improper topic. Nicky, on the other hand, appears to have displayed her characteristically scientific mind already during her early childhood by supplying herself with the necessary information from a children's encyclopaedia. Neither Roberta nor Nicky highlight the role of others in telling them about sex(ual intercourse) but instead foreground their own agency, for example in stave 11 when Nicky says: 'I read it', or, one stave later, when Roberta asserts: 'I just sort of knew'.

Similarly to Nicky, Jane's knowledge about sex is not depicted as innate but instead as the consequence of her own efforts to learn new things.

Extract 13: I don't know how I learned about sex

(13)
Nicky   she **told** you (d')she sit you
Jane   = m[y mum] told me (.)
Roberta   [and then]

(14)
Nicky   down
Jane   no cause I (.) no n[o (no)]   [I asked her]
Elizabeth   [my cousin] tol[d me (xxxxxx)]

(15)
Jane   what **rape** was yeah (-)
Elizabeth   (-) oh God {amused}<u>you learnt</u>

(16)
Jane   no because I was
Elizabeth <u>about it in a really **abrupt** way</u>{laughing}

(17)
Jane   watching the **ne:ws** (-) and I've heard this word rape

(18)
Jane   yeah they were saying (they'd) **raped** this woman

(19)
Jane   %(and I didn't know what does it mean rape)% (-)

(20)
Jane   (a::nd) she told me...

Nicky interprets Jane's utterance in stave 13 as stressing the initiative of Jane's mother 'd[id] she sit you down', but Jane's subsequent objections and explanations highlight her own agency in the pursuit of early sexual knowledge. Thus, it turns out that Jane first learned about sex when she was watching the news and asked her mother for the meaning of the word 'rape'. Young Jane had clearly not expected that her questioning of the word 'rape' would lead to a lesson of parental sex education, nevertheless, this short narrative provides evidence of Jane's own agency and thirst for knowledge as well as of the liberal stance of Jane's mother towards early sex education. The act of watching the news as a, presumably, pre-pubescent child, also highlights the significance of knowledge for a child like Jane, and being confronted with such explicit grown-up information about sex without, it seems, being particularly disturbed about it, shows little Jane's maturity as well as her lack of inhibition about sex at an early age.

Challenge of 'naive/innocent-girl-position'

The significance the girls attribute to adopting knowing positions is also evident in their talk about finding out about pregnancy and the 'facts of life' as children. Extracts from this 'reproductive paradigm' (West 1999: 534) show that the girls are clearly opposed to displays of naivety. This explains why in the following example Nicky's attempt to construct herself as an innocent child when reproducing a conversation with her brother is thwarted by the other members in the group.

Extract 14: I don't know how I learned about sex

(29)
Nicky   >and we're talking about< I was lik:e (1.5)

(30)
Nicky   five six yeah (-) and he used to go "how do you

(31)
Nicky   get pregnant" .hh and then I said "is it because (.)

(32)
Nicky   they hold hands and they make a wish"
?Elizabeth   {snort/chuckle}

(33)
Nicky   and like my brother [(xxxxxxxxxxxxx no that's what
Elizabeth   [you didn't really believe that
?Roberta   [(xxxxxxxxxxxxxxxxxxxxxxxxx

(34)
Nicky   I honest]ly thought when I was like five yeah=
Elizabeth   did you]
Roberta   xxxxxxx)   =that's

(35)
Nicky   =erm (.) and they used to laugh at me
Roberta   quite sheltered=

When Nicky reveals the unrealistic views about procreation she had as a child in stave 32 the other girls do not judge this innocence positively. Thus, Nicky's depiction of herself as naive is openly challenged by

Elizabeth in staves 33–34 'you didn't really believe that did you'. Roberta, whose first reaction is indecipherable due to its simultaneity, also expresses her surprise when referring to Nicky's view as 'quite sheltered' (stave 35). As my discussion of the 'cool girl' positions in Chapter 2 showed, the subject position of the sheltered and naive girl is not one that is encouraged by the group. It would conflict with the group's efforts to construct themselves as knowledgeable and is thus rejected.

A less extreme degree of naivety or child-like innocence, however, finds acceptance from the group as Nicky's following claim about her views of kissing and pregnancy shows.

Extract 15: I don't know how I learned about sex – continued

(36)
Nicky   and say one day you'll find out=and I used to think

(37)
Nicky   you get pregnant from kissing and I thought that's

(38)
Nicky   [what it was] .hhh an[d then] and then I l:ooked it
Jane   [yeah I know]
Elizabeth   [m:hm:]

(39)
Nicky   up [I just found it in the encyclo]paed[ia
Elizabeth   [oh God
Roberta   [no I never thought stuff like that]

(40)
Nicky   (and I was)]   and I was so (shock]ed)
Jane   (I used to know)
Elizabeth   that's such] a classic way **you** would learn to (f-)]

Nicky's revelation about her naive beliefs regarding kissing and pregnancy in stave 37 is accepted by Jane and Elizabeth (in stave 38) but is still rejected by Roberta (in stave 39). In the remaining staves Nicky then makes an effort to reposition herself. In staves 38 to 39 she invokes a discourse that emphasises her scientific knowledge, repeating that she took it into her own hands to inform herself about sex with the help of an encyclopaedia. Thus she portrays herself as scientifically orientated, a stance that is recognised by Elizabeth in stave 40. Nicky is identified as a (natural) 'scientist' by the other girls on several occasions, which explains Elizabeth's reaction. Nicky reinforces this position in the extract below.

Extract 16: I don't know how I learned about sex – continued

(41)
Nicky   {swallows}   I went into school and I said
Jane   (.) (there w- there was)

(42)
Nicky   (.) to Paola (-) "do you know what happens" (-) and she

(43)
Nicky   goes what d'you mean and I (-) like (.) {amused}described

(44)
Nicky   it in a really like {laughing}crude way (-)

In staves 39 and 42 Nicky modifies her initial innocence, expressed in staves 32 and 37, and her emotional reaction in stave 40: 'I was so shocked ...'. By describing sex to her friend in a 'crude' way Nicky takes up a position as uninhibited and 'knowing' (future scientist) in relation to her friend Paola, and, by extension, in front of her present circle of friends.

None of this talk about their first knowledge of human reproduction leads to a discussion about contraception or sexual desire as in the group of Pat and her friends. This, however, is clearly not due to the girls' prudishness or shelteredness in relation to sexual knowledge.

Being uninhibited about sex talk

The girls' knowledge about sex tends to be paired with a display of coolness and a lack of inhibition about the potentially embarrassing (and even taboo) nature of sex talk. The following example shows an explicit attempt by one of the girls at presenting herself as knowledgeable and uninhibited rather than as prudish and naive in her reminiscing about talking to her mother about sex.

Extract 17: I don't know how I learned about sex – continued

(65)
Elizabeth   and my mum goes "do you know what sex is" (-) and I

(66)
Elizabeth   go "**yup**" and she goes "what" and I go .hh {cool}"<u>the</u>

(67)
Elizabeth   <u>man puts his willie</u> (.) <u>in the woman's fanny</u>" and

(68)
Nicky   {laughs}
Jane   {laughs}
Elizabeth   she goes "yeah"
Roberta   {laughs} {amused}<u>hhhh</u>
?   {chuckle}

The fact that Elizabeth knew about sex before her mother told her, and, even more so, the explicitness of this knowledge, illustrated by her use of slang words for the male and female genitalia (the latter predictably labelled more coarsely than the former), present Elizabeth as an uninhibited child, a subject position which is supported by her cool tone of voice in staves 66–67. Like Jane, Elizabeth also portrays her mother as very liberal by signalling that she was not shocked by her daughter's knowledge about sex.

Elizabeth reinforces both her own and her mother's display of being uninhibited about sex talk in the following staves.

Extract 18: I don't know how I learned about sex – continued

(69)
Nicky   {chuckle}
Elizabeth   yeah bu[t]
Roberta   do you wanna sit down   [y]ou are making me

(70)
Elizabeth   [I remember] my cousin told me (all about) she goes
Roberta   [(nervous)]

(71)
Elizabeth   {bossy}"<u>just **don't** tell your mum (alright)</u> **don't** <u>tell</u>

(72)
Elizabeth   <u>your mum</u>" and my mum came and I go {excited}"<u>guess what</u>

(73)
Elizabeth   <u>Sam has been telling me all about what sex is and</u>

(74)
Nicky   my brother
?Jane   %(xxxxx)%
Elizabeth   (about) **sperms**" *{amused}*.hhh
?Elizabeth   *{chuckle}*

(75)
Nicky   showed me with a (.) banana what ha<u>ppens and it</u>

(76)
Nicky   <u>really threw me up</u>*{amused}* [<u>yeah</u>]
?Jane   (xxxxxxx)
?Elizabeth   [*{loud squeak}*]

Elizabeth shows off her terminological and factual/scientific knowledge about sexual reproduction and sperms in a way that Coates
(1999) found typical of the talk of white middle-class girls as young as
12/13 years old. Thus Elizabeth emphasises both the good relationship
between her mother and herself and their liberal stances in relation to
sex. This anecdote encourages even Nicky to match Elizabeth's liberalism and lack of inhibition. However, whereas she succeeds in portray-
ing one member of her family as equally uninhibited as Elizabeth's
mother (staves 74–75), her own appalled reaction to her brother's
graphic explanations of intercourse positions her at a distance from
Elizabeth's uninhibited stance (stave 76). Nevertheless, Nicky's previous reactions to Roberta's and Elizabeth's explicit and implicit challenges of her child-like innocence foreground a more mature stance
(informing herself in an encyclopaedia, staves 38–39, Extract 15) and
more a daring or cool self (describing sex in a 'crude' way, see staves
43–44, Extract 16), which shows that even Nicky recognises and
acknowledges the group's opposition to the innocent or naive girl
position.

Boundaries of childhood sex talk: personal experiences

Again, however, the group has established clear boundaries of this
most personal type of sex talk. These are reached when Elizabeth
attempts to direct the conversation towards the future and their
personal sex life.

Extract 19: I don't know how I learned about sex – continued

(80)
Nicky   my mum had trust[ed us
Roberta   [my brother on- only started to

(81)
Nicky   [(not alone)-]
Roberta   [tell me about] his sex life like (-) this gap year

(82)
Nicky   (1) did he (tell you xxxxxx)
Elizabeth   *(1) (xxxx) what time did he have like how old was
*+*sucking noise – eating mints*

(83)
Elizabeth he when he first did it
Roberta   like (-) fifteen or something

(84)
Elizabeth {sucking noise}]   I'm gonna be about
Roberta   (or)]   (.) something like that

(85)
Elizabeth twenty I expect .hhh   {sucking noise}
Roberta   (1.5) (%right%)   oh God

(86)
Roberta   (it was just so amazing when my brother went to France)

After Roberta reveals that her brother was fifteen years old when he first had sex (see also Extract 7), Elizabeth self-discloses about when she expects to have her first experience of sexual intercourse (staves 84–85). However, this rare self-disclosure is not mirrored by anyone else, which constitutes a marked lack of reciprocity in comparison with the intimate talk of Pat and her friends. Neither do the other girls in this group attempt to develop this topic further by commenting on Elizabeth's prognosis about her future sex life in any other way. It is particularly interesting that Roberta, who has a boyfriend, does not display any more interest in a hypothetical discussion about their future sex lives than the others, as her abrupt topic change indicates.

This exchange is significant in two ways. Firstly, it shows that the group does not encourage the development of sex talk into a more personal direction. Secondly, this group norm is respected or even reinforced by Roberta, who has a steady boyfriend, which suggests that the girls' avoidance of personal sex talk cannot be explained by a lack of experience in relation to boyfriends or sex. This extract suggests that the girls do not want to discuss their personal sex life with each other, even if this discussion is a hypothetical one. It does not seem that the girls' reluctance to proceed with Elizabeth's topic is caused by a moralistic discourse about young active female sexuality, and there is certainly no indication that the girls are concerned about their reputation in their community, as is the case with the Bangladeshi girls (Chapter 6). However, despite not adopting prudish, sheltered or premaritally chaste positions, Roberta and her friends do not position themselves as sexually active. It is likely that the girls want to keep this aspect of their identity more private, which is not only due to their awareness of the tape recorder. Instead the data in this chapter contains evidence of the girls' identity practices and positions being affected by and orienting to other, more dominant norms, which are related to their private-school and upper-middle-class background. These norms are responsible for the girls' foregrounding of their rational academic mind over their sexualised desiring bodies in their discursive accomplishment of young femininities.

Conclusion

The sparse sex talk of Roberta and her friends does not only identify boundaries of what the girls perceive as normative vs. deviant sexuality, but also allows for their negotiation of group norms and identity positions well beyond the realms of sexuality. Thus, when the girls approach topics such as paedophilia, pornography and male promiscuity in their academic debates and 'lesbian' advances in their playful teasing they do not construct themselves as naive, embarrassed or moralising but rather highlight the symbolic capital that knowledge, liberalism and lack of (sexual) inhibition constitute in their group. Roberta and her friends do not hesitate to speak about the sex life of other people they know and present themselves as enlightened and liberal when discussing their childhood knowledge about sex. However, the girls refrain from approaching the topic on an explicitly personal level and there is no self-disclosure about their own sexual experiences, practices, desires or anxieties. Thus, the sex talk in Roberta's group is both more marginal and less face threatening than either the playful accusations of 'having been through it' among the Bangladeshi girls or the direct questions about each other's sex life characteristic of Pat and the other East End girls. Although they willingly engage in academic or other non-personal sex talk, their lack of conversations about sex on an intimate level suggests that the girls construct themselves as 'knowing but not doing'. This lack of personal sex talk cannot, I believe, be explained by a lack of actual sexual experience (see also Introduction to Part II). It is of course possible that the girls felt inhibited to talk about sex (in a personal way) due to my status as a member of staff at their school. On the other hand, the girls felt free to talk about other highly confidential issues such as (soft) drug-taking on tape, an admission which would have resulted in their immediate expulsion had it become known (see Chapter 2). I believe it is more revealing to consider the girls' (lack of) sex talk from a discourse analytic perspective. Whereas in both working-class groups in my study there were signs of what I called a 'pro-sex discourse', these private-school, upper-middle-class girls were not affected by any (peer or youth culture) pressures to present themselves as sexually active at their age. Instead, their talk was dominated by their desire to construct themselves as knowledgeable, in relation to sex as well as to art, scientific and societal issues. Thus, the girls appeared to evaluate their status in the 'academic market' more highly than in the 'heterosexual market', which dominates the practices and identities of many of their (pre) adolescent peers (Eckert and McConnell-Ginet 2003: 27). This focus on 'knowledge' appears to be a central reason for the girls' lack of talk about sex-related issues, such as contraception and the 'right time' for sex. Walkerdine et al. (2001: 194), who followed the trajectory of various groups of young working-class and middle-class women growing up in Britain, highlight the relationship between young middle-class femininity and sexuality on one hand and academic knowledge and achievement on the other. They conclude that '[t]he regulation of feminine sexuality for middle-class girls has to be understood as part of a wider regulation of their achievement and academic success. Nothing is allowed to obstruct the academic path...'. Like Walkerdine et al. (2001: 184–94) I believe that this foregrounding of the rational mind over the sexual/fecund body is central to the discursive construction of young femininity in the friendship group of Roberta and her private-school, upper-middle-class girls.

8
Conclusions

In this book I not only wanted to capture what three different groups of adolescent girls talk about, but I was also interested in the way the girls conduct their talk. Above all, I was interested in how they position themselves and are positioned in this talk, or, in other words, in the discursive and interactive construction of identities within the girls' friendship groups. Although the girls often spoke about similar topics (like school, sex, their families), the three groups' positioning in relation to these topics frequently differed; they drew on a range of different discourses, and/or negotiated discourses and subject positions differently within their interactions.

My micro-analytic exploration of the girls' interactions on a discourse level allowed me to identify several local identities within the three friendship groups. Roberta, Elizabeth, Nicky and Jane frequently presented themselves as cool and real, as socially aware and knowledgeable but unpretentious private-school girls. Ardiana, Dilshana, Rahima, Hennah and Varda foregrounded their tough and 'bad' girl identities in some instances, mostly in their teasing and sex talk, at other times they presented themselves as respectable 'good' girls. Pat, Jenny, Natalie and Susan frequently constructed themselves as sheltered and loved daughters, but they also switched between positions of responsible adults and self-determined or even rebellious teenagers.

By focusing my analysis on the different discourses, stereotypes, cultural concepts, and types of cultural capital that were invoked (and negotiated) by the girls in their talk I also demonstrated that some of these local positions reflect and affect socio-cultural meanings, practices and identity categories of a higher order and that gender and adolescent identities have to be seen in relation to ethnicity and social class. It was this dialectic relationship between one level of identity and another that became of particular interest to me in this book. My discussion of the girls' talk shows that different levels of identity constantly interact with one another. The following concluding discussion brings together my findings about this connection from both Part I and Part II in this book.

The relevance of social class to the girls' construction of adolescent femininities was both implicit and explicit in the talk of Roberta and her upper-middle-class friends. The girls' awareness of (their own) social status is apparent in many of their conversations about poems and mines, dance clubs and clubbers, London's West and East End, state-schools and 'middle-class' schools with their respective expectations for students (e.g. A-levels and future university degrees for the latter). In these conversations the girls seek to distance themselves from their socially unaware and pretentious fellow students at their elite school for girls, who, as I argue, represent a stereotypical upper-middle-class, private-school femininity for Roberta and her friends. At the same time the girls also distance themselves from what they perceive as tough working-class areas and stereotypical working-class femininities as their talk about Hackney clubs and 'Sharons' shows. The girls seek to assume a mid-position on the social scale, a positioning which is indexed in their talk about musical preferences, their alignment with 'real' adolescents, and above all, their accomplishment of cool girl identities, that is, of a tame non-conformity which places them at a distance from a sheltered upper-middle-class femininity. However, their social class identity is reproduced in other ways. The foregrounding of rational mind over active female (hetero)sexuality, is, as Walkerdine et al. (2001) argue, central to the reproduction of young upper-middle-class femininity. This is particularly striking in the girls' (limited) talk about sex, but the girls' performance of academic selves is central throughout their conversations, and balances their display of alternative types of cultural capital (Bourdieu 1983, 1984) such as coolness. Thus it is likely that the alternative (cool, real and socially aware) upper-middle-class femininities which the girls construct in their group talk do not constitute a challenge to the girls' actual social status, but instead are expressions of what Skeggs (2004) sees as the new middle-class lifestyle of 'cultural omnivores'.

In the other two groups, both from a working-class area in the East End of London, social class is never spoken about explicitly. I argued that this absence of explicit talk about social class should not be interpreted as an indication of the irrelevance of social class to the identity performances in the talk of these two groups. The talk of Pat's group in many ways captured what Skeggs (1997: 74) described as working-class women's 'multitudinous efforts *not to be* recognised as working class' due to the mostly pathological discourses of working-class femininity. My analysis shows how this disidentification from working-class femininity, which has been found in a range of non-linguistic studies about (young) working-class women, is achieved interactively and discursively. The interactive and discursive negotiations are complex, they often require a careful balancing of teenage voices of adventure and rebellion with positions which show that the girls have appropriated their mothers' or other authoritative voices (Bakhtin 1981; Maybin 2007). What struck me was that the girls frequently position themselves in opposition to classed subject positions like that of the neglected daughter in single-parent families, the vandalising truant, the (pregnant) school dropout, the sexually hyperactive 'slag', the future teenage mother. By constructing themselves as sheltered and loved by their (single) mothers and (distant) fathers, as compliant with (parental) authority, and as responsible about their education as well as about boys and sex, Pat and her friends frequently disidentify from these stereotypical notions of working-class femininity and instead engage in performances of respectable middle-class femininity.

Interestingly, the second group of working-class girls, from the same state school in the East End of London, in some ways displayed an interactive and discursive behaviour, which aligns them with practices and stances indexing ladette or young working-class femininity. Ardiana, Dilshana, Hennah, Varda and Rahima frequently adopt the most pronounced anti-school and truanting stances among all three groups, with several of the girls in the group prioritising 'having a laugh' over serious school work. The girls also engage in verbal toughness in the form of extended sequences of competitive teasing. I argued that, similar to the use of non-standard grammatical and phonological forms by American 'burnout' girls, the competitive teasing constitutes a resource for the Bangladeshi girls to accomplish toughness. These tough femininities may not be valued by Pat and her friends, which also indicates that there is no pre-determined link between working-class femininity and toughness, but they are clearly valued by other girls within their (working-class/ladette) peer group. I also suggest that they are of particular value to Ardiana and her friends because they position them in opposition to the stereotype of the timid, quiet and studious Asian girl.

However, Ardiana, Dilshana, Hennah and Rahima also negotiate a range of cultural discourses which index their Muslim Bangladeshi femininities. In their talk about love, boyfriends, dating, kissing in public and sexual experiences the girls invoke discourses of female respectability with inflections of ethnic and religious culture. In all three groups the girls at times align themselves with one or the other variation of 'respectable femininity' in their sex talk. In Roberta's upper-middle-class group this alignment is, however, frequently balanced by a self-positioning as knowing, uninhibited and cool in 'academic' or impersonal sex talk, and in Pat's group the girls balance moralistic discourses of respectable femininity with their desire to determine when, where and with whom they should have sex to make 'the first time' a worthwhile and even enjoyable experience for them. In Ardiana's group the emphasis on respectable femininity is very strong, it is shaped by a discourse of pre-marital chastity and is associated with Muslim Bangladeshi norms. The girls' spontaneous talk and the interview data contain several examples which highlight their awareness that social interaction between young women and young men, and even more so sex before marriage, are seen as inappropriate or even shameful by many members of the Bangladeshi community. In the girls' spontaneous talk this is most explicit when Ardiana suggests that kissing in public is 'alright [...] in front of a white person' or when Dilshana playfully subverts the voice of adult Bangladeshi speakers who liken kissing in public to 'watching free cinema'. Unsurprisingly, the level of explicitness about cultural norms in relation to young Muslim Bangladeshi femininity is even higher in the interviews between Hennah and myself (see also Cameron 2009 on spontaneous talk vs. interviews). Here Hennah frequently invokes norms of religious (rather than ethnic) culture when she problematises talk about romantic love and pre-marital dating or even socialising with boys, highlighting the relevance of the concept of 'shame' for daughters and parents alike within the Muslim Bangladeshi community.

The girls' awareness of (different) cultural norms about young women's (sexual) respectability is also implicit in their preference for playful frames (Bateson 1987/1972; Goffman 1974) such as teasing and boasting when they talk about these sensitive topics. In these playful frames the girls can align themselves with discourses and subject positions which they know are problematic for other members of their community and even for some of the girls within the group. In the teasing and boasting the girls can present themselves as sexually experienced or 'bad' girls, they can tease each other about 'having been through it', and boast about public displays of kissing. The risk of aligning themselves with these positions, which the girls see as the norm in the white community, is mitigated by the inherent ambiguity of their playful teasing and boasting. The playful frames allow the girls to show respect for their own and each other's face needs within the group. I argued that by switching between different frames and cultural discourses the girls not only negotiate different positions with respect to sexual experiences and norms, but they also (re)negotiate their femininities as both British and Muslim Bangladeshi.

One topic which dominates the talk of Ardiana and her friends, but is completely absent in the other two groups, is marriage. I dedicated an entire section to this topic, showing how the girls negotiate a range of different discourses to achieve a consensus in the form of what I interpret as a modified discourse of arranged marriage. This discourse emerges in the course of the girls' complex negotiations of different traditions of marriage and allocates a significant match-making role to the families of the girls but at the same time highlights the girls' agency as they insist on husbands who they consider compatible with their 'British' or 'Londoni' Bangladeshi identities.

However, in the subsequent interviews with my in-group 'informant', Hennah at times distanced herself from my (post-modern) celebration of cultural hybridity with regard to the topic of arranged marriage. I used an extract from the interviews in which Hennah's opposition to my interpretation is very clear to reflect on the boundaries of micro-linguistic data. Roberta and her friends' interactive/discursive negotiations of 'cool' or non-conformist private-school femininities need to be seen in relation to the girls' relatively secure trajectories into university educated, upper-middle-class lives, and Pat and her friends' discursive disidentifications from stereotypes of young working-class femininities are constrained by the lack of certainty about similar (higher-education/middle-class) trajectories. Similarly, Ardiana and her friends' relatively effortless synthesising of linguistic practices and discursive positions needs to be seen in the context of norms of ethnic and religious culture which, according to Hennah, may be considerably less flexible or compatible in the girls' lives outside their friendship group than their stances within their talk. As Deborah Cameron (2009: 15) argues 'to make sense of what [speaking subjects] are doing as creative, agentive language-users, we also have to consider the inherited structures (of belief, of opportunity or the lack of it, of desire and of power) which both enable and constrain their performances'.

In this book I contemplated both signs of agency and of structure in the identity performances in the talk of young women. I started by looking at the local positioning of the girls, but found that a full understanding of some of these positions cannot be gained by turning away from (interacting) macro-categories of identity. I also showed that even essentialist notions of ethnicity and class should not be ignored by researchers interested in the (gender) identity performances of young women, as they constitute important resources for the girls' discursive (dis)identification. Structures of belief can shape the positioning of young women, for example in the form of stereotypes about working-class femininity or discourses of cultural incompatibility. And structures of opportunity and power, for example in the form of legitimate cultural capital (academic/high culture knowledge), can reaffirm the performance of traditional upper-middle-class femininities, which the display of alternative cultural capital, such as coolness, may disrupt. But in conversational data these structures are rarely entirely static; dominant discourses or essentialising stereotypes are invoked, negotiated and resisted interactively by speakers. My exploration of spoken data from three groups of adolescent British girls captures some of the many different subject positions that young women adopt in their discursive and interactive negotiations, focusing on local and supra-local resources for the construction of young femininities in girls' talk, and on the interplay between gender, ethnicity and social class.

Notes

1 Girls' Talk as a Resource for Identity Construction

1. The term 'discourse' captures the dialectical relationship between language use and social practices and structures on a more abstract level (e.g. see Fairclough 2003). My analysis in this book focuses on concrete types of discourse, or discourses, that is 'ways of representing aspects of the world' (Fairclough 2003: 124) or, in my own words, different types of language use which reflect, affect and constitute social and cultural practices. I view discourses as carrying ideologies, but again, the relationship is bidirectional; discourses do not just contribute to the reproduction of ideologies, but they also constitute resources for language users to challenge ideologies.
2. Fairclough (2003: 23) defines 'social practice' as 'intermediate organisational entities between structures and events'. He later continues 'social events are causally shaped by (networks of) social practices – social practices define particular ways of acting ... ' (25). Like Fairclough I see social practices as constituting normative influences over events and actors, as being in a dialectical relationship with discourses, that is, as being shaped and constituted by discourses as well as shaping and constituting discourses.
3. For a critical review of terminology see also Cameron 2005a, 2005b, 2009.
4. Although the terms 'subject position', 'position' and 'self' can imply very different conceptualisations of identity, I use them synonymously (in both singular and plural forms) from a postmodern, constructionist perspective throughout the book. For a summary of (historically) different theories and understandings of identity and selfhood (e.g the rational self of the Enlightenment or the individualistic self of Romanticism) see Benwell and Stokoe 2006, especially 17–47 and Hall 1992, especially 275–91.
5. Pat and her friends recorded their talk for me about six months earlier than Ardiana and her friends. Both groups of girls were in year 11 at the time of the recording, but they were not of the same year cohort.
6. School records indicate that all four girls were living in one-parent families, however, it is possible that two of the girls, Susan and Jenny, may actually have (step-)fathers living within their household.
7. Although I had originally been concerned about this change to my research design, I later accepted it as a consequence of the different role school plays in the life of this group of private-school friends. Whereas the other two groups found time for their talk at school, this was not the case for Roberta and her friends, and the girls therefore had to change the setting to accommodate to their natural space for doing friendship talk: their own bedrooms at home.

2 Cool and Socially Aware Private-School Girls

1. Beverley Skeggs (1997) differentiates between legitimate cultural capital, e.g. knowledge of high culture, formal education which allows individuals to accumulate larger scale, institutional power, tradable into both economic and symbolic capital, and other cultural capital, e.g. working-class men's 'macho physical hardness' or 'working class femininity', which is de-legitimised, restricted in its value to more local, interpersonal contexts and 'cannot be traded as an asset; it cannot be capitalized upon [...] and its power is limited' (Skeggs 1997: 9, 10).
2. See also Harris (2004: 20) and Hey (1997: 118) on the significance of a display of consumer lifestyle for the 'can-do girls' or middle-class girls respectively
3. In a current DJ directory (of 173,702 DJs) only 1 out of the 50 top DJs listed is a woman (The DJ List 2007). This imbalance and the connotations of masculinity in DJing are likely to have been even more pronounced in the late 1990s when the recording took place. Even a successful DJ like Anne Savage talked about DJing as 'male dominated' and a 'boys' club' in 2002, despite having been voted number 2 'female DJ' in the world (BBC Radio 4, 2002).
4. A Channel 4 programme about the 'The Best and Worst places to live in the UK' branded Hackney as the worst place in the UK as recently as October 2006.

3 Sheltered but Independent East End Girls

1. The conversations I recorded between the girls confirm that Pat and Natalie live with their mothers in single-parent families, but the way Susan and Jenny speak about their families could suggest that there are (step-)fathers within their households.
2. Roberta and her friends speak about mothers in general about once every 2 minutes 54 seconds, but this percentage includes a majority of references to the mothers of other girls. The girls in Roberta's group speak about their own mothers less than about the mothers of other girls.
3. Note that Roberta and her friends (Chapter 2) use the term 'sheltered' differently, to refer to their privileged and socially unaware colleagues at their posh private school.
4. Roberta and her private-school friends speak about other girls' mothers and fathers more than about their own, which is not the case in the other two groups. Equally noteworthy is the fact that only in Ardiana's Bangladeshi group do the girls mention their fathers more often than their mothers, although this is partly due to one of the girl's repeated complaining about her dad.
5. Kodz et al. (1997) from the Institute for Employment Studies describes the intended use of the NRA as follows:

> The NRA is a document, in a nationally recognised format, for individuals to set out their skills, experience and achievements. The NRA aims to recognise and value individuals' learning and helps them plan and manage their own development. As such it helps to promote lifelong

learning and provide a vehicle to create a better-skilled workforce. For employers, the NRA has key uses in recruitment and staff development.

The actual usefulness of the NRA (e.g. in comparison to GCSEs and A-level exam results) has frequently been doubted by students and employers alike.

6. For an in-depth discussion of young schoolchildrens' appropriation of authoritative voices which index dominant institutional discourses or educational perspectives see Maybin 2007, especially pages 152–3.

4   Tough and Respectable British Bangladeshi Girls

1. It is essential to acknowledge that Hennah's views and positions may or may not have been representative of the entire group. Nevertheless, hers is a more 'insider' view than my own and I argue with Larson (1997: 459) that this dialogue between (the perspectives of) researcher and researched 'makes understanding of the life world and lived realities of others possible'.
2. Shashmia is a member of the group who was so rarely at school during my recordings that she features in none of the extracts I discuss here.
3. This divergence between my own emphasis on ethnic culture and Hennah's on religious practice is discussed further below.
4. In Chapter 6 I will discuss this discourse of respectable femininity, linked to notions of *sharam* and *izzat*, in the context of the girls' sex talk.
5. In Pichler 2001 I use the term 'bicultural identities' to capture my interpretation of the girls' switching between conversational frames and cultural identities. The progression of my work and my problematisation of essentialist notions of culture later led me to adopt the concept of 'hybridity'.
6. I offer my apologies for this simplistic and outdated summary of a 'sociologist' stance towards the 'torn-between cultures' discourse, based on Watson 1977.

5   Self-disclosing Sex Talk: Self-determined Girls

1. There are other interesting reversals of this gendered subject/object symbolism. In one of these further examples Pat positions both Susan's boyfriend and Susan herself as active and desiring subjects. Although Susan is amused by Pat's formulation, she concurs, positioning her relationship with her (sexually experienced) boyfriend as a symmetrical one, in which she is not experiencing any pressure.

Extract 19: asking for sex

(1)
Susan   I **spoke** to him about it and everything

(2)
Pat   [he hasn't] asked you has he
Susan   he don't act really (.) [(xxxxxx)]

(3)
Pat   asked has he asked you for sex have you asked
Susan   **no**

(4)
Pat   [him (for sex)]
Susan   [asked me] *{laughs}* asked me .hh **no** (.) he s-
Jenny   *{- -laughs- -}*

(5)
Susan   I **spoke** to him about it and everything

2. Throughout this extract there is background noise from a second, simultaneous conversation. Only Jenny's conversation about her boyfriend was clear enough to transcribe, although some of the utterances by other speakers were still not intelligible.
3. For a critique of the academic and public overemphasis on this concept see Ahmad 2003 and Chapters 4 and 6 in this book.

6 Playful Sex Talk: 'Good Girls' and 'Bad Girls'

1. Please note the different transcription conventions for the ethnographic interviews, displayed at the beginning of the book.
2. It is important to note that the purpose of Ardiana's request is to ensure that the question (and the following answers) are on tape. Thus she addresses not only the girls present in the conversation, but also the tape recorder and, ultimately, me. It almost seems as if Ardiana was switching into a discourse which she expects to be familiar to her audience, that is, a white female researcher. However, there are many other extracts of data from this and further conversations which suggest that Ardiana's resistance to a discourse which values emotional restraint in public is not merely a performance for a white audience.

7 Impersonal Sex Talk: Knowing Girls

1. Halliday's 1985 study of transitivity, that is, the (systemic linguistic) study of how actions/processes are represented and how these representations or transitivity choices contribute to creating a worldview or ideological perspective in a text (Mills 1995: 143), has informed the work of feminist linguists exploring gender relations in representations of heterosexual romance (Mills 1995) and in the representation of actions by complainants and accused in rape trials (Ehrlich 1998).

Bibliography

Aapola, Sinikka, Gonick, Marnina and Harris, Anita (2005) *Young Femininity. Girlhood, Power and Social Change*. Basingstoke: Palgrave Macmillan.

Ahmad, Fauzia (2003) Still in 'in progress?': methodological dilemmas, tensions and contradictions in theorizing South Asian Muslim women. In Nirmal Puwar and Parvati Raghuram (eds.) *South Asian Women in the Diaspora*. 43–66. Oxford: Berg.

Ahmad, Fauzia, Modood, Tariq and Lissenburgh, Stephen (2003) *South Asian Women and Employment in Britain. The Interaction of Gender and Ethnicity*. London: Policy Studies Institute.

Alberts, Janet Kaye (1992) An inferential/strategic explanation for the social organisation of teases. *Journal of Language and Social Psychology* 11 (3): 153–77.

Alexander, Claire (2000) *The Asian Gang*. Oxford: Berg.

Amos, Valerie and Parmar, Pratibha (1981) Resistances and responses: the experience of black girls in Britain. In Angela McRobbie and Trisha McCabe (eds.) *Feminism for Girls. An Adventure Story*. 129–52. London: Routledge and Kegan Paul.

Antaki, Charles and Widdicombe, Sue (eds.) (1998) *Identities in Talk*. London: Sage.

Anwar, Muhammed (1998) *Between Cultures. Continuity and Change in the Lives of Young Asians*. London: Routledge.

Archer, Louise (2001) 'Muslim brothers, black lads, traditional Asians': British Muslim young men's construction of race, religion and masculinity. *Feminism & Psychology* 11 (1): 79–105.

Archer, Louise (2002a) Change, culture and tradition: British Muslim pupils talk about Muslim girls' post-16 'choices'. *Race, Ethnicity and Education* 5 (4): 359–76.

Archer, Louise (2002b) 'It's easier that you're a girl and that you're Asian': interactions of 'race' and gender between researchers and participants. *Feminist Review* 72: 108–32.

Archer, Louise, Halsall, Anna, and Hollingworth, Sumi (2007) Class, gender, (hetero)sexuality and schooling: paradoxes within working-class girls' engagement with education and post-16 aspirations. *British Journal of Sociology of Education* 28 (2): 165–80.

Austin, John Langshaw (1962) *How to Do Things with Words*. Cambridge, MA: Harvard University Press.

Bakhtin, Mikhail ([1929]1984) *Problems of Dostoevsky's Poetics*. Ed. and trans. Caryl Emerson. Minneapolis: University of Minnesota Press.

Bakhtin, Mikhail ([1935]1981) Discourse in the novel. In *The Dialogic Imagination: Four essays by M.M. Bakhtin*. Ed. Michael Holquist, trans. Caryl Emerson and Michael Holquist. Austin: University of Texas Press.

Bakhtin, Mikhail M. ([1953]1986) The problem of speech genres. In *Speech Genres and Other Late Essays*, 60–102. Ed. Caryl Emerson and Michael Holquist. Trans. Vern W. McGee. Austin: University of Texas Press.

Ballard, Roger (1994) Introduction: the emergence of Desh Paradesh. In Roger Ballard (ed.) *Desh Paradesh. The South Asian Presence in Britain*, 1–34. London: C. Hurst & Co.

Barker, Chris (1997) Television and the reflexive project of the self: soaps, teenage talk and hybrid identities. *British Journal of Sociology* 48 (4): 611–28.

Barker, Chris (1998) 'Cindy's a slut': moral identities and moral responsibility in the 'soap talk' of British Asian girls. *Sociology* 32 (1): 65–81.

Barrett, Rusty (1999) Indexing polyphonous identity in the speech of African American drag queens. In Mary, Bucholtz, A.C. Liang, and Laurel Sutton, (eds.) *Reinventing Identities: The Gendered Self in Discourse*. 313–31. New York: Oxford University Press.

Basit, Tehmina (1997) *Eastern Values, Western Milieu: Identities and Aspirations of Adolescent British Muslim Girls*. Aldershot: Ashgate.

Bateson, Gregory (1987[1972]) A theory of play and fantasy. In Gregory Bateson (ed.) *Steps to an Ecology of Mind. Collected Essays in Anthropology, Psychiatry, Evolution and Epistemology*. 177–93. Northvale, NJ: Jason Aronson Inc.

Bauman, Gerd (1997) Dominant and demotic discourses of culture: their relevance to multi-ethnic alliances. In P. Werbner, and T. Moodod, (eds.) *Debating Cultural Hybridity: Multi-cultural Identities and the Politics of Anti-Racism*, 209–25. London: Zed Books.

Bennett, Andy (2001) *Cultures of Popular Music*. Buckingham: Open University Press.

Benwell, Bethan and Stokoe, Elizabeth (2006) *Discourse and Identity*. Edinburgh: Edinburgh University Press.

Bhopal, Kalwant (1999) South Asian and arranged marriages in East London. In Rohit Barot, Harriet Bradley and Steve Fenton (eds.) *Ethnicity, Gender and Social Change* (117–34). Basingstoke: Macmillan – now Palgrave Macmillan.

Borthwick, Stuart and Moy, Ron (2004) *Popular Music Genres*. Edinburgh: Edinburgh University Press.

Bourdieu, Pierre (1984 [1979]) *Distinction: A Social Critique of the Judgement of Taste*. Trans. R. Nice. London: Routledge.

Bourdieu, Pierre (1986 [1983]) The forms of capital. In J.G. Richardson (ed.) *Handbook of Theory and Research for the Sociology of Education*. 241–58. Westport, CT: Greenwood Press.

Boxer, Diana and Cortés-Conde, Florencia (1997) From bonding to biting: conversational joking and identity display. *Journal of Pragmatics* 27 (3): 275–94.

Bourdieu, Pierre (1991) *Language and Symbolic Power*. Cambridge: Polity Press.

Brah, Avtar (1996) *Cartographies of Diaspora*. London: Routledge.

Brah, Avtar and Minhas, Rehana (1985) Structural racism or cultural difference? Schooling for Asian girls. In Gaby Weiner (ed.) *Just a Bunch of Girls. Feminist Approaches to Schooling*. 14–25. Milton Keynes: Open University Press.

Brown, Penelope and Levinson, Stephen (1987) *Politeness*. Cambridge: Cambridge University Press.

Bucholtz, Mary (1996) Geek the girls: language femininity, and female nerds. In Natasha Warner, Jocelyn Ahlers, Leela Bilmes, Monica Oliver, Suzanne Wertheim and Melinda Chen (eds.) *Gender and Belief Systems: Proceedings of the Fourth Berkeley Women and Language Conference.* 119–31. Berkeley, CA: Berkeley Women and Language Group.

Bucholtz, Mary (1999). 'Why be normal?': language and identity practices in a community of nerd girls. *Language in Society* 28: 203–23.

Bucholtz, Mary (2003) Theories of discourse as theories of gender: discourse analysis in language and gender studies. In Janet Holmes and Miriam Meyerhoff (eds.) *The Handbook of Language and Gender.* 43–68. Oxford: Blackwell.

Bucholtz, Mary and Hall, Kira (2004) Theorizing identity in language and sexuality research. *Language in Society* 33: 469–515.

Bucholtz, Mary and Hall, Kira (2005). Identity and interaction: a sociocultural linguistic approach. *Discourse Studies* 7 (3): 585–614.

Burns, April and Torre, María Elena (2004) Shifting desires: discourses of accountability in abstinence-only education in the United States. In Anita Harris (ed.) *All about the Girl. Culture, Power and Identity.* 127–37. New York: Routledge.

Butler, Judith (1990) *Gender Trouble: Feminism and the Subversion of Identity.* New York: Routledge.

Cameron, Deborah (1998) Performing gender identity: young men's talk and the construction of heterosexual masculinity. In Jennifer Coates (ed.) *Language and Gender: A Reader.* 270–84. Oxford: Blackwell.

Cameron, Deborah (2001) *Working with Spoken Discourse.* London: Sage.

Cameron, Deborah (2003) Gender and language ideologies. In Janet Holmes and Miriam Meyerhoff (eds.) *The Handbook of Language and Gender.* 447–67. Oxford: Blackwell.

Cameron, Deborah (2005a) Relativity and its discontents: language, gender, and pragmatics. *Intercultural Pragmatics* 2–3: 321–34.

Cameron, Deborah (2005b) Language, gender and sexuality: current issues and new directions. *Applied Linguistics* 26 (4): 482–502.

Cameron, Deborah (2009) Theoretical issues for the study of gender and spoken interaction. In Pia Pichler and Eva Eppler (eds.) *Gender and Spoken Interaction.* 1–17. Basingstoke: Palgrave Macmillan.

Cameron, Deborah and Kulick, Don (2003a) *Language and Sexuality.* Cambridge: Cambridge University Press.

Cameron, Deborah and Kulick, Don (2003b) Introduction: language and desire in theory and practice. *Language and Communication* 23: 93–105.

Cameron, Deborah and Kulick, Don (eds.) (2006) *The Language and Sexuality Reader.* London: Routledge.

Cheshire, Jenny (1997) Linguistic variation and social function. In Nikolas Coupland and Adam Jaworski (eds.) *Sociolinguistics: A Reader and Coursebook.* 185–98. Basingstoke: Macmillan – now Palgrave Macmillan.

Coates, Jennifer (1996) *Women Talk. Conversation between Women Friends.* Oxford: Blackwell.

Coates, Jennifer (1999) Changing femininities: the talk of teenage girls. In Mary Bucholtz, A.C. Liang and Laurel A. Sutton (eds.) *Reinventing Identities. The Gendered Self in Discourse.* 123–44. Oxford: Oxford University Press.

Coleman, John C. (1980) *The Nature of Adolescence.* London: Methuen.

Community Relations Commission (1976) *Between Two Cultures.* CRC.

Cramb, Auslan (2002) It was my fault says mother of arranged marriage girl, 16. *Daily Telegraph* (25/04/2002).

Dale, Angela, Shaheen, Nusrat, Kalra, Virinder and Fieldhouse, Edward (2002) Routes into education and employment for young Pakistani and Bangladeshi women in the UK. *Ethnic and Racial Studies,* 25 (6): 942–68.

Drew, Paul (1987) Po-faced receipts of teases. *Linguistics* 25: 219–53.

Duckworth, Ted (2007) *Dictionary of English Slang.* //www.peevish.co.uk/slang/ accessed 11/06/2007.

Dwyer, Claire (2000) Negotiating diasporic identities: young British South Asian Muslim women. *Women's Studies International Forum 23* (4): 475–68.

Eckert, Penelope (1993) Cooperative competition in adolescent 'girl talk'. In Deborah Tannen (ed.) *Gender and Conversational Interaction.* 32–61. Oxford: Oxford University Press.

Eckert, Penelope (2000) *Language Variation as Social Practice. The Linguistic Construction of Social Meaning in Belten High.* Oxford: Blackwell.

Eckert, Penelope and McConnell-Ginet, Sally (1992) Think practically and look locally: language and gender as community-based practice. *Annual Review of Anthropology* 21: 461–90.

Eckert, Penelope and McConnell-Ginet, Sally (1995) Constructing meaning, constructing selves: snapshots of language, gender and class from Belten High. In Kira Hall and Mary Bucholtz (eds.) *Gender Articulated. Language and the Socially Constructed Self.* 469–508. New York: Routledge.

Edelsky, Carole (1993) Who's got the floor? In Deborah Tannen (ed.) *Gender and Conversational Interaction.* 189–226. Oxford: Oxford University Press.

Eder, Donna (1990) Serious and playful disputes: variation in conflict talk among female adolescents. In Allen Grimshaw (ed.) *Conflict Talk.* 67–84. Cambridge: Cambridge University Press.

Eder, Donna (1993) 'Go get ya a french!': romantic and sexual teasing among adolescent girls. In Deborah Tannen (ed.) *Gender and Conversational Interaction* 17–31. Oxford: Oxford University Press.

Edley, Nigel and Wetherell, Margaret (1997) Jockeying for position. The construction of masculine identities. *Discourse and Society* 8 (2): 203–17.

Ehrlich, Susan (1998) The discursive construction of sexual consent. *Discourse and Society* 9 (2): 149–71.

Eisenberg, Ann R. (1986) Teasing: verbal play in two Mexican homes. In Bambi B. Schiffelin and Elinor Ochs (eds.) *Language Socialization across Cultures.* 182–98. Cambridge: Cambridge University Press.

Fairclough, Norman (2001) *Language and Power* (2nd edition). Edinburgh: Longman/Pearson.

Fairclough, Norman (2003) *Analysing Discourse. Textual Analysis for Social Research.* London: Routledge.

Fikentscher, Kai (2003) 'There's not a problem I can't fix, cause I can do it in the mix': On the performative technology of 12-inch vinyl. In René T.A. Lysloff and

Leslie C. Gay Jr. (eds.) (2003) *Music and Technoculture.* 290–315. Middletown, CT: Wesleyan University Press.

Finch, Janet (2007) Displaying families. *Sociology* 41 (1): 65–81.

Foucault, Michel (1980) *The History of Sexuality.* Harmondsworth: Penguin.

Foucault, Michel (1989/[1972]) *The Archaeology of Knowledge.* London: Routledge.

Frazer, Elizabeth (1988) Teenage girls talking about class. *Sociology* 22 (3): 343–58.

Frazer Elizabeth (1992) Talking about gender, race and class. In Deborah Cameron, Elizabeth Frazer, Penelope Harvey, M.B.H. Rampton and Kay Richardson (eds.) *Researching Language. Issues of Power and Method.* 90–112. London: Routledge.

Frith, Hannah and Kitzinger, Celia (1998) 'Emotion work' as participant resource. A feminist analysis of young women's talk-in-interaction. *Sociology* 32 (2): 299–320.

Frosh, Stephen, Phoenix, Ann and Pattman, Rob (2002) *Young Masculinities.* Basingstoke: Palgrave – now Palgrave Macmillan.

Gardner, Katy and Shukur, Abdus (1994) 'I'm Bengali, I'm Asian, and I'm living here': the changing identity of British Bengalis. In Roger Ballard (ed.) *Desh Paradesh. The South Asian Presence in Britain.* 142–64. London: C. Hurst & Co.

Gavron, Catherine (1997) *Migrants to Citizens: Changing Orientations among Bangladeshis of Tower Hamlets, London.* Unpublished PhD Thesis, University of London.

Gay, Leslie (2001) Rap, Hip Hop, and the Mainstream. *The school of music at the University of Tennessee, Knoxville website.* 1–3. http://www.music.utk.edu/rock/rap.html (accessed 05/03/02).

Ghuman, Paul A. Singh (1994) *Coping with two Cultures. British Asian and Indo-Canadian Adolescents.* Clevedon: Multilingual Matters.

Ghuman, Paul A. Singh (2003) *Double Loyalties. South Asian Adolescents in the West.* Cardiff: University of Wales Press.

Goffman, Erving (1974) *Frame Analysis.* New York: Harper and Row.

Goodwin, Marjorie Harness (1990) *He-Said-She-Said: Talk as Social Organisation among Black Children.* Bloomington: Indiana University Press.

Goodwin, Marjorie Harness (1999) Constructing opposition within girls' games. In Mary Bucholtz, A.C. Liang and Laurel A. Sutton (eds.) *Reinventing Identities. The Gendered Self in Discourse.* 388–409. Oxford: Oxford University Press.

Griffiths, Vivienne (1995) *Adolescent Girls and Their Friends. A Feminist Ethnography.* Aldershot: Avebury.

Gumperz, John (1982) *Discourse Strategies.* Cambridge: Cambridge University Press.

Günthner, Susanne (2000) *Vorwurfsaktivitäten in der Alltagsinteraktion: grammatische, prosodische, rhethorisch-stilistische und interaktive Verfahren bei der Konstitution kommunikativer Muster und Gattungen.* Tübingen: Niemeyer.

Hall, Stuart (1980): Encoding/decoding. In Centre for Contemporary Cultural Studies (ed.): *Culture, Media, Language: Working Papers in Cultural Studies, 1972–79.* 128–38. London: Hutchinson.

Hall, Stuart (1990) Cultural identity and diaspora. In John Rutherford (ed.) *Identity: Culture, Community, Difference.* 222–37. London: Lawrence and Wishart.

Hall, Stuart (1992) The question of cultural identity. In Stuart Hall, David Held and Tom McGreen (eds.) *Modernity and its Future.* 273–325. Cambridge: Polity.

Hall, Stuart (1997) The spectacle of the 'Other'. In Stuart Hall (ed.) *Representation: Cultural Representations and Signifying Practices.* 223–90. London: Sage in association with the Open University.

Halliday, M.A.K. (1985) *An Introduction to Functional Grammar.* London: Edward Arnold.

Hammersley, Martyn (2006) Ethnography: problems and prospects. *Ethnography and Education* 1 (1): 3–14.

Harris, Anita (2004) *Future Girl. Young Women in the Twenty-first Century.* London: Routledge.

Hasund, Ingrid Kristine and Stenström, Anna-Brita (1997) Conflict talk: a comparison of the verbal disputes between adolescent females in two corpora. In Magnus Ljung (ed.) *Corpus-based Studies in English. Papers from the Seventeenth International Conference on English Language Research on Computerized Corpora.* 119–32. Amsterdam: Rodopi.

Hennink, Monique, Diamond, Ian, and Cooper, Philip (1999) *Ethnic and Racial Studies: Young Asian Women and Relationships: Traditional or Transitional?* 22 (5): 867–91.

Hewitt, Roger (1986) *White Talk, Black Talk.* Cambridge: Cambridge University Press.

Hey, Valerie (1997) *The Company She Keeps: Ethnography of Girls' Friendship.* Buckingham: Open University Press.

Hey, Valerie (2001) 'Beacon girls: the moral high ground and managing aspiration in public and private lives; some feminist reflections', unpublished paper presented at *A New Girl Order?* conference, London, 14–16 November.

Holland, Janet (1993) *Sexuality and Ethnicity: Variations in Young Women's Sexual Knowledge and Practice.* Women, Risk and AIDS Project (WRAP) Papers. London: Tufnell Press.

Holland, Janet, Ramazanoglu, Caroline, Sharpe, Sue and Thomson, Rachel (1998) *The Male in the Head. Young People, Heterosexuality and Power.* London: Tufnell Press.

Hollway, Wendy (1983) Heterosexual sex: power and desire for the other. In Sue Cartledge and Joanna Ryan (eds.) *Sex and Love: New Thoughts and Old Contradictions.* 124–40. London: Women's Press.

Hollway, Wendy (1984) Women's power in heterosexual sex. *Women's Studies International Forum* 7 (1): 63–8.

Hollway, Wendy (1995) Feminist discourses and women's heterosexual desire. In S. Wilkinson, and C. Kitzinger, (eds.) *Feminism and Discourse: Psychological Perspectives.* 87–105. London: Sage.

Holmes, Janet (2007) Social constructionism, postmodernism and feminist sociolinguistics. *Gender and Language* 1 (1): 51–66.

Hoyle, David (1998) Constructions of pupil absence in the British education service. *Child & Family Social Work* 3 (2): 99–111.

Hutchby, Ian and Wooffitt, Robin (1998) *Conversation Analysis. Principles, Practices and Applications.* Cambridge: Polity Press.

Jackson, Carolyn (2006) 'Wild girls?' An exploration of 'ladette' cultures in secondary schools. *Gender and Education* 18 (4): 339–60.

Jackson, Susan M. and Cram, Fiona (2003) Disrupting the sexual double standard: young women's talk about heterosexuality. *British Journal of Social Psychology* 42: 113–27.

Jamdagni, Laxmi (1980) *Hamari, Rangily Zindagi: Our Colourful Lives*. Leicester: National Association of Youth Clubs.

Kehily, Mary Jane and Pattman, Rob (2006) Middle-class struggle? Identity-work and leisure among sixth formers in the United Kingdom. *British Journal of Sociology of Education* 27 (1): 37–52.

Kelbie, Paul (2006) Mother appeals for safe return of daughter, 12, feared abducted by father for forced marriage. *Independent* (30/08/2006).

Keltner, Dacher, Capps, Lisa, Kring, Ann M., Young, Randall C. and Heerey, Erin A. (2001) Just teasing: a conceptual analysis and empirical review. *Psychological Bulletin* 127 (2): 229–48.

Kenway, Jane (1990) Privileged girls, private schools and the culture of 'success'. In Jane Kenway, and Sue Willis, (eds.) (1990) *Hearts and Minds: Self-Esteem and the Schooling of Girls*. 131–56. London: Falmer.

Kenway, Jane and Willis, Sue (eds.) (1990) *Hearts and Minds: Self-Esteem and the Schooling of Girls*. London: Falmer.

Kodz Jenny, Atkinson John, Hillage Jim, Maginn Andrew, and Perryman Sarah (1997) Employers' use of the National Record of Achievement. *Report 328, Institute for Employment Studies*. http://www.employment-studies.co.uk/ pubs/ summary.php?id=328. (accessed 28/07/08)

Kulick, Don (2000a) Gay and lesbian language. *Annual Revue of Anthropology* 29: 243–85.

Kulick, Don (2000b) No. *Language and Communication* 23: 139–51.

Kulick, Don (2003) Language and desire. In Janet Holmes and Miriam Meyerhoff (eds.) *The Handbook of Language and Gender*. 119–41. Oxford: Blackwell.

Labov, William (1966) *The Social Stratification of English in New York City*. Washington, DC: Centre for Applied Linguistics.

Labov, William (1972) *Sociolinguistic Patterns*. Philadelphia, PA: University of Pennsylvania Press.

Labov, William (1972a) The transformation of experience in narrative. In *Language in the Inner City: Studies in Black English Vernacular*. 354–96. Philadelphia: University of Pennsylvania Press.

Lampert, Martin D. and M. Ervin-Tripp, Susan, (2006) Risky laughter: teasing and self-directed joking among male and female friends. *Journal of Pragmatics* 38: 51–72.

Larson, Colleeen (1997) Re-presenting the subject: problems in personal narrative inquiry. *Qualitative Studies in Education* 10 (4): 455–70.

Lawler, Steph (2000) *Mothering the Self. Mothers, Daughters, Subjects*. London: Routledge.

Leech, Geoffrey N. and Short, Michael H. (1981) *Style in Fiction. A Linguistic Introduction to English Fictional Prose*. London: Longman.

Lees, Sue (1993) *Sugar and Spice: Sexuality and Adolescent Girls*. London: Penguin

Levinson, Stephen (1983) *Pragmatics*. Cambridge: Cambridge University Press.

Mac an Ghaill, Mairtin (1994) *The Making of Men: Masculinities, Sexualities and Schooling*. Buckingham: Open University Press.

Manning, Elizabeth (1997) Kissing and cuddling: the reciprocity of romantic and sexual activity. In Keith Harvey and Celia Shalom (eds.) *Language and Desire: Encoding Sex, Romance and Intimacy*. 43–59. London: Routledge.

Martin, Karin (1996) *Puberty, Sexuality and the Self. Girls and Boys at Adolescence*. New York: Routledge.

Maybin, Janet (2003) Voices, intertextuality and introduction to schooling. In Sharon Goodman, Theresa Lillis, Janet Maybin and Neil Mercer (eds.) *Language, Literacy and Education: A Reader*. 159–70. Stoke on Trent: Trentham Books in association with The Open University.

Maybin, Janet (2007) *Children's Voices. Talk, Knowledge and Identity*. Basingstoke: Palgrave Macmillan.

McDermott, Elizabeth (2004) Interviewing and the class dynamics of 'talk'. *Women's Studies International Forum* 27: 117–87.

McElhinny, Bonny (2003) Theorising gender in sociolinguistics and linguistic anthropology. In Janet Holmes and Miriam Meyerhoff (eds.) *The Handbook of Language and Gender*. 21–42. Oxford: Blackwell.

McRobbie, Angela (1978) Working class girls and the culture of femininity. In *Women take Issue. Aspects of Women's Subordination*. 96–108. London: Hutchinson.

Mendoza-Denton, Norma (1999) Turn-initial no. Collaborative opposition among Latina adolescents. In Mary Bucholtz, A.C. Liang and Laurel A. Sutton (eds.) *Reinventing Identities. The Gendered Self in Discourse*. 273–92. Oxford: Oxford University Press.

Miller, Jody and Glassner, Barry (1997) The 'Insider' and the 'Outside': finding realities in interviews. In David Silverman (ed.) *Qualitative Research. Theory, Method and Practice*. 99–112. London: Sage.

Miller, Peggy (1986) Teasing as language socialization and verbal play in a white working-class community. In Bambi B. Schiffelin and Elinor Ochs (eds.) *Language Socialization across Cultures*. 199–212. Cambridge: Cambridge University Press.

Mills, Sara (1995) *Feminist Stylistics*. London: Routledge.

Mills, Sara (1997) *Discourse*. London: Routledge.

'Mina' (1997) My first date. In Nadya Kassam (ed.) *Telling it Like it is. Young Asian Women Talk*. 9–12. London. Livewire Books, The Women's Press.

Mirza, Munira (2006) Religiosity and Politics of Identity. Paper contributed to *Multicultural Britain: From Anti-Racism to Identity Politics?* Cronem Conference, Roehampton University, London.

Modood, Tariq, Beishon, Sharon and Virdee, Satnam (1994) *Changing Ethnic Identities*. London: Policy Studies Institute.

Moore, Susan and Rosenthal, Doreen (1993) *Sexuality in Adolescence*. London: Routledge.

Morrish, Liz and Leap, William (2007) Sex talk: language, desire, identity and beyond. In Sakis Kyratzis and Helen Sauntson (eds.) *Sexual Identities and Desires across Cultures*. 17–40. Basingstoke: Palgrave Macmillan.

Ochs, Elinor (1992) Indexing gender. In Alessandro Duranti and Charles Goodwin (eds.) *Rethinking Context: Language as an Interactive Phenomenon*. 335–58. Cambridge: Cambridge University Press.

Orellana, Marjorie Faulstich (1999) Good guys and 'bad' girls: identity construction by Latina and Latino student writers. In Mary Bucholtz, A.C. Liang and Laurel A. Sutton (eds.) *Reinventing Identities. The Gendered Self in Discourse*. 64–82. Oxford: Oxford University Press.

Peterson, Richard A. and Kern, Roger M. (1996) Changing highbrow taste: from snob to omnivore. *American Sociological Review* 61: 900–7.

Phillipson, Chris, Ahmed, Nilufar and Latimer, Joanna (2003) *Women in Transition*. Bristol: Policy Press in association with the University of Bristol.

Pichler, Pia (2001) The construction of bicultural femininities in the talk of British Bangladeshi girls. In Janet Cotterill, and Anne Ife, (eds.) *Language across Boundaries*. 25–46. London: British Association for Applied Linguistics.

Pichler, Pia (2006). Multifunctional teasing as a resource for identity construction. *Journal of Sociolinguistics* 10 (2): 226–50.

Pichler, Pia (2007a) 'This sex thing is such a big issue now': sex talk and identities in three groups of adolescent girls. In Sakis Kyratzis and Helen Sauntson (eds.). *Sexual Identities and Desires across Cultures*. 68–95. Basingstoke: Palgrave Macmillan.

Pichler, Pia (2007b) Talking traditions of marriage: negotiating young British Bangladeshi femininities. *Women's Studies International Forum* 30 (3): 201–16.

Pichler, Pia (2008a) Gender, ethnicity and religion in spontaneous talk and ethnographic-style interviews: balancing perspectives of researcher and researched. In Kate Harrington, Helen Sauntson, Lia Litosseliti, and Jane Sunderland (eds.) *Gender and Language: Theoretical and Methodological Approaches*. Basingstoke: Palgrave Macmillan.

Pichler, Pia (2008b) Hybrid or in-between cultures: traditions of marriage in a group of British Bangladeshi girls. In Jose Santaemilia and Patricia Bon (eds.) *Gender and Sexual Identities in Transition: Cross-cultural Perspectives*. Cambridge: Scholar Press.

Pichler, Pia. (2009) 'All I've gotta do is wank on about some bollocky poem': cool and socially aware positions in the talk of London private school girls. In Pia Pichler and Eva Eppler (eds.) *Gender and Spoken Interaction*. Basingstoke: Palgrave Macmillan.

Pollen, Roseanna (2002) *Bangladeshi Family Life in Bethnal Green*. Unpublished PhD thesis. University of London.

Pomerantz, Anita (1984) Agreeing and disagreeing with assessments: some features of preferred/dispreferred turn shapes. In John Heritage and J. Maxwell Atkinson (eds.), *Structures of Social Interaction*. 57–101. Cambridge: Maison des Sciences de l'Homme and Cambridge University Press.

Preece, Siân (2006) *Talking Posh, Acting Posh? The Construction of Gendered Identities and Identifications in the Talk of Multilingual Undergraduate Students on an Academic Writing Programme*. Unpublished PhD Thesis. London: Institute of Education.

Preece, Siân (2009) 'A group of lads, innit?' Performances of laddish masculinity in British Higher Education. In Pia Pichler and Eva Eppler (eds.) *Gender and Spoken Interaction*. Basingstoke: Palgrave Macmillan.

Preece, Siân (forthcoming) *Language and Identity in Higher Education: Gender, Multilingualism and Widening Participation*. London: Palgrave Macmillan.

Press, Andrea (1991) *Women Watching Television: Gender, Class and Generation in the American Television Experience*. Philadelphia: University of Pennsylvania Press.

Puwar, Nirmal (2003) Melodramatic postures and constructions. In Nirmal Puwar and Parvati Raghuram (eds.) *South Asian Women and the Diaspora*. 21–42. Oxford: Berg.

Raleigh, Veena Soni, Almond, Charmaine and Kiri, Victor (1997) Fertility and contraception among ethnic minority women in Great Britain. *Health Trends* 29 (4): 109–13.

Rampton, Ben (1995) *Crossing: Language and Ethnicity among Adolescents*. London: Longman Group Limited.

Rampton, Ben (2001) Critique in interaction. *Critique of Anthropology* 21 (1): 83–107.

Rampton, Ben (2002) Stylisation and the meaning of social class. Paper presented at the Sociolinguistic Symposium 14, Ghent.

Rampton, Ben (2003) Hegemony, social class and stylisation. *Pragmatics* 13 (1): 49–84.

Rampton, Ben, Tusting, Karin, Maybin, Janet, Barwell, Richard, Creese, Angela and Lytra, Vally (2004) UK linguistic ethnography: a discussion paper. *UK Linguistic Ethnography Forum*. http://www.lancs.ac.uk/fss/organisations/lingethn/ (accessed 15/06/05).

Reay, Diane (1998) Rethinking social class: qualitative perspectives on class and gender. *Sociology* 32 (2): 259–75.

Reay, Diane (2000) A useful extension of Bourdieu's conceptual framework: emotional capital as a way of understanding mothers' involvement in their children's education? *Sociological Review*, 568–93.

Rich, Adrienne (1983) Compulsory heterosexuality and lesbian existence. In Ann Snitow, Christine Stansell and Sharon Thompson (eds.). *Powers of Desire: The Politics of Sexuality*. 177–205. New York: Monthly Review Press.

Richardson, L. (1990) *Writing Strategies: Researching Diverse Audiences*. Newbury Park, CA: Sage.

Sacks, Harvey, Schegloff, Emanuel A. and Jefferson, Gail (1974). A simplest systematics for the organisation of turn-taking for conversation. *Language* 50: 696–735.

Sauntson, Helen and Kyratzis, Sakis (eds.) (2007a) *Language, Sexualities & Desires. Crosscultural Perspectives*. Basingstoke: Palgrave Macmillan.

Sauntson, Helen and Kyratzis, Sakis (2007b) Introduction: Language, Sexualities and Desires. In *Language, Sexualities & Desires. Crosscultural Perspectives*. 1–16. Basingstoke: Palgrave Macmillan.

Savage, Mike, Bagnall, Gaynor and Longhurst, Brian (2001) Ordinary, ambivalent and defensive: class identities in the northwest of England. *Sociology* 35 (4): 875–92.

Schegloff, Emanuel (1991) Reflections on talk and social structure. In Deidre Boden and Don Zimmerman (eds.) *Talk and Social Structure. Studies in Ethnomethodology and Conversation Analysis.* 44–70. Cambridge: Polity Press.

Schegloff, Emanuel (1997) Whose text? Whose context? *Discourse and Society* 8 (2): 165–87.

Schieffelin, Bambi B. (1986) Teasing and shaming in Kaluli children's interactions. In Bambi B. Schiffelin and Elinor Ochs (eds.) *Language Socialization across Cultures.* 165–81. Cambridge: Cambridge University Press.

Sealey, Alison (2005) Linguistic Ethnography: an Applied Linguistic Perspective. Paper contributed to Linguistic Ethnography Colloqium at the British Association of Applied Linguistics Conference, Bristol.

Sebba, Mark (1993) *London Jamaican: Language Systems in Interaction.* London: Longman.

Segal, Lynne (1997) Feminist sexual politics and the heterosexual predicament. In Lynne Segal (ed.) *New Sexual Agendas.* 77–89. Basingstoke: Macmillan – now Palgrave Macmillan.

Shain, Farzana (2003) *The Schooling and Identity of Asian Girls.* Stoke on Trent: Trentham Books.

Sidnell, Jack (2003) Constructing and managing male exclusivity in talk-in-interaction. In Janet Holmes and Miriam Meyerhoff (eds.) *The Handbook of Language and Gender.* 327–52. Oxford: Blackwell.

Silverstein, Michael (2004) Cultural concepts and the language-Culture nexus. *Current Anthropology* 45 (5): 621–52.

Skeggs, Beverly (1997) *Formations of Class and Gender.* London: Sage.

Skeggs, Beverley (2004) *Class, Self, Culture.* London: Routledge.

Smart, Carol and Neale, Bren (1999) *Family Fragments?* Cambridge: Polity Press.

SOED *Shorter Oxford English Dictionary* (1993) Oxford: Oxford University Press

Springhall, John (1998) *Youth, Popular Culture and Moral Panics: Penny Gaffs to Gangsta-Rap 1830–1996.* Basingstoke: Macmillan – now Palgrave Macmillan.

Stokoe, Elizabeth (2003) Mothers, single women and sluts: gender, morality and membership categorisation in neighbour disputes. *Feminism and Psychology* 13 (3): 313–44.

Straehle, Carolyn A. (1993) 'Samuel?' 'Yes, dear?' Teasing and conversational rapport. In Deborah Tannen (ed.) *Framing in Discourse.* 210–30. Oxford: Oxford University Press.

Swann, Joan (2002) Yes, but is it gender? In Lia Litosseliti, and Jane Sunderland, (eds.) *Gender Identity and Discourse Analysis.* 43–67. Amsterdam: Benjamins.

Swann, Joan (2009) Doing gender against the odds: a sociolinguistic analysis of educational discourse. In Pia Pichler and Eva Eppler (eds.) *Gender and Spoken Interaction.* Basingstoke: Palgrave Macmillan.

Tannen, Deborah and Wallat, Cynthia (1993) Interactive frames and knowledge schemas in interaction: examples from a medical examination interview. In Deborah Tannen (ed.) *Framing in Discourse*. 57–76. Oxford: Oxford University Press.

Talbot, Mary (2003) Gender stereotypes: reproduction and challenge. In Janet Holmes and Miriam Meyerhoff (eds.) *The Handbook of Language and Gender*. 468–86. Oxford: Blackwell.

Tannen, Deborah (ed.) (1993) *Framing in Discourse*. Oxford: Oxford University Press.

The DJ List – DJ Directory (2007) http://www.thedjlist.com/djs (accessed 03/10/07).

Tolman, Deborah (2005) *Dilemmas of Desire. Teenage Girls talk about Sexuality*. Cambridge, MA: Harvard University Press.

Toop, David (1991) *Rap Attack 2: African Rap to Global Hip Hop*. London: Serpent's Tail.

Volosinov, Valentin Nikolaevich ([1929]1973). *Marxism and the Philosophy of Language*. Trans. L. Matejka and I.R. Titunik. Cambridge, MA: Harvard University Press.

Walkerdine, Valerie (2003) Reclassifying upward mobility: femininity and the neo-liberal subject. *Gender and Education* 15 (3): 237–48.

Walkerdine, Valerie and Lucey, Helen (1989) *Democracy in the Kitchen: Regulating Mothers and Socialising Daughters*. London: Virago.

Walkerdine, Valerie, Lucey, Helen and Melody, June (2001) *Growing up Girl. Psychosocial Explorations of Gender and Class*. Basingstoke: Palgrave – now Palgrave Macmillan.

Warde, A. Tomlinson, M. and McMeeking, A. (2000) *Expanding tastes? Cultural omnivorousness and social change in the UK*. CRIC Discussion Paper. Manchester, Centre for Research on Innovation and Competition. University of Manchester.

Watson, James (1977) *Between two Cultures: Migrants and Minorities in Britain*. Oxford: Basil Blackwell.

Weeks, Jeffrey (1981) *Sex, Politics and Society: The Regulation of Sexuality Since 1800*. London: Longman.

West, Jackie (1999) (Not) talking about sex: youth, identity and sexuality. *Sociological Review* 47 (3): 525–47.

Weatherall, Anne (2000) Gender relevance in talk-in-interaction and discourse. *Discourse and Society* 11: 290–2.

Wetherell, Margaret (1995) Romantic discourse and feminist analysis: interrogating investment, power and desire. In Sue Wilkinson and Ceila Kitzinger (eds.) *Feminism and Discourse*. 128–44. Psychological Perspectives. London: Sage.

Wetherell, Margaret (1998) Positioning and interpretive repertoires: conversation analysis and post-structuralism in dialogue. *Discourse and Society* 10 (3): 293–316.

Whelehan, Imelda (2000) *Overloaded. Popular Culture and the Future of Feminism*. London: Women's Press.

Wight, Daniel (1994) Boys' thoughts and talk about sex in a working class locality of Glasgow. *Sociological Review* 42 (4): 703–37.

Willis, Paul (1977) *Learning to Labour: How Working Class Kids Get Working Class Jobs*. Farnborough: Saxon House.

Wilson, Amrit (1978) *Finding a Voice. Asian Women in Britain*. London: Virago Press.

Wolfson, Nessa (1997) Speech events and natural speech. In Nikolas Coupland and Adam Jaworski (eds.) *Sociolinguistics: A Reader and Coursebook*. 116–25. Basingstoke: Macmillan – now Palgrave Macmillan.

Yedes, Janet (1996) Playful teasing: kiddin' on the square. *Discourse and Society* 7 (3): 417–38.

Index